RAVYNSCROFT

Richard Edgar

For Ravyn with love

Cover design thanks to Mary M. Clark

CHAPTER ONE

Gone Walkabout

It was... some kind of a holiday, maybe? Sunday, I was pretty sure, so I rolled over to go back to sleep. In those days I slept with my hair down... which makes it almost unmanagable. It's so much easier to braid it at bedtime, shake the braid loose in the morning, or wind it up around my head while I shower. So of course part of it was over there under... something.

I woke up enough to figure out it was wrapped around the other pillow, which was conspicuously vacant. I was pretty sure we had, like... given rug burns on elbows and... stuff... A lingering scent. Rumpled sheets.

Odd. She was not an early riser, most of the time. The cat hit me up for breakfast and left her in peace, knowing which tactic was more likely to result in food in the actual bowl. He was... also missing in action. So I guess Rachael fed him.

I propped myself up on my elbows and tried to remember. Elbow. Right. The non-dominant hand one (would that make it submissive? Rachael would love that joke...) was a little sore to lean on.

My mind flooded with a hundred details from work that I was going to have to figure out very soon. But not today, thank you very much. A vision of Rachael, grading the endless pile of essays under the lone lamp that stood next to the couch.

"You go," she would say. "I'll be up... later," after a pause to weigh, at least in her own mind, the pile of ungraded papers against the hours left before they were due back to their authors.

"Love you," I would say, crossing the room to kiss that spot atop her head where the part was before she cut her hair short and spiked it. The product was expired by the evening time, and so the spikes were unoffensive. She didn't look up.

Now and then, sure, I can live with that. As an every night thing, I had to wonder.

One year after Christmas, Rachael and I had brought the little ladder up to the bedroom, put hooks at intervals into the crown moulding around the ceiling, and put a string of Christmas lights up. I would leave them on when I went to bed first; she had told me once I looked sexy in their light. She turned them out when she came to bed.

They were on that morning when I woke up.

The satin robe was missing. It's really only fun when both of us are around, so whatever. The weather was warm, too warm for the big winter-weight robe, so whatever. T-shirt, shorts, whatever. But I repeat myself. Coffee. There was some in the thermos. So I took a mug full out to the patio to watch the neighborhood wake up. The cat had a mouse; he had reached the stage in his hunt when he was consuming it.

Which reminded me of a vet appointment, where we had worried aloud about him eating the wildlife. Mice, in particular.

"35 calories," said the breathlessly cute vet we could hardly talk to.

We had to laugh.

"Seriously," she said. "Don't worry about it. We'll check for parasites, but it's fine. They're supposed to hunt and eat what they catch."

Hm. Perhaps some breakfast, now that I had a wit or two to rub together. Rachael's car was not in the driveway. There's probably a note here someplace, or an e-mail. She goes walkabout sometimes, to get her head straight. Or maybe an early morning trip to the grocery store if something particularly irresistible had intruded on her dreams. She did a trip to the store once in search of plums to make jam. The jars are still on the basement shelf.

On the desk was a neat stack of envelopes, addressed and sealed. She'd been writing checks to the various folks we pay bills to. I would need to find stamps, but I appreciated the practical sitting down and writing out the checks. But there wasn't one for me.

One wonders. This one did, at least.

I texted her, but her phone was off. Which, okay, but.

Practical stuff. The dogs needed walking, and the cat needed disabusing of the notion that it was okay to stalk Gus when he was on his leash, being a good dog.

We always talked about all kinds of stuff, hypotheticals mostly. We're both very wordy people. It would annoy me that she does words for a living, and so sometimes we'd be having a serious conversation, like, oh, maybe, would we have met and gotten together if one or the other (or both!) were male? What's the etiquette when the partner comes out as transgendered and you're at least a little bit bi? Go with it? Or run away screaming? What if just being straight is an actual thing?

And then she annoyed me by analyzing the "being a thing" thing and when it became a thing and who used it first in print and for what and while she was fascinated, it was about as much fun for me as watching Freddy (the cat) eat the mouse he caught. Crunch crunch crunch.

There was this guy she had known in high school, John something. The one that got away, I gather. Which is odd, because, guy, and we were hella gay, at least together. The net is a big place, though, and it's actually possible to find people years later.

But... no, surely. She'd be home again today or tomorrow or in a week and it would be... fun, catching up.

She's an adult, right? I trusted her. Though that thought coming to mind just then made me wonder...

No. Nope, nope, nope. Never. Mercy. Incendiary mercy.

Aaaand Gilbert and Sullivan was running through my head now.

"What never?" "No, never!" "What, never?" "Well, almost never."

And, "Mercy even for Poobah."

Who says lesbians aren't into show tunes?

I did find the note in my briefcase when I got to work on Monday. Sealed in an envelope just like the bills I had put in the mailbox by the entrance to our building, with the one word, "Ravyn" on the outside, stuffed in alongside my laptop.

No time to read it when I found it, so I leaned it against the screen of the computer in my office and flitted off to class. Those details of the experiment also wanted into my attention, so I had to pay close attention to the lecture to get the equations to behave themselves on the board. The point of junior-level physics is showing people that, given a few simple ideas you can write out as equations, it is actually possible to solve some problems with just your wits, a pencil, and some paper.

And me without my wits.

Already there were four lines of equations on the blackboard when I realized I was in trouble, so we made it into a game. "I think I've made a sign error somewhere," I admitted.

The geekboy who has all the answers couldn't find it. The woman student who's more careful than I am on exam problems? She's good, to the point that I would grade her exam first and use it to correct mistakes in the key. "Um, Professor Perkins?" she said, shy to a fault. "Over there?" she said, pointing at the first panel. "Second line down, in the magnetic term? Shouldn't that be a minus sign?"

Sure enough, I had violated Lenz' Law, which shows up in this particular batch of equations as a single minus sign, which I had omitted. "Remind me to talk sometime about what the equations do without that minus sign," I said. But first, we talked through the rest of my algebra, changing stuff, in another color so people could follow along and correct their notes. "Okay, that's gonna work, I think," I said, finally able to envision the next three steps. And it rolled over and let me stroke its belly fur and purred for me. Good equations.

~

Next up, just after class, was a group meeting with all my grad students, a few undergrads we'd hired to work there, the post-doc I hired with another prof I'm collaborating with, and whatever other hangers-on we had accreted. We have a pet theoretician in the group, and he was away that term, but his student might be there.

So this is where the chica gets to demonstrate her mastery of the auto mechanics part of physics: building custom hardware to make a measurement nobody's ever done before. It's a little easier nowadays, being a better mechanic than the students, because most of the geek boys wasted their youth on computers instead of actually fixing cars, so I can keep up with the guys based on my somewhat delayed practical education. But also, all that computer expertise makes the robotics part much easier, though we tend to argue over programming languages and data hacks more than vacuum greases nowadays.

We do these things standing up in the common area of the lab, so we don't drone on too long, and so we can walk over to look at the equipment if we need to. There was no big screen or anything in there, so it's not a presentation thing. Aaaand my hair was a fright because I hadn't figured out that with Rachael away I didn't have to seduce her with mounds of the stuff on the pillow, so I could put it up at night. And of course being a teaching day I was wearing a dress, which is just not very practical as a laboratory garment, the white coat cliché to the contrary notwithstanding. Loose garments (and hair) get caught in equipment. Not to mention getting down on hands and knees and looking up at that pesky vacuum gage on the bottom of the chamber? It really sucks if you're the little person in the dress. I did keep extra clothes in my office for this reason, but there was no time to change.

I explained some of my night terrors to people, about things breaking down in creative ways only their little milled aluminum hearts could come up with, and got several of the guys thinking my way about how to mitigate that. The one guy who's clever with things mechanical agreed to talk to the guy in the shop about our problem, and how to fabricate a particularly tricky part for the mechanism.

"Cool," I said, pushing sleeves up to the elbows, flipping big hair and tugging at my little dress.

"I didn't think anybody says *Cool* any more," said Jason, in the moment between topics.

"Pff," I pffed. "I'm old, remember? I just forgot to grow up." And it's true, he's easily a head taller than I am. "What's next?" I added, again revealing my age by quoting *West Wing*.

And then we went out to lunch, to continue the discussion of details without the hardware in front of us. It's hard keeping up with people whose legs are much longer, and most of them I have trained to walk at a pace I can match, but again the dress was a disadvantage. It's stretchy, which means the wardrobe malfunction mechanism produces catastrophic failure. What Rachael used to call a *Voop* where your boobs drop through the waistband, or the skirt decides a lower energy state would be all bunched up above your hips.

Which, y'know, if it's just her and me, can be fun.

But it would be unprofessional. Like not wearing pants to work or never getting a haircut. Which I think is fine, if one can manage her assets, but it can be a distraction for everyone concerned. I guess. I have no insight and little interest into the workings of the male mind and the gaze attached to it.

Anyway, all that to explain why it was nearly 2pm before I had a chance to sit down with the envelope. Which had been bothering the far corners of my consciousness all morning, though it promised to quell some of the worry about where Rachael was and what she was doing.

My tummy was earpy when I finally sat down at my desk and looked at her handwriting on the envelope. *Ravyn*, it said, with the tail on the y underlining the first three letters of my name.

Dear Ravyn,

Lemme start by saying that I love you. Don't ever forget that. Please don't ever forget that.

So the other day... month... whatever... the internets turned up friends of friends from high school and there was John. Who made the teenager Rachael's stomach drop and her heart beat faster, watching him with the girls who mattered. He's... widowed now, with a kid who's, what, 18? I think? He was a year or two ahead of me in school.

I'll be in Vermont, gathering my wits. Seeing how the other half live. I'll be back in a week or two.

I love you,
  Rachael.

"Slumming, is the word you're groping for, Raitch," I said aloud. And then I got out the tissues and had a good cry. Because I knew it was too good to last. Hadn't I always known it was too good to last? Because I think we both knew neither of us has what you'd call a fixed gender identity. It's a little hard to be a committed lesbian when you're not even sure you're a woman. So it's a little odd with that under the hood that Rachael would go for a (presumably) straight guy. Who probably can't think with his big head when there are tits and quims on offer, so he won't even notice she's genderfluid or even queer.

"Dammit, Janet," I said to nobody who was there. Renee and I had a friend in high school named Janet, and we used to say that to each other when she wasn't around. I learned years later when somebody dragged me out to *Rocky Horror* that it was a quotation.

Maybe it really was all too good to last. You know, the dancing through gender-space together, backward and in heels. Taking turns, which of us was Fred and which was Ginger. Not that either of us would wear heels. Silly footbinding torture devices that make male shoe tycoons rich while we suffer. I don't mind being little, and I rather like being honest about just how little I am. That said, it's good Rachael bought us a library kick-stool for the kitchen.

Maybe... Maaaaaybeee... whenever she comes home, I can show her just how mindboggling it is to have somebody that actually knows what they're doing.

CHAPTER TWO

Mint Tea

Rachael's car is quiet, so it wasn't until I heard the car door slam that I knew she had returned.

I had pondered this conversation most of the time she was gone. It's so hard to know, and looking back, everything is so poignant, so maybe it's best that I just stumbled out the back door, narrowly missed stepping on Freddy, the cat, and then bounced down the steps like the girl who had once picked up this fabulous woman in a coffee shop.

"Heeeey!" I said, or something equally dorky. Dorkily eloquent, maybe.

She looked up and smiled, tiredly, handed me an armload of stuff, winced, and said one word in greeting: "Ibuprofin."

It's... that time; perhaps she hadn't thought to be away this long and forgot. Better living through chemistry, says the advertising slogan, and in this case it's totally true.

I mean, arguably this was the most important conversation of my life, and I came to regret everything about it that I could recall. I so wanted to remember; and I can't forget. I so needed to forget, and I can't remember. The tired smile. The twitch of her eyes. The headache line between her eyes, under the unibrow, duly plucked.

"Can I wash your stuff?" I asked, and she nodded. So I took her laundry bag to the basement and started a load. Cold.

"I'm sorry," she said, from her spot lying on the couch with a forearm across her eyes. "I'm all..."

"Achey," I suggested.

"Yeah."

So I let her doze off, fed the laundry machines as required, made a bottle of cold mint tea. The drugs would bite presently, but they won't be rushed.

"Better?" I asked, on my way upstairs with the laundry basket, to sort and fold.

"Much. You're too good to me," she said. "Lemme just..."

"I coulda washed that stuff you're wearing," I said, just for something to say. The laundry basket wasn't even cold and here it was filling up again.

"And you will, when there's more to go with it," said Rachael.

I had considered seducing her at the door when she arrived, and watching her change while I folded her clothes brought to mind other times, in this room, including what would perhaps become the last one.

The last time.

When I already knew she was going, but ignored it as loudly as I could.

When, changing, I stopped to stretch, standing on tip toes to reach the overhead beam that supported the roof in the extension of our bedroom.

Right where she was when I looked up. "Not tonight, you have a headache," I said, just for something, anything, to fill the air.

"You are too good to me," she repeated. She shrank back to her normal size, turned away, put on summer afternoon clothes.

"I made some mint tea," I said.

"Thank you. That'll help."

We went down to the kitchen, where I dispensed ice into two tall glasses, followed by the promised medicinal. Pharma is nice, to be sure, but there are always side effects. Rachael had brought some mint home from her mom's place after the funeral, and planted it in the yard. She carefully figured out how to dry it to make tea that took the edge off those days, almost magically. I waited while the breeze riffled the half-open curtains.

"Ravyn," she said at last. I was chewing up an ice cube, something she had told me many times set her teeth on edge.

I wanted to say *please don't say it i know i know i know how can i change how can i be the girl you want to spend your life with do we need different I dunno what exactly*. But my mouth was rubbery and cold. I blame the ice chips.

"You are too good for me. You deserve somebody..."

I tried to interrupt but no sound came out.

"...who knows she's gay," said Rachael. "I..." She stopped to blot tears with the back of her left wrist. She snorted, said "fuck it," and wiped snot on the back of her hand, laughing through tears. "I am not that person," she said when she could voice a whole sentence. "I'm so, so, sorry."

"So that's it," I think I said. There was a sensation sitting there politely in the half light of the living room that the sun, when it set in a few minutes, would never rise again. That we... that we were no longer a we. That I... was hurtling into the darkness way faster than I could react given the reach of my headlights. That, being a physicist I had to try to put into terms of headlight angle over reaction time, compared to gathering speed, breakneck speed, fatal speed.

Except time just kind of stopped. Stuff continued to happen, but not in any particular order. Causality was broken. Nothing mattered any more. Nothing ever had mattered, it seemed, and though I knew in my head that was wrong, still the absence of time surely implied...

"What now?" I think I asked. Practical to a fault, the thing that popped into my head was this. It seemed somehow important to help out with whatever she needed to do. "Somebody we know just moved, I think; was it Joanne? She probly has lots of boxes."

"You own the house," she said. "I'll find a place in town."

"Not with Bob?" I asked, voice shaking.

"John," said Rachael. "No, he lives too far away. Vermont, the sign said."

"The dogs love each other. You should keep them," I said. Dammit, Ravyn, your marriage is ending and all you can talk about is boxes and animals.

She nodded. "It'll make finding an apartment harder, but sure. I'd miss them."

She would miss the dogs. What kind of an alien had I married? I couldn't know then, but I would miss Rachael terribly. The dogs were always happy to see me during those poignant visits to bring her that one more thing I had found. But they're dogs. Simple souls, both of them obviously, clearly, bonded to Rachael as their person, once I was not a part of their daily lives.

She turned to go into her place, calling the dogs, who went with her, leaving me standing on the sidewalk out front, with a knife through my heart and too many tears in my eyes to find the car keys.

There's an echo in the dining room, and a pile of unused packing paper for dishes, which sat on the floor there for weeks. Freddy bit the fuck out of my hand while I was trying to open his food can. If I were impulsive, I would have throttled him right there, or drowned him in his water bowl. I'm sure he missed his other person as much as I did.

But no, I left him gobbling his food while I went to wash out my wounds, find disinfectant, and another big glass of tea, courtesy of Eleanor Cohen's mint plants. I chewed up the ice cubes with mad abandon. I dabbed tears with the back of my wrist, Rachael-style. And then laughing as I cried, said, "fuck it," and wiped snot on the back of my hand.

Silly is good, Rachael and I used to tell each other. If silly makes the marriage go, this kind of super-poignant gallows humor maybe makes the divorce work. Laughing while I cried gave me hiccups, which I hate. Lying in what had been our bed until earlier that summer, weeping, twitching when my diaphragm jumped, and then chuckling... everything all at once. Which fits, somehow, with the fact that time had stopped the day of Rachael's headache.

CHAPTER THREE

The Walking Dead

In some ways it was like going to college, alone in the city, missing my people. The one in particular who's always been there, for whatever I needed, would hold me when I needed to cry, would laugh with me when I needed to laugh. Who... made me complete, in some way I hadn't thought about until the darkness, the drop into nothingness, was approaching my toes where they stood, there on the edge of forever.

Or something. I'm sure Rachael would be amused by the poor words I thought up to describe it. A poet I am not.

And I thought about what I did when I went to college. Cried myself to sleep, quietly, every night, so as to not disturb my roommate. Missing Renee sooo much. Everybody else seemed to be as sad as I was, so I fit right in, morose teenagers when morose was in fashion.

When this had gone on for weeks, Annie sat me down one afternoon, just the two of us, in our little desk chairs at the foot ends of our beds.

"So...," she said.

"So?" I said when nothing further came out of her mouth.

"I have a little piece of advice for you, Ravyn," said Annie. "You're lonely, everybody here is lonely."

I nodded, fussed with my hair, and nodded again.

"We're here, your other people are... not."

A nod.

"There are lots of people here you could get to know, and while it'll never be the same as it was..."

Understatement of all time, since Renee is me and I am her and nobody else has ever been either of us. But in that moment I decided not to tell people I had a sister, let alone an identical twin, who was so much more than... anything they would imagine.

"...it can still be pretty wonderful," Annie added. "You... look at girls," she said.

I glanced right into her eyes, which were looking into my soul. I nodded again. If I opened my mouth to say anything I'd probably cry, or at least squeak, so I didn't.

"Well, you're in luck. We live in a women's dorm. There's plenty of eye candy," said Annie. "And I'm going to the library. Laters."

And I didn't do anything with that for a long time, but it did kind of rattle around in my head, pop up in my monologue from time to time, notably when I happened to notice a cute girl in the dining hall or walking to class or wherever. They're not Renee, none of them are.

None of the people I see now, when I can stand to peek over the tops of my sensible shoes, none of them are Rachael, either.

We had friends, Rachael and I, most of whom we'd made as a couple. Young faculty types have to work hard, long hours, trying to prove themselves, that their departments should invest a rare position in not just anybody, but in meeeee, because I'm going to have lots of very cool ideas and stuff in the years to come. Goddamn. They totally bought it. For both of us, each on her own merits.

Friends, right. Most people in this world are straight. We fought our way into the network; it seems there's a place for committed gay couples. The atmosphere is more or less stable if it's all composed of diatomic molecules, neatly bound to each other and not available.

And then she moved out.

And, like it or not, I was a free radical in a world of couples. To change metaphors, the roots I had grown, to share in her joys and loves, were exposed to the world.

We also had friends among the lesbian coupled people. And if you think straight society is destabilized by a divorce, think about this: a single lesbian is a potential mate for either partner of every other couple in the group. Some of them wanted to stay friends, but as a group, they dropped me, and I suppose Rachael (but I couldn't afford to care), as if I were sending electric shocks through the system. And the safety net, which I had thought was these very people, let me fall through.

The physicist in me noticed the disconnect, and I had to wonder what we had been thinking, and how very wrong that operating theory was, if it can be violated so completely by what is, after all, not such an unusual happening. Or maybe it's just that coupled society is for couples. It sounds like a tautology, but the flip side has teeth: if you're not any longer in a couple, you're not welcome. Please take your things and go, before anybody else gets ideas. And maybe it was especially scary since Rachael left me because she's bi and wants... men. Every lesbian wife's nightmare, I guess.

I became the walking dead.

It was harder, in some ways, than it was in college. There everybody was single, mostly; some of them were dating, of course. Some of them were *Dating* dating, like, and my mind was duly boggled every time that came to my averted attention. The mouth opened, thinking to make an acerbic comment. The mouth closed again, leaving it unsaid.

Now, it seems, absolutely everybody is involved in a Relationship of some description. The general theory of relativity or relationships or whatever seems to only understand straight marriages. As generalized, just a little, to account for people like us, coupled gay people, with, in some times and places, even some legal protections.

I think maybe we had it right at age twenty, very cautiously getting to know everything about somebody, several somebodies, before making any kind of a commitment. But of course biochemistry tries to short circuit all that so you tiptoe gently along the unstable rim of the volcano, feeling the warmth without, you hope, being scorched. I understand that: genes just wanna get duplicated, so that means they figured a way to make girls want to go out and get laid. And then to make people want to nest, together, in case there are kids. It's odd, at this end of me, thinking about the cynical other end having her way with me, whatever veneer I use to cover it all up, to civilize the lusts.

But damn, the bed was empty at the end of the day. And the sense of hurtling full speed through the darkness without headlights scared me to death.

If only. But no, I have no active death wish. If the wall wants to rush out of the darkness and smash me, let it. At least the pain will be different.

So I kept on keeping on. Get up (feed the cat), go to work, tinker with stuff, give lectures as if I'm sleepwalking. Go home (feed the cat), find something, anything, to eat for myself. I miss Rachael's creativity in the kitchen. Sit staring at the darkening room through the evening until bedtime (with a treat for the cat). I miss Rachael's... well, everything, especially at night. Put my hair up, with tears in my eyes, because she's not there to run her fingers through it. The tinkering with stuff is hard. Paying attention is like trying to look around a huge, glaucomic dark... *thing*... in the middle of my field of vision. And the dreams... hurtling through the dark, waking with a start to see it really is just as dark, but that the trouble breathing has to do with the cat on my chest.

"What are you, a succubus?" I ask him. And I roll over, making him find a different way to snuggle up to steal body heat, and I go back to sleep wondering what the difference is between an incubus and a succubus. And whether whichever one was female would visit the dreams of lesbians in the night. I could ask Rachael. She would know.

"Well, you're in luck," Annie had said. "We live in a women's dorm. There's plenty of eye candy." Why is this echoing in my otherwise empty head now? Forming itself into letters dancing in rows, curling into a ring and nesting in that black hole in my vision.

Well, I was in luck, kind of. When I graduated at last and left all the dorm girls behind, nearly all of them planning to straighten up and... Well, be straight, to tell the truth. There was lots of male attention in grad school, endless fascination among young scientists trying to understand how the mathematics of stretchy membranes worked, and how it applied to... gravitation and electrodynamics, was the plan, but they found applying it to wrapping female bodies more immediately interesting. There are so many of them; they're available; I could have whatever I wanted. And I'm not one to walk by the candy store when the door is open. I didn't even need to know, really, what it was that I wanted.

And now let me pause for a shudder and blow my nose and wonder what kind of an alien I was then, as opposed to the person I grew up to be.

With, to be sure, a lot of help and influence from Rachael. We sat in the coffee shop, which unlike the candy store you can smell from the next block down, even with the door shut, and bitched by the hour about the impossibility of forming relationships in the modern world. Not noticing that we were doing it, amid the bitterness. Somehow leading with our dislikes and vulnerabilities made it easier, being together, being pretty sure we both knew the least attractive parts of the other.

CHAPTER FOUR

Girls' Night Out

So, yeah. The cat kept getting me up for breakfast. I think for a while he was as upset that one of his people had moved out as I was, and my attempts at petting or other care, including feeding, often resulted in biting, sometimes with blood.

Maybe it's a form of self-harm. Who knows.

I'm happy to report that I didn't murder him, or even make him go without his dinner.

Since the agony of getting out of bed was done by the time the cat was face-down in his bowl, one might as well hit the shower, or try to make coffee or whatever. It was really hard to care, but I did all that. Titrating the coffee was difficult without herself to consult, in large part because I was doing the experiment before coffee in the morning. One day it would be strong enough to grow hair on my boobs, and in all the other places I don't want hair growing. The next, cleverly remembering at least that it had been too strong, if not exactly how many beans went into the grinder, it would come out watery.

Orange juice comes in a carton already mixed. Hooray. We were not so much juicy persons, but it was easy and nutritious and I could do that while the coffee cooked. Whatever you call that snorting thing the machine does.

I had to re-learn to wash my own hair, but that was a skill just a few years unused and so it came back to me. I managed to arrive at the lab more or less put together and equally more or less ready for the day, pretty much every day, pretty much on time. It was a struggle. I suppose it will be a struggle forever, or until I retire, whichever comes first. Oh, another dip into my bag for a new bandage for today's cat wound.

Seriously, why didn't I strangle him on general principles?

I mean, there's a sad little place behind the bushes where the previous generation of critters were interred, under spare paving stones. The present generation may well follow, whether for natural causes or not.

The tears and the sniffles were for the cat, honest. Not about the fact that the yard was Rachael's fief, to do with as she wished. It was becoming apparent that her love for morning glories was not compatible with growing anything else in the vegetable garden. "Bindweed," I had sniffed, telling her about the dwarf variety that grows wild throughout the mountains back home, wrapping everything in its viney tendrils.

Maybe with careful tending one could get it to bind the tomatoes to the trellis, and then remove its leaves. It grows a lot faster than the tomato plants do, though.

Anyway. I was at work; I should be figuring out today's lecture. I had regained enough of my wits to be able to do algebra successfully for an hour in front of an audience. So that was a thing.

But I still hadn't figured out that showing up to the Monday Elevenses lab meeting in a dress was a bad thing. I tried to remember how I did that before Rachael uprooted my life... imploded it. Whatever. And there's quite a maze of rabbit warrens down that way that I never found my way out of. Just make up something new, girl; you used to be kinda creative, right? I remember that... Maybe I didn't have a Monday morning class last term? I forget.

There's this thing you can do with a beer can or similar; I did a demo for the labbies with a gallon can that had some kind of solvent in it but was now empty. You get a vat of water, a burner, and pliers or something. Put a little water in the bottom of the can, heat over the burner for a few minutes until most of the air inside is replaced with steam. Then you upend the can into the water, and it implodes with great force. The deal is that the steam inside suddenly condenses to water, and so the air pressure outside collapses the can.

That's kinda how I felt. Spluttering with my face underwater, but mostly just crushed.

I mean, I had to respect Rachael's assessment of her identity. We're queer, it's what we do. Well, maybe she's not, but still. Which means there's really no call for anger; it was just incredibly sad, left curbside waiting for a bus that doesn't run any more. For a streetcar named Desire that's been out of service since 1936. How quaint. There might be replicas, but they won't punch my ticket.

And there's the after-lunch time for sitting at the desk, ostensibly working. The time I had used to finally read Rachael's note. The time when the bottom dropped out of my stomach, not to return.

The guys in the lab went and found one of the few female professors who walked me down the hall to the ladies' room and helped me put my face together again after I quit blubbering. I hardly knew Andrea, but she took good care of me. I guess everybody needs a friend now and then.

"You're coming out with me. We'll have beer. Eat something sinful."

"Yes'm," I said.

"I'll get JJ," she said, naming the third and last female member of the physics department.

"Not too far, I hope," JJ was saying when we met her at the elevator. "I'm a little lame."

"I have a car. I'll go get it," said Andrea. "You two can chat in the lobby til I pull up in front of the building."

"It's funny how small the small world is," I said.

"It'd be funnier if it wasn't so sad," said JJ. She found a bench to sit on and thudded heavily into place. Which is quite a feat, given that she's no heavier to look at than I am. She's just my height, which is not much, only Chinese, so her hair is straight. Mine is a cloud of unmanageable curls.

"I'd ask why the bum leg, but it might not be polite," I said.

"I'd ask why the puffy eyes, but it might not be polite," said JJ, smiling crookedly.

"Nah, it's okay," I said. "I appreciate people willing to listen. I was holding it in just fine until this afternoon. The guys in my lab found me weeping at my desk and went to find Andrea."

"Well, good for them," said JJ. "For knowing they were out of their depth, dealing with their professor in tears, and for coming up with a viable solution. Creative problem solving is a skill that's kind of neglected in graduate education."

"Yeah, they're going to have to learn to be counsellors somewhere if they go on to be faculty people," I said.

"Andi's good at that kind of thing," said JJ.

"I hardly know her," I admitted. "Except in the sense that everybody knows all three of us: female physics professors. Collect them all."

Andrea's car appeared in the window, so I helped JJ to her feet and supported her on the way out.

"So, you're wondering, of course," I said, when we had beer. "After years of... being together, the sudden famine when Rachael moved out is... kind of overwhelming. I've been trying to find poems to express it."

"That bad?" said Andrea, grinning. "Somehow I can never find that one perfect poem again when I want it."

"Google is your friend," JJ drawled.

"I'd rather try to remember it myself," I admitted.

"Encyclopedia Ravyn," said JJ.

"Another obsolete resource," said Andrea.

"Andi, our friend is not obsolete," said JJ.

Which Andrea thought was hilarious, and nearly choked on her beer laughing about it.

"I'm... not sure how to take that," I admitted. "So I'll just babble for a bit."

"That works," said JJ. "I'm getting annoyed at Benny. My Significant Other."

"My... guy... is just so frustrating sometimes," said Andrea. "Also named Ben. How confusing."

"At least my... I guess she's my ex, now... isn't named Ben," I said. With a smile. How... odd... to smile at something just because it's amusing. "Rachael. Moved out three weeks ago."

"Yikes," said JJ. "I mean, I think about leaving Benny, before he, like, rolls over and dislocates my hip again."

"Again?" said Andrea. "I think if Ben ever hurt me, physically, I mean..."

"Yeah, this is three. I think I qualify for a frequent flyer card at the Ortho office," said JJ. "I know the drill. Emergency room, x-rays, nope, just... And they pop it in with a few good drugs and I limp around for a while."

"And I was going to whine about how empty my bed is," I said. "I guess everybody has their problems."

"Yeah, I guess," said Andrea. "You all know Ben."

We did. He's one of, like, fifty male faculty people in the department. The one who scored with a woman professor.

"He's... kinda... single-minded," said Andrea.

"As in, not the marriagable type?" said JJ.

"Oh nononono," said Andrea. "Not that I've asked..." She blushed. "Dammit, JJ, you've got me all confused."

"I'll just whine for a bit while Andrea gathers her wits," I said.

"He's, like, so focused on whatever's going on in his lab," said Andrea.

"Benny's kind of oblivious, and he's really big. Weighs easily twice what I do," said JJ.

"Rachael and I were such a thing, for a while," I said.

"More beer?" said the waitress.

"Food," I said, and we studied the menu for a while. We ordered when the second round of beer arrived.

"That's not sinful enough," said Andrea. "She wants fries with that."

"I guess I want fries with that," I told the waitress.

"Anyway, she's gone now, and somehow I don't want to do anything any more," I said.

"The waitress? You hardly know her," said JJ.

I stuck my tongue out at her. She laughed.

"Rachael would have asked what I was going to do with that tongue," I said, suddenly staring at the foam in my beer glass.

JJ and Andrea laughed nervously. "Yeah, that's a place I never want to go," said JJ. "Again," she added, with an evil gleam in her eye.

Andrea looked at her and blushed.

"You have my attention," I said. "I had no idea you guys were..."

JJ drew the proverbial bell curve on a napkin with the pen she borrowed from me. "Kinsey scale," she wrote across the bottom. She added "Gay" at one end, and "Straight" at the other. "Hardly anybody's out here at the three sigma ends of the scale," she said.

We looked into each others' eyes for a very long moment.

"I should go see if Ben ate anything tonight," Andrea said, recovering from her latest embarrassment. And incidentally staking a claim to heterosexuality.

"Yeah, Benny's probably drinking beer in front of the television," said JJ.

"I'll just go home to my rocking chair, and my bitey cat, I guess." I was fighting with another sob caught in my throat.

"We should do this more often. And not on a school night," said Andrea. "Physics girls' night out or whatever."

"Or whatever," said JJ. "Yeah, we should."

"I'm free," I said. "Every night, pretty much."

They each put a hand on top of one of mine, and we went our separate ways.

CHAPTER FIVE

The Attempted Madman

So I was in a choir. Kind of a cool experience, doing complicated things, together, and creating something that's much more than any one person could do alone. For the glory of God, I might have told you then. It's kind of like love, in a group sense.

And then my life imploded. Rachael is Jewish, so she didn't come with me to church, but anybody who knew me there knew I was married to her. But We Don't Talk About That, and so beyond the whispering, there was no way to say anything. One of the guys asked how Rachael was doing, and I said, "I don't know. She moved out last month."

Face fell. "I'm sorry I asked," he said. And that was that.

I was a little annoyed when one of the ringers, the paid section leaders in the choir, came in a week or two after and was all in tears because her husband had left her. And the director was all ears and comfort and call me anytime you need to talk.

The young clergy dude is all about families and how bad it is to be alone. So I sat down one day with my appointment calendar and attempted to do some numbers. There are a few boxes full of people in my week. Three lectures. Office hours, but nobody shows up for most of them. The Monday Elevenses lab meeting to talk about what everybody's doing on our joint research projects; what we're doing ourselves. The office door is open and now and then somebody comes by. Either one of the labbies with a question, somebody wanting some kind of committee work, whatever. Church for a few hours on Sunday. So that's, what, ten hours a week, maybe, when there's somebody else in the room with me? And then I go home to an empty house. By actual count, I spend 94 percent of my time alone.

So after I had a sore throat for a couple weeks and couldn't sing, I just kinda never went back. But the guy had a point; I do need people around. They say single people die younger, and I can totally see it: nobody there to do the Heimlich maneuver if you choke on your food. Just for one. I checked out a local bar. It was... not a good match. So on Friday I purposely rode the train the wrong way (having come in on the train instead of driving for exactly this reason... what, me? premeditated?), got off not too far from where Rachael's new apartment was, and tried out a bar in that neighborhood. A place where well over half the people are female. My tribe, I guess.

"What's up?" said the bartender. She's kinda young... I mean, most of my undergrad students are probably younger, but. Asymmetrical hair in unnatural shades (plural) some of which show only when she whirls around to go serve people on the other side of the bar.

"Girlfriend dumped me," I said.

And she checked me out and I'm pretty femme, so there's that.

"Let me just..." she said, pulling down a glass from the overhead rack, several bottles of variously ambered liquids, a bit of soda, a squirt of hot sauce, a twist of citrus she'd been slicing up while I watched. "Voilá. I call it the Attempted Madman."

I pawed in my purse for some cash.

"On the house," she said.

"Thanks," I said. Taking a sip, I closed my eyes and let the volatiles waft capsaicin through my sinuses. "An excuse to have tears in my eyes," I added. Wallet found, I left a generous tip.

And eventually I stumbled back to the subway station for the trip home, walked through suburbia, alone, to a cold house empty of everyone but the cat who thought it was way past dinnertime.

"Sorry buddy," I said, but he was grunting face down in his food bowl.

All of which got me a Saturday morning hangover. I hadn't had one of those in years. Now and then Rachael and I would go out dancing or whatever, but not for a while now, and then not at all. Like, never again. These tears weren't Tobasco-enabled.

But it's Saturday, Rachael is not around to be annoyed by the way I do the same thing at the same time every week, so I did my laundry and went grocery shopping. The usual Saturday morning interlude has been cancelled until further notice.

I had some trouble putting together a shopping list, or imagining what I might want to eat next week. Or even what I might want to eat that day. But it's Saturday so I went. Food shopping was an us-thing, bouncing ideas for things to cook and eat off each other, wondering whether we have the ingredients, enhancing each others' memory of what's in the cupboards. She had a grand collection of dried beans, for example, that is still there and I have no idea what to do with all that, beyond soaking and slow-cooking. Presumably with spices or something.

I was not hungry. I broke down in tears in the spice aisle, wondering which, if any ever again, of those little bottles of exotic substances would need replacing. A too-helpful clerk hovered for a while, and eventually decided leaving me alone was the best thing. Probably right.

And I ended up not buying much at all. "Spectacular failure," I told the cat when he greeted me, with a load of groceries I could carry in both arms in one trip in from the car, and still find a hand to unlock the door. He seemed unconcerned. There are more cans of his favorite in the box, so he's fine. If I could eat the same thing every day, it might help with the never wanting to eat thing. I ended up having wine and cheese and crackers for dinner. At least the cheddar was sharp.

CHAPTER SIX

Bathroom vs. Cat

"You know," I told the cat who was occupying all the choice real estate on the too-small bathroom floor, making me climb over him and around the door to get to the john, and then again to get to the shower. And yet again to dry off and find my robe, and with a contortion around the door that insists on swinging right where he's sleeping (or he insists on sleeping where it swings), "I could totally take the door off its hinges."

So I went and found a hammer and a nail and took the pins out and the bathroom is now doorless. "I live alone. I don't need a bathroom door, and besides it's always been in the way."

Now Rachael would probably tell you if you asked, if she's still talking about me, that I'm something of an exhibitionist. So being able to see what the cat was up to in the kitchen while I was in the bathroom was a good thing. He didn't seem to care if I was dressed or not, as long as I fed him regularly and didn't shriek too loud when he clawed me.

And then I had a guest over. OK, I picked up a girl in a bar. A girl, as it happens, who was unable to use a bathroom with no door. So we got the door out again, wrestled it into place, put the pins in, tapped them home, and latched it while she did her business and I ran water in the kitchen so I couldn't hear.

"Well, okay," said Jenna, when we were getting out of the shower and trying to figure out how to dry ourselves or each other, not step on the cat, and not whack our elbows on the open door, "I'll admit the door is in the way, at least when it's open."

"I was kinda proud of my solution," I said. "And there's hardly room for one person's feet, let alone two of us."

"Unless we're really chummy," she said, with a smile. "You could have latched the door before we... started," she said.

"The cat hates closed doors," I said.

"You are officially pussy-whipped," said my companion. Guest. Miz Right Now.

"He's very vocal and violent when he doesn't get his way," I said.

"Yeah, I had a boyfriend like that once," she said. "I dumped his ass."

"Adult humans mostly land on their feet," I said. "If I turned the cat out, he might survive on bunnies and birds..." Do adult women talk about bunnies? I've been talking to the kitty too much.

"OK, OK, I get it. He stays. I'll try not to step on him."

Mighty generous for a one-night stand, if I say so myself.

"I think you have a bathroom cat partly so you can watch people like me do contortions," said Jenna. "Naked, of course."

"Girl has a point," I said, grinning at her.

I took the door off again after she left.

CHAPTER SEVEN

Unsent Letter

Dear Renee,

Since we both know I'm never gonna mail this, I'll just tell you what's been going on the last, what is it? Fifteen years? Twenty? We each of us went her own way, thinking it would be better that way. We'd been prisoners in each others' lives in ways that were all too real. I dunno. Maybe that was the right thing. You kept Dad's name; I took Mom's, so unless somebody knew both of us, we could have separate academic careers.

In, as it happens, almost the same subfield. Yeah, not a success-oriented plan.

But from time to time curiosity wins out, and google knows all and sees all. Well not all, but an astonishing amount. I haven't tried it on myself. So you're all married and stuff; I found a wedding picture. With your husband. What a peculiar word. I don't think I'll ever say "my husband" out loud. We seem to have come down on the opposite sides of that border.

Presuming you do this now and then, you've learned that I married a woman, eloped to Provincetown, how romantic. From time to time Rachael and I would muse about what it would be like, being straight. Not that we ever would... but bi with a minor in straight might be doable. And now she's gone and done it.

It's... so sad, being a failure at the one most important relationship of my life. Not to mention what must be the second most important, with you. Or with the parents, but that's not at all uncommon for queer people. I think they'd understand, mostly, or at least be supportive. But it's easier not to ask that of them.

And so the house was full of boxes for a while, separating our stuff. She found some guy with a pickup truck and moved out. To, oddly enough, a neighborhood that has a reputation for being full of lesbians. There are rainbow flags on half the houses. It feels almost like Ptown, just walking down the street, not being a minority.

I dunno. Maybe buying a house in Whitebread Suburbia was a mistake. Hanging out with people more like ourselves might have been a good thing.

Anyway. I used to be single, right? So how hard can it be, remembering how to do things for myself? Raitch and I used to tell each other we didn't have to do the hard parts of life alone any more. Well, this is one of the hard parts, and I have never been so alone.

Life goes on, mostly. It's sad, and I cry a lot, and then I wash my face and go back to work. I think it was during a college vacation that you told me your motto was "Work a little harder, feel a little less bad." So I'm doing that. I keep having ideas for the lab, so that's something. I'm not looking forward to that grant renewal proposal, but then I never have.

I bought a brush to wash my back. How sad is that?

I went to the coffee shop, and the barrista reminded me so much of the one that got away, who as it happens Rachael was also making eyes at. This girl is not much older than Susie was then, so I might as well date undergrads. It's better not to get my undies in a bunch. (Rachael sometimes refers to undergrad students as "undies"... It was a joke, but like all things Rachael, it's poignant now.)

The cat (of course we have a cat... I have a cat...) is adapting to the new situation. He bites. I haven't killed him yet. I'm kinda proud of that.

I'm sure you're familiar with this, but nearly everybody in the department is male. And some of them think I should find them attractive (I don't). Some of them have a kind of hurt puppy look in the eyes that makes me reconsider my life choices. And then I remember the last time I felt this sad and lonely, on my own for the first time ever, and I have to shudder and laugh at myself and ask what was I thinking.

The skinhunger is something that doesn't go away, ever. Most of the friends I had were our friends, and they're gone now, unable to cope with the reality that is a failed relationship. I wonder who I've dropped for reasons like that, when we were together.

So even a city this size is a small town in some ways. A month or two ago I dragged myself into the coffeeshop hoping for a pick-me-up (and, to be honest, to have another look at the barrista, if she was working). Wiped the fog off my glasses, turned around with my merch, and there was Rachael, at the only table with an unoccupied chair.

"Um, hi," she said.

"Hi," seemed the thing to say in return. She pushed the chair out with her toe, so I slid into it.

She smiled. "You make it look easy, flying a dress into confined space like that."

So, yeah, she's looking at my clothes and the way I move inside them. Should I be flattered? Or just infinitely tired, that this my former lover, has joined the rest of the world, ogling my legs in a dress arguably too short for a mature woman my age.

"Thank you," I said, trying to be ambiguous.

"Are you, like..." said Rachael, stopping to blush. "...seeing anybody?" she finished.

I shook my head no. "You?"

"No."

"What about... Bob?"

"John," she said. "He's... far away."

I nodded, trying to be sympathetic.

"It's gonna be hard," I admitted, "walking out that door alone."

"We shouldn't," said Rachael. With a twitch of one eyebrow and the corner of her mouth, telling me she wasn't so sure about that.

"We shouldn't," I agreed. But, um, apparently she's changed how she drinks her coffee in the morning. Or I forgot, which would be a good thing.

Anyway. Not mailing this.

love,
    Ravyn

CHAPTER EIGHT

Left-Handed

Summer seems to have come again. I see on the usual social media that it was this time of year that my lamented housemate would be out getting her hands and knees dirty putting together the garden. Perhaps I should start thinking about that. There are a few peas from last summer that dried before I found them; I could plant them. And watch them get overrun by morning glories.

Or are they mourning glories? They're deep blue, like the geysers in Yellowstone, with some hellish chemical or other. Living on a corner lot there's no place for a vegetable garden but right next to the sidewalk on the south side of the house, which as it happens is also right next to the front entry. Not a place to be crawling around with tears on my face, remembering the amazing stuff Rachael used to pull out of the dirt here.

Maybe some dirt from wiping away the tears, to make mud. Some kind of aboriginal ritual, hiding my face from the evil spirits. Or maybe it's just further degradation. From time to time people have said I would come to a bad end. Groveling in the mud or something; I never did understand what that was about. See the sights of the neighborhood, cautionary tales. If you color outside the lines, live outside the walls, this could be you.

Or, hey, if I just put up a trellis, the morning glories will claim it. They're kind of pretty. And they're no bother, and if they die back because I forgot to water, no worries. They'll just wait for next year.

Maybe Rachael had it right. Downsizing from this way too big for just me kind of a house, getting away from the spooky emptiness of all the space. Where we used to... read together. Practice music. Do art. Snuggle with the critters.

Cry.

I can still do that by myself.

It'd probably be cheaper in some ways than this place. But it would involve getting my act together, fixing the house up, finding somebody who wants to buy it, selling half my furniture, donating more books than even I can believe I own, and moving.

With a bitey cat who owns this particular neighborhood.

Well, he won't live forever. He's middle-aged like I am, but being an outdoor hunter, he'll probably have a date with a car mid-hunt or something. Perhaps a coyote. I'll miss you, furball, but perhaps not as much as I should. Your demands for regular mealtimes kept me getting out of bed in the deeps of the winter.

Aaaanyway. It's not quite time yet, but there's a renewal proposal to write, to keep my lab running for another few years, pay the grad students and the post-doc, buy computers, stuff like that. Pay for the esteem of my much larger and overwhelmingly male colleagues. I should start sketching out ideas, perhaps recruit the post-doc and even some of the grad students to help with that. They need to know this part of the career path, so it's even educational.

Somewhere I have the one I turned in last time, promising... what did I promise, anyway? To love and to cherish, in sickness and health, as long as...

No. Not that.

Well, I did promise that. It's hard to figure out what that means now that she doesn't want any of that any more.

We were going to make a measurement, see if a certain atomic system knows right from left, even a little bit. Mostly atoms are held together with electrical and magnetic effects, which don't know right from left. But there should be a smidgen of the Weak Interaction in play as well, and it's exclusively left-handed. Like Rachael.

Like Rachael, dammit.

So we bought some exquisitely sensitive equipment, figured out how fast the laser pulses needed to be, how to synch them with the puffs of gas full of target atoms, and it didn't work. We're still not entirely sure why, but maybe we can promise to find out in the renewal grant. Well, it worked, but if we got the math right, the effect isn't there at the expected strength. Or there's something else masking it. Or there's something subtly wrong with the equipment, or our opinion of its sensitivity.

It's half past July. The proposal is due in mid-September sometime.

It's hot out, and even though there are no classes to teach in the summer, somehow the Ravyn who comes out of the closet most mornings wants to wear a sundress or something. So that I can be cool on the commute, I guess, and then spend all day in air conditioned labs and offices with male colleagues who don't agree on many things, but wearing pants to work seems to be one of them.

Apparently the department sent out a flyer to the kids who've been here a year, reminding them they have to hook up with a research group soon. There have been several timid knocks at the door, wanting the half-hour lecture about what we do in my lab and whether there's a place for a very green grad student. Most of them vanished, never to be seen again.

Except Margaret. Just as in my day, everybody, including me, knew all the female students by name. So I tried very hard to give her exactly the same information I'd given to the guys, but instead of running away screaming, she smiled and asked if there was something she could do to help.

"Well, we're trying to figure out this problem," I started... "How's your perturbation theory? Do they teach that in first year Quantum?"

"Sort of?" said Margaret. She named the textbook, so I told her which chapter to study next in the second half of the book, and she smiled again.

"Let me introduce you to the guys," I said. "I'm sure you were expecting that they're all guys."

"Kinda, yeah," she said. "I mean, everybody knows who all the women are and where they're working, and if you had a female... group member, I haven't heard of her. Not counting you, of course."

"I don't count," I said, intending to be funny, but a tear escaped from my eye. We ended up laughing at me instead of my humor, but that can work.

CHAPTER NINE

Dear Renee

Dear Renee,

I really need somebody to talk to, but nobody seems to be willing to listen. That other letter I wrote without sending was therapeutic, so let's try it again, shall we?

Hello, long lost sister.

But enough about you, let's talk about me. (I knew you would laugh.)

So this cute grad student just starting her second year came looking for a job the other day. And oddly enough, despite having a grad student already plus a post-doc I kinda share with the group theoretician, suddenly I feel all responsible again.

For a year or so since Rachael left, I'd stand in front of my closet and put on whatever came to hand. As often as not it was something girly, because... who knows why, really. Missing Rachael made me feel girly? I dunno.

The bifold doors of my closet have full length mirrors on them. Every now and then I have to wash the cat oils off the part by the hinge where he amuses himself marking things while he's waiting for me to find my robe already and feed him his breakfast. Normally, in the Before, I would use the mirror to check myself out, make sure my hair looked good, outfit matched and draped and all. Maybe arrange the doors just so and look at myself in profile, to fix things. See how the curls skate off my boobs or whatever.

When Rachael left, I stopped looking at myself in the mirror. Didn't seem to be a point, somehow. Maybe if I didn't look, I wouldn't see myself suffering. Pretty much everybody else in my life seemed to think so, at least.

I was having a session with Jason, the post-doc I mentioned, and he kinda looked at me, like right in the eye.

"Ravyn," he said. "It's not my place to say this, but I'm gonna say this."

"Okay," I said, wondering, kinda shrinking inside my dress, inside my skin somehow.

"My mom died, what, two? Yeah, two years ago already. Wow," said Jason. "And I learned to recognize other people carrying grief. Ask yourself what it is you're grieving, what love continues beyond anything you could have imagined."

And I looked into his eyes, and I couldn't say anything, but I nodded. Thinking about how madly in love I still am with Rachael, in some ways, despite hating her in others. I mean, I can't hate her for being bi; as you know, I'm bi myself. Maybe for promising me... everything, and then being unable to deliver. Again, not so different from me, but I wasn't the one who called it off. Does that even matter? I dunno.

"Calling it grief is interesting," I said, at last, wiping a tear from my eye. That day I had long sleeves, pulled over my hand and wiping my eye with the back of my wrist. "Thank you, Jason."

"Sure," said Jason. "Now about that equation... what's the Hamiltonian supposed to look like?"

And I laughed, choked back the lump in my throat, and we figured out whatever he was stuck on so he could continue his work.

"Thank you, Ravyn," he said, in just the same tone of voice I had used.

"Seriously, I'll buy you a drink sometime, and you can tell me anything," said Jason.

I nodded, again unable to speak.

Oh, so where I was going with the closet thing...

Since Margaret started in the lab, I started really looking at myself in the mirror. Going back to caring what I'm going to wear, which Ravyn is coming out of the closet. Which is to say, naked. We really do look a lot alike, you know? I had to remind myself that the naked chica in the mirror is me, not you. I... checked.

I knew you would laugh. But it's not so funny, is it?

outdoor spigot in the basement this year (I did! Woo!), water the new blueberries. Whew. Done.

I kicked off my shoes and hosed down my legs, which were a little pink. Sunscreen. Right. That would also probably be why my shoulders hurt when my hair brushes them. It was up, the hair, but it is up no longer, having discombobulated itself part way through the job. That tube top I bought in, what, 1995? Not gardening apparel. Seems I remember chiding Rachael for the ground-in mud in the knees of her jeans after she did this job. Smart girl, wearing long pants. And leaving her wife to deal with the muddy jeans.

Ah, love. I wasn't gonna think about that today. I wonder if she left a bottle of aloe lotion here someplace? Hm. Best get my nose as well. Or maybe I should have waited til after my shower washes it all away. Except, probably, the part in the middle of my back, if there is any there to begin with. Applying lotion is much the same problem as washing, except I can't imagine using a wash cloth. Moisturizing in the winter would help; it's very itchy then. I am not nearly as flexible as I used to be. Nor do I have a partner to help with my back.

And I wasn't gonna think about that today.

I never was very good at holidays. We did stuff when Renee and I were kids, family stuff. Went with my grandmothers on Memorial Day to decorate the headstones in the family plot, though I think none of them were veterans. Other holidays, other things that had to be done. Thinking up something clever for Renee was hardest, because we spent all our time together anyway, and she really could read my mind, almost. So I learned to think about that only during those times at school when we had different classes. And of course coming up with something so absurd she wouldn't have thought of it, only to find a return gift very much in kind. I miss my sister, still, after all these years.

With Rachael, there were also all the Jewish holidays to observe. She was not fooling around with that stuff, though she wasn't particularly observant most of the time. When we were grad students and first together, the rabbi at the campus center hooked us up with a couple of gay men for Passover, with that twinkle in his eye. She made me read the bits for the youngest child, because she's ooooold... like two months older than I am.

Anyway. Memorial Day, and I planted the garden, got myself sunburned wearing silly clothes to do it in. I guess that could be a thing. I could do without the sunburn. Or without the echoey emptiness of my house and my life, and the lack of hands to apply lotion to soothe the hurts.

I wasn't going to think about that.

Who am I kidding. I wallow in thinking about that, all the time. I used to think life was about joy and happiness. Shit got real, yo, as Rachael put it. Now, it's about pain. And for better or worse, this pain is mine. I don't see it going away; it may change form, but it'll always be there... the love of my life decided she didn't want to be that. Nothing personal; I just don't fit her preference any more. Categorically excluded from my own life. That part of that relationship will always be dead.

Happy holidays. Not.

CHAPTER ELEVEN

Maybe I Mentioned...

Dear Renee,

This worked pretty well the last two times, and the cat thinks if I do something twice, it's like that for always. So here we are again, me writing and not sending, you not receiving or reading. Deal? Deal.

I dunno how it is in your department; I suppose I could look it up; but here out of the fifty-odd faculty and senior scientific staff, three of us are women. And my, aren't they odd, I hasten to add, since I missed sticking it into parentheses. I wrote parasynthesis the first time. Sounds like it should mean something, maybe even something in physics. Sorting out the para-hydrogen from the ortho- or something. Microwaving the one to turn it into the other. Can you remember which is which? I never could. I wonder if we could make a maser out of it.

Anyway. Every year the building folks want to rewax the floors, and we have to carefully negotiate when they want to come so somebody can be there to make sure nothing that'll interact with wax fumes is open on the bench, and so we can at least see what got bumped and might need to be realigned. I drew that delightful task, and ended up chatting the afternoon away on a Saturday with Margaret, my latest student. She's... very green. She can do some calculations, and she's been working with the guy Jason who runs our models, trying to figure out how the code works. She spent half the afternoon whining about revision control systems, about which I know nothing of use, except that in principle they're a good idea, being able to go back to the previous version when your bright idea fails. I wish we could do that in hardware sometimes.

We found an older version of a control circuit in the corner while we were picking up stuff for the janitors. So I guess maybe that cabinet is like the repository of old circuitry or something. It's without its documentation, but I remembered it, and managed to find the notebook where I wrote out the draft, so that's something. Hooray for inscribing dates (with a year!) on the circuit board itself.

Anyway. They were done by mid-afternoon, so we went for coffee, and I demonstrated just what a fouffy cloud of hair I can generate on a windy day. "Observe," I told her, as the tie came loose, and rather than lose that, I let the wind have its way with me.

Need I say that Margaret keeps her hair short. Rachael cut hers a year or so before...

Yeah, so I wasn't going to think about that.

Maybe I should be writing these letters to nobody to her instead of you. There's more chance she'll find them someday, if only because she's less ancient history than you are. Or, who knows, perhaps in a fit of... what is this that I have? Somebody suggested calling it grief, which it is, at least partly. Perhaps in a fit of something something I'll stuff this stuff in an envelope and then into a mailbox.

Not.

Or I could get a therapist or something, just to have somebody to talk to about things.

That would be sensible. So it's not gonna happen. Besides, they'd never know the backstory, because while I might tell them some of the later history, the ancient stuff with you is... Difficult, shall we say.

So, yeah, no.

Oh. So maybe I mentioned JJ, who's one of the other two women in the department. We agreed, on the one occasion that we had dinner together (in one of those "they don't serve food there, do they?" joints, yes thanks for not asking that) that we should do that more often. She was kind of limping the other day at some kind of a faculty meeting, so I asked, and we're doing it again. I'm not sure if she invited Andrea along or not.

This is me, being all adult and sociable and stuff. This is me, trying not to care that the cat will scold me for feeding him two hours late tonight. This is me, stopping the writing of this letter that'll never be sent, so I can go be sociable.

Laters,
      Ravyn.

PS, okay I'm back.

So JJ did indeed invite Andrea along, and we did a department faculty girls' night out. Not that anybody else is allowed to call us girls. I've been on committees with JJ from time to time, and our work is just similar enough to be confusing in detail. Andrea I hardly know at all.

"Call me Andi," she said, and I was immediately reminded of Andy whom you'll remember from high school. Pimplefaced geek with puppy eyes that made me go kinda weak in the knees, and you laughed at me because of it. But I teased you right back about Janet.

And I swear JJ told us her actual name, but within about a minute I'd scrambled it. "Cannot parse; unable to remember," I told her, and she laughed.

"JJ will do just fine," she said. Her last name, Jong, also starts with a J. I suggested calling her JjJ, but no.

Two hours into the evening, and this time we chose a venue that actually served us food, I started thinking about going home.

"That seems like a wise decision," said JJ. "You're not going to do it, are you?"

"Probably not," I admitted. "And how is it you know me so well already?"

"Just thinking about the empty apartment I'm living in, and what good company I'm in now, and..." she said.

"All those empty rooms in my house..." I said.

"Lemme buy you another round," Andi suggested, so we did.

There was a little too much looking into each others' eyes while we drank Andi's liquor. Thinking about some of the messes I've gotten into over the years, doing exactly that.

And so when JJ asked, "What are you thinking?" I told her.

"Yeah," she said. "I'm sure you're right." And she flipped her long straight hair over her shoulder, shook the cobwebs out of her mind, and smiled for me.

It was all I could do to resist mirroring all her gestures back to her.

"Um, all right," said Andi. "I really do hafta go home now, or Ben's going to..."

"Yeah," I said.

"Yeah," said JJ.

The glance lingered... a bit too long...

I'm sure you know exactly what I mean, Renee?

love,
    Ravyn.

CHAPTER TWELVE

Comes a Day...

Some days are just intensely frustrating. It's hard to guess which ones they'll be. But I'm a lot less resilient than I was, so maybe they happen more often now.

Anyway. Getting up and out the door is a ritual I can do most of the time. I managed to get to work without even thinking about packing a lunch. Huh. Lecture went okay; my hair… Gah. Prolly shoulda washed it a day or two ago. It was in that awful in-between state where it won't stay out of the way and doesn't want to be bound and gagged because it's slightly too oily for the fastener. Knowing when to wash it is critical, and I used to have this intuitive feel for the passing days and knew when it was time. I guess I missed that. Dress was a little frumpier than it needed to be, and wanted a bit more attention than I could spare it.

The weekly group meeting went okay. Jason's getting some interesting results out of the computer, now that we figured out how to translate what the particle physics folks do into something an ordinary atomic quantum mechanic can understand. And we have most of the detector working that should measure that asymmetry he's going to calculate. So that's good. Ahmed's making good progress studying for his prelims. Margaret has hit the ground running and only fallen flat on her face once. The guys were happy to help her up, show her how to do things, make her feel better by telling her stories of worse mistakes they've made.

And then just before lunchtime I got this e-mail from the journal about our latest paper, which was sent out for peer review to an anonymous referee and is now back with their comments. There were a bunch of really silly suggestions, mostly consisting of adding references to work that's really not relevant but has one particular name in the author list that keeps coming up again and again... Gee, I bet Dan is the referee. He's in, what, Chicago, I think? A guy I see now and then at conferences who's doing research that's broadly similar to ours. And he picked on Ahmed's English mercilessly, even though it's his second or third language and we helped him clean it up a lot. But fundamentally the referee missed the point. I'd have to convene the group again sometime soon so we could figure out how to respond.

Lunchtime. Urge to kill. Perhaps I should go out, what with the lack of having brought food along to eat. And what with the need to cool off a bit before firing off some regrettable e-mail in anger. So I looked up JJ's phone number in the department directory. This was way back when those were printed on multi-colored paper, so you'd know who was in what category. My department is way too status conscious.

"JJ Jong," came her voice.

"Hey, it's Ravyn," I said. "I find myself without food at lunchtime, and I wanna take out a contract on a certain anonymous referee... If you're free, would you have lunch with me?"

She laughed. "Sure. Dial M for Murder. I'm under J in the department phone list, but that's pretty close."

So we walked to a nearby sushi joint that has fusion food... Whatever can be cut up in little bits and served raw in a rice roll.

"Tell me all about your referee," she said, when we'd marked up the menu and sent it in to the kitchen.

I explained at some length the vengeance I would like to wreak upon him, his children, and his children's children, unto the fourth and fifth generation. And how annoying a bad hair day is. And maybe (our food had been delivered) that extra-strong snort of wasabi was just the thing because I'm certainly not crying, noooo, there's no crying in physics.

"There is when I do it," she said. "Sometimes." That smile, that staring into my eyes, that looking long and hard to see where the pupils of her eyes end and the black irises begin. That hand pushed across the table without looking at it to find mine.

She put her napkin in my other hand, and I caught the tear trying to escape from my eye, which broke our mutual seductive stare. Because that's what it was, really.

"Ooo," squeaked Margaret, who'd just arrived with a group of male grad students. "It's professors Perkins and Jong."

We, very slowly, spread our fingers and pulled our hands apart. Because while thoughts of flirtation and mutual seduction were going through my mind, and, I hoped, JJ's, they were so not ready for the cold light of attention from the grad students.

"Hi," said JJ, waving. "How strange to meet up with people we know in a sushi joint even though it's cold outside." I'm with her on that, typically wanting hot soup or something when the winter turns cruel.

I was staring at those fingers, remembering what it was like having them between my own.

"Ravyn," she said, and I came partially out of my reverie. "Say hello to the nice grad students."

I pawed enough hair out of the way to do that. Margaret seemed pleased. The guys... are guys. Who knows, beyond the perpetual drool young men seem to have when I'm around.

Unlike Rachael who was left-handed, JJ wanted her right hand to eat with, so there was no more hand-holding across the table. Not to mention public displays of as-yet untested affection.

"How's things?" I asked her, when the grad students were mostly out of earshot.

She shrugged most of her upper body, including, I swear, her waist-length hair. Focus, Ravyn, and stop watching the waves in her hair. Which is straight, apparently unlike the owner. Mine is kinky, again unlike the owner.

"I found an apartment that'll do for a while," she said. "I'm done getting smooshed by a supersize Hawaiian."

"We talked about that at the girls' night out," I said.

"Oh right," she said. "And the part about not wanting to go home to an empty..." Whatever she was about to say apparently started with a B, but hey, she's allowed to change her mind. "Apartment," she ended up.

"Yeah," I said. "There are lots of unused bedrooms at my house. I'm not sure how Rachael and I managed to fill it up, just the two of us. And, to be honest, a small zoo."

We put on our coats and started back to the department. Her hair behaves itself. She left it under her coat no problem. Mine... Well, static from the lining of my coat would send it right around the bend, so I pulled it through my neck scarf. She... watched. As did all the guys at the other table. They always watch me. She, on the other hand...

"One thing about apartments is that they come with heat," said JJ. "Which means I pay for it in the rent, not that they actually supply it."

"Gah," I said, or something equally eloquent. "It's cold. My boots are squeaking on the snow."

"Could I... " said JJ, and stopped. "Like, borrow a room til they fix it?"

I turned to her on the street and smiled. "Of course," I said. "I'd like that," I added, trying not to go on and trying not to take her head between my hands and kiss her. On the street. Two blocks from the department. Where absolutely everybody knows both of us.

"This is me, keeping my hands to myself," I said.

"Thank you," said JJ, but she was smiling and staring into my eyes.

At quitting time, we suited up and walked to my car. I drove her to her apartment and waited while she brought out an armload of stuff. Then we went to my house. I turned up the heat, fed the cat, and helped bring in her things, which we dumped in the east bedroom. I found a bunch of hangers, but somehow there are never enough. I also found some sheets and a blanket, so we put the bed together.

"That blanket might not be warm enough," I said. "And I'm using the only warmer one."

She made a point of laughing, bending over, popping up with her face in her hands, flipping hair, and then saying, "Well, maybe we'll just have to share body heat."

"You're hot," we both said together, and we laughed again.

We stared into each others' eyes. She put her arms around my neck; I put mine around her waist. There was a long pause, just there. Whoever she wanted, I would be that girl. *Desire* is such an ordinary word. "And, sure, there's room for two," I found myself saying. I had seen her unpack wooly pajamas.

"This is me, not keeping my hands to myself," I murmured in the doorway.

"They're cold," she said, clamping one of them in her armpit. "Muuuuch better."

"Which hip was it you hurt?" I asked.

"Right one. And it was all his fault," she said. "What was I thinking? And which side of the bed are you used to?"

"Yeah, that'll never work," I said, with a laugh. "We both want the one by the door."

"Well, you should change your ways, because Rachael is not me."

"You should change your ways, because I'm not a 300 pound Hawaiian."

"With a cock. What was I thinking?"

"I mean, it can be okay, mostly; even feels good under..." some circumstances, I didn't get to say.

"She said *under*," said JJ.

"But it's not like having a girl in your bed," I said, ignoring her.

"There's nothing like having a girl in your bed," said JJ.

CHAPTER THIRTEEN

You Need, I Have

"There's nothing like waking up with a girl in your bed," I said in the gray dawn.

"Unless it's having a girl in your shower. Let me wash your hair," said JJ.

"I guess it's kinda overdue," I admitted. "One loses track of time."

"Maybe we can use your hair kinkiness for a calendar somehow," she said, grinning. "Am I a physicist or what?"

So we fed the cat and showered together.

"I didn't know how hungry my skin was," I told her over coffee.

"It's been too long since I had my hands on a woman's skin," said JJ.

"It's been too long since a woman touched me," I said. We stared into each others' eyes for too long; my coffee was cold when I thought to take another sip.

"Are you busy tonight?" my mouth said.

"I can be," said JJ, smiling. "Meanwhile, work. Gotta do it. You have a referee to slay."

"Don't remind me."

"Ravyn," said JJ, suddenly serious. "Thanks for taking me in."

"I have room, you need a bed..."

"And a girl in that bed," said JJ. "May I kiss you again?"

"After... you have to ask?" For the record, it's really hard to kiss someone when both of you are smiling.

"There's an advantage to not being girly enough to wear makeup," said JJ. "You can kiss your girlfriend without wearing her lipstick the rest of the day."

And there it is... From one night room to bed together to girlfriends... All in one emotion-packed day. "Girlfriends," is what I said out loud.

Complicated emotions flickered across JJ's face. "I mean, not to presume or anything," she said, "but it's okay with me if it's okay with you..."

Which, I had to laugh. "I love you, too, JJ," I said. It started out as a wry joke on the tentative way she pushed herself forward. By the time I got to the end of the sentence... I wasn't sure anymore.

"Can I stay for a few days?" asked JJ. "I'll call my landlord today and find out about the heat."

"Anything you need," I said.

She startled and stared seriously into my eyes for a long moment. And then she laughed. "You rock, as the kids say these days."

All the emotions there are came through me at once, and I suppressed the urge to say "Nuh uh!" like the five and ten and fifteen year old Ravyn had done with her sister. "Thank you," is what I said. "Now the practical stuff. I can drive you to campus. Do you need to go home first? Will you need more stuff from there tonight? And what do you like in your coffee? I usually stop at the drive-through..."

And JJ was laughing in three octaves, at the absurdity of moving in by stages, her gratefulness that I was there to catch her when she needed it, and the amazement of new love. Because whatever lies we told ourselves about it being a one time thing, there are some powerful nesting hormones unleashed when you first sleep with a woman. In past lives I managed that by always having multiple partners. With Rachael I just went with it, and we see where that ended up. And Renee... Oh dear, I've been recovering from her all my life, it seems like.

There's serious stuff going on here, so it's important to laugh.

"Speaking of practical," said JJ, "I cannot believe you wear a dress in weather this cold."

"The pantyhose Rachael bought me are nice and warm," I said. "And you're absolutely the only person in the world I could say that to."

"Honey," she said, after laughing, "we need to find you some more women friends."

"Seems like it'd be easier, being a lesbian in academia and all," I said.

"Well, we can start with Andrea," said JJ.

"And I wonder how often our names just come up in conversation, simply because we're female and in physics."

"We could sit down sometime and talk through all the stupid lines our various colleagues have tried out on us," JJ suggested. "If there's enough together time to get through them."

"I'd like that. The together time. Not necessarily the colleague thing."

"I try not to sleep with physicists," said JJ. "Except, astonishingly, you, it seems."

"I'm glad you made an exception for me."

"Ravyn, you are the exception to all the rules. The counterexample to every proposition."

"She said *proposition*," I chuckled.

"Love to," said JJ. She leaned over for a kiss before we got out of the car. The windows were snowy and mostly fogged. "Tonight."

"Um, sure," I said in parting, at the elevator. With a handful of mail and a backpack and trying to open my coat to let in the warm air, without getting hair caught in the zipper.

"One thing at a time," I was saying to myself when Margaret walked by my office. "Backpack off, check. Put down the mail."

"I'll hold that if you like," said Margaret.

"Unzip coat, but first, it seems, get hair out of the zipper." I narrated all that as I did it. Margaret laughed. "Long hair is a lifestyle, I tell you," I added.

"I can see that," she said. "If you give me your key I'll open your office." An hour or so later I found the stack of mail, neatly sorted by size, on my computer keyboard. How thoughtful. This kid will go far.

CHAPTER FOURTEEN

A Good Day

We had a good day, my group and I. I shared the referee's report, and when everybody had read it, and the paper we wrote that it referred to, and the annotations from the journal editor, we had an impromptu meeting. My co-authors, Jason and Ahmed, and Margaret, who joined the group since we wrote up this paper and sent it in.

"First thing," I started, "The referee is always right, perhaps especially when he's wrong."

"Explain," said Margaret.

Jason picked up the challenge. "The referee has arguably read the paper as carefully as anyone will, and if he missed the point, the writing's not good enough, or the evidence not compelling enough, to make it clear what we're trying to say."

"Exactly," I said. "Second, they recommend we refer to about half a dozen papers, and you'll probably notice presently that the author lists of those all intersect. I think we know who our anonymous referee is. But we have to respond, which means looking at all of those papers to see if they pertain to anything we did."

So they divvied up the list, after scanning the titles on the laptop Ahmed had brought along. He's nothing if not thorough.

"Third," I said, turning to Ahmed, "Let me apologize for what he said about your English, my friend. We should make him spend ten thousand years in purgatory, writing papers in Arabic. But again, he has a point, and maybe we can learn something by sharpening up the English, making it more idiomatic."

Ahmed nodded.

"Maybe Margaret can help you with that."

"I'm not covering my hair," was the first thing Margaret said in response.

Ahmed laughed. "No need. I'm not that kind of Muslim."

"And then there's the one objection of some substance. Jason, maybe you and I can figure out how to respond to that."

"OK, sure," said Jason. "I think he's wrong, but..."

"But we can't prove it. Yet." I smiled deviously. "Everybody know what they're doing?"

"Yup." "Yes, Professor." "Totes cool," they said. I'll let you figure out who said what.

Lunchtime. The phone rang. "Ravyn," I said.

"JJ," it said. "I happen to know you forgot to bring your lunch."

"I haven't had time to notice, but you're right," I said.

"Andi and I will be by your office in ten minutes. Wear a coat."

"Yes, Mother," I said, but I was chuckling when they arrived.

"I cannot believe you wear a dress in weather this cold," Andi said, as I pulled my hair through my coat collar.

"The pantyhose her wife bought her are warm, she claims," said JJ.

"Some kinda wool blend with high tech fibers? Or something like that," I said.

"Better be warm because it's wicked cold outside." Andi is the only person I've met who's from around here, and uses the local dialect.

"And how is it that JJ knew you forgot your lunch?" Andi wanted to know when we had our coats off and were seated.

"We kinda..."

"Heat's out..."

"Extra rooms..."

"Slept together," said JJ. "And whatever we did this morning didn't involve putting food in a bag to bring along."

"Whatever we..." Andi repeated.

We smiled for her.

"Jesus," she squeaked.

"Nope. He's a boy, last I heard," I said.

"Oh my fucking god," said Andi.

"Goddess, and you're right," said JJ. "Not that we're divine, either of us."

"It's just..." said Andi.

"Just..." I prompted after a long pause.

"I'm kinda..."

"Bi?" said JJ. "Isn't everybody? Everybody who's female, at least. Dunno about the guys."

"Yeah," said Andi. "Also kinda annoyed at my current straight relationship, and the other partner. Who would otherwise be sitting where you guys are, taking up as much space as the two of you together."

"I had a guy literally twice my size," said JJ.

"I had way too many guys, back in the day," I admitted. "And then I fell in love with a girl, married her, got dumped. So I'm living in solitary splendor in a house that's way too big for just me and one cat, and a whole lotta echoes. Also everything is so fucking sad and poignant and stuff."

I got a pat on each hand for that.

~

Since JJ was staying again that night, we stopped by her chilled apartment to get more stuff, including the blanket off her bed. "Options," she said, smiling and nodding.

"Options," I agreed.

I put together some pasta for our dinner, found half a bottle of wine in the fridge.

"Thanks for putting me up," said JJ.

"Thanks for holding me," I said.

"Once we got your hands warmed up, it was nice," said JJ. She started rubbing my hands between hers, trying to get the circulation to warm them up.

"Tea?" I said.

"Something without caffeine," said JJ.

And so I held a teacup in my hand, which was more effective at getting it warm. Wrapping it around JJ would also be effective, but I do understand not wanting cold hands on your body.

"I saw how you were looking at Andi," said JJ.

"I thought I was being subtle."

"You were almost drooling," she said, grinning. "But it's fine. She's very attractive. And, apparently, bi. Who knew?"

"Well, she looks at me sometimes. I thought it was just incredulity for the one out lesbian in the department, but there's some hint of wanting to be the girl there by your side, y'know?" I looked at JJ for a moment.

She smiled. One of those smiles that gets me laid.

"With Rachael..." I started. "Is it okay to talk about my ex?"

"You can talk about anything you want," said JJ.

"We used to compare notes on women we found attractive. And men," I said. "She had a list of celebrities she said she would do. So I played along and voted yea or nay on hers, adding a few of my own."

"Seems like a fun game," said JJ. "Not having had a long-term relationship with another woman, it's out of my ken, but it sounds harmless enough."

"Well, until she left me for a man," I said. I was proud that I didn't even sniffle. "Anyway, is talking about Andi like that? Somebody who, hypothetically, we might, kinda sorta, um..."

"I'm not very... monogamous," said JJ. "I never really understood the American uptightness about sex and the obsession with who's fucking whom. Does my language offend?"

"You can use any language you want," I said. "Though if you cuss at me in Chinese I might ask for a translation."

"Anyway. I have no idea how she feels about it, but if Andi asked, I might just go with her," said JJ. "Not so very unlike what I did with you." And she smiled that sexy smile again.

"Even though with your blanket there's no need to cuddle, thermodynamically I mean?" I babbled.

"Hush," she said, smile continuing.

"I'm going to kiss that smile off your face and, and, um, show you my toybox," tumbled out of my lips. Was I reacting to her being non-monogamous by being extra seductive? I dunno.

"Deal," said JJ, and she laughed. "You show me yours, I'll show you mine... sometime. It's in my freezing apartment at the moment."

There's that moment when the veneer of light humor wears through and the smiles fade. Mine did before JJ's, but by the time I leaned in for a kiss, she was seriously into it. Her fingers got tangled up in my hair, which triggered a few giggles, but the evening returned to the serious side of the border. Until various... items... being operated by unfamiliar... hands... malfunced, and we just had to collapse into a lump of laughing lesbians.

"Not the involuntary body response I was going for," said JJ, wiping tears of mirth from her eyes. "But I'll take it."

Sometimes you just have to laugh at how silly it all is.

"You're very cute when you totally lose it," JJ said, much later, when we stopped off in the kitchen for rum on the way back from the bathroom. We snuggled on the couch for a while and managed to consume our drinks without choking (it's very volatile), getting our hair in them (it was everywhere else), or flashing each other too much.

"It's remarkably hard to keep a female body inside a satiny robe," said JJ.

So I took her out of it. "It's chilly. We should go back to bed."

"You should show me how that thing is supposed to work," she said, on the way up the stairs. "The toy. Or the robe. Either one."

Thankfully the next day was a Saturday, so it didn't matter all that much that sleeping together didn't involve that much actual sleeping.

"Can I have your wifi password?" JJ asked in the morning. The late morning.

"Um, sure... I wonder what it is..." and while I searched my laptop for it, I was teasing her. "D'you think it's a good idea, sharing wifi on our first sleepover?"

"Second," said JJ. "I just didn't go home in between. Well, I did, but only to get stuff."

"Like a blanket so you wouldn't have to sleep with me," I said, glancing up from the screen.

"No trouble," said JJ, laughing.

"Here," I said, reading the numbers to her.

"Just wanna check and see if the heat's on again at my place," she said.

"Your thermostat is on the internet. Why am I not surprised." It wasn't a question.

"Well, no. But I did have a spare thermocouple and a USB interface," said JJ. "And as you know, one thing leads to another, and ook, it's still 45 in my living room."

She was beside me on the couch, so I glanced at her screen. There was a graph on it. "And you were bored so you wrote a script to sample the thermocouple and plot the results."

JJ flipped her hair out of her line of sight. "Yeah. I guess I'm a nerd."

"Ya think?" I said. "I mean, yeah, I know how to do all that stuff, but why?"

"Because I wanna deduct x number of days from my rent?" said JJ.

"And when your landlord tosses you out, you'll just have to move in here," I said.

We looked at each other for a long moment. She shut the lid on her computer. She shut the lid on my computer. She stacked the two of them on the desk. "I'd like that," she said in a very small voice, climbing into my lap and using her open-fingered hands to comb the hair out of my face.

When we had kissed, my mouth opened and said, "Let's see if I can replace that little girl voice with a full-throated adult woman's."

We stopped by JJ's still-cold apartment that afternoon while we were out shopping for food and wine. She packed yet more clothes, and pulled *The House at Pooh Corner* off the shelf. In the car on the way home, she found the spot. "'Do I look like a horse?' said Piglet," she read. "People keep calling me a little horse."

I had indeed called her a little hoarse after... testing her voice. When we could have been eating lunch like civilized women.

The, what was it, third day? That she was there, I gave her the official tour of the house. She had figured out the way from the upstairs bedrooms, of which there are three, but only two with beds fully furnished with sheets and stuff, plus another small room Rachael used as an office sometimes, or a music room or an art studio. There's an attic with two more finished rooms that could sleep a few more people in a pinch. The main floor has the living room, which is small but has a glorious bay window facing south that admits lots of sun on a cold winter's day. And the dining room, featuring the table Rachael's mom gave her, but that she had no room for in her apartment. And the kitchen, with 1970s decor and funky cedar shingles on the wall, and the only bathroom, inconveniently nowhere near the stairs coming down from the bedrooms. Book shelves in every room, some of them empty since Rachael moved out and I didn't have the heart or the energy to move my own library in. And there's a small mud room near the bathroom just inside the back door. Plus a basement where there are tools and laundry machines and heaters and stuff. There's a small yard and a garage, which just then was mostly ice-encrusted. So yeah, a bit big for just me to rattle around in.

It was... odd... having her around my house. I had lived here with Rachael, of course, until she left, and then I'd been here alone for, what, a year or more. I'm resisting the urge to add up how many days. But I would come around the corner and there would be JJ, communing with her laptop on Rachael's corner of the couch, a few papers spread out, and a graph or two on her screen. Not like what Rachael did there, which was to grade endless stacks of purple prose. Or maybe it was blue and became purple with the addition of a few milliliters of red ink.

And then JJ would look up and smile, and her Chinese face is so different from Rachael's Jewish one, that even though the smiles might be similar, the parallel was broken and I was back in the now.

And then JJ caught a wave of grief crossing my face, shut her laptop, stacked it and the papers on the end table, folded her glasses on top, and patted the couch next to her, inviting me to join her.

"It's such a Rachael-like gesture," I said, between sobs. "I'm sorry I'm such a mess."

"Oh, hush," said JJ, "You can cry all you need to. There's plenty of sad stuff in our lives."

So she lay me down, because it's easier to hug that way, and held me while I cried. Not missing Rachael, exactly; more like missing the person I was when she was around.

"Yeah, I miss the Chinese girl who fell for the big Hawaiian guy," said JJ. "Now? I'm just kind of continuing. Existing. Not exactly living."

"If we're, like, living together, we should make each other a deal," I said, sitting up and gathering steam.

"Oh?"

"Living, each of us, as opposed to just getting by. So we can do it together."

"I like the sound of that," said JJ. "Aaaand I kind of feel as if I'm imposing, joining you in your bed every night. Let me invite you to mine."

I... smiled. Damn, that smile has gotten me laid so many times.

~

The cat was confused. I think he uses the bed in that room in the night sometimes, and then comes to join me in the grey hours of the morning, hoping to wake me up to serve his breakfast. I remember finding him snuggled on top of the covers in the kerf between us, stretched out full length, back to JJ and belly snuggled up against me. It proved to be difficult for him to get out of that position when I started chuckling at him.

"We've been having a threesome with a male," I told JJ when he woke her up. "He's a kitty, and he's been fixed, so not to worry."

"Wait, what?" seemed to be the only thing to say to that.

I decanted a very annoyed feline from the bed, my hands under his arms like a small child. "I'm a little surprised I'm not bleeding," I murmured, snuggling up to JJ's body, in the space vacated by the cat. "I like your shampoo," I said, inhaling through my nose, somewhere behind her ear.

"You're going to make me wake all the way up, aren't you?" And she sat up, clicked on the lamp, put her hair in order, and turned to face me, arms crossed under her boobs. "What's this about shampooing the kitty?"

So I told her what we'd been up to while she was sleeping. "Tomorrow, if you want, we can shampoo each others' pussies…"

"Ooookay then," she said. "You're very strange. I like that in a lover." She turned out the lamp.

There was something about her arms around me in the night that had me in tears again by morning. Which she magically transformed into tears of joy, but they were still running down my face. Apparently I really really missed having a woman in my bed. You'd think I would be aware of this, but it wasn't til there was another one that I even noticed.

CHAPTER FIFTEEN

Snow Day

Dear Renee,

It occurs to me that I have no idea what your home address is. If I were mailing these little therapy letters, I could of course send them to your office, but that's... probably hostile.

So here it is midwinter. It's snowing outside, and friend JJ has no heat in her apartment, so she's... visiting, shall we say.

I hafta say it's nice having somebody else around. Each day we've stopped by her cold apartment to get another armload of stuff. Pretty soon she'll be all moved in, and then they'll fix the heat and we'll have to take all that stuff back. She has this unrequited relationship with the landlord. You provide a warm, habitable place for her to live, she pays you for it. But there seems to be some issue, whether it's that the heating system needs a swift dismantling, or social, attempted contract fraud. Dunno. But if the heat of her anger could warm the apartment, she'd be all fixed up.

Hope is fading with the light, though. Which leaves me with a longer-term guest.

This actually suits me just fine, at least so far. There's been more weeping lately than I thought I could do; figured I was done with that, but there's something about that somebody else sitting at the far end of the couch working. Or, yes, waking up in my bedroom. Not enough blankets. That's my story and it's even true for that first night, before we brought one of hers over.

I guess we'll have to go out and dig the cars out, at least. And the sidewalk. Once it's done snowing. It'll be nice to have help; maybe my assortment of variously shaped snow shovels will provide two that are useful today. I'll have to try to remember the surveying stuff relative to the fenceposts, and tell JJ about where the chips in the curb stones are. They like to catch the blade if you cut too close to the cement. And I hope I got enough of the weeds pulled out of the sidewalk cracks.

"So is Danny..." I asked

"Benny," said JJ.

"... out there someplace contemplating a snowbank?"

"He was smart enough to move back to Hawaii. He was only in the North Country because of my job."

"Sometime I want as much of your story as you'd like to share," I said. Trying to smile encouragingly.

"Sometime," she said. Her smile was a little crooked. Maybe it's too soon.

We did manage to time food shopping before the storm, so we have stuff to eat. And the network is almost like being there, so we've taken turns using the big screen on the desktop computer, mostly using laptops. The cat seems to have figured out she's a pushover, so he climbs into her lap and stretches out purring between computer and girl. Under the wrists, unlike another cat I knew who wanted to sack out on top of your wrists while you typed.

It seems to have stopped snowing, and the blue and white stuff on the map between here and there has mostly gone. Back in an hour or two...

We managed to get astonishingly wet, but it was fun having help. I was standing in the kerf I had shoveled out, resting, shovel in hand, when JJ came along. To admire my work, I thought.

"I know I shouldn't," she said, "but..." and I was on my back in snow over my head, while lying down at least. She swiped my shovel and went back to working on the driveway.

My coat was full of snow anyway, so I took it off and used it for a scoop, dumping it over her head. There was much shrieking and laughing and cussing in at least three languages.

The driveway is only 80% shoveled.

"It was almost 90," JJ points out. "But sooomebody had to dump snow back in where I had shoveled it out."

"And somebody is all soggy," I said. The broom was (of course) nowhere near the back door, so little bits of snow are now melting on the kitchen floor, and soaking through our socks when we step in them.

But it's nice and warm in the house. The snow is mostly out of the way; we're more or less ready for tomorrow. We dumped jeans into the dryer, to replace the towels it was warming for us. They might be done by bedtime.

And I only got a little teary a couple of times, remembering winters past when it was Rachael's car I was digging out, and Rachael who remembered about putting the broom by the door. And Rachael who knew where all the best weather forecasts could be found on the net.

JJ knows all that stuff, too, and even has them weighted for reliability. She also is dreaming up ways to calibrate the bathroom scale, which she resolutely refuses to believe. She's a physicist, all right.

Anyway. Somebody wants to snuggle. What a wonderful thing.

til next time I write a letter I won't send...

love,
    Ravyn

CHAPTER SIXTEEN

Civilized Party

Dear Renee,

...or should I call you Diary, since I'm not ever sending you this stuff.

Clever rhetorical question without the question mark, don't you think?

Anyway. So yeah, moping around was kind of impacting my work. I do manage to get myself together and in the office, every day, without much thinking about it. It's when I stop to think that it's hard. Which route to take. I used to have a kind of intuitive feeling for the traffic based on... subtleties. I knew something was up when they had a bridge close on the highway, even though we don't go that way. Now? Just get in the car, Ravyn, and drive. Traffic is what it is. Refill the car when it gets empty, listen for expensive sounding noises that are not part of the sound track coming from the tunes.

As you know, we used to be fascinated by the grand sweep of what you can only see not sweeping when you open the hood. Listen to the beats of the engine or whatever. I had a mechanic tell me he put a stethoscope on a wheel bearing once, after I'd told them it was clicking between 15 and 20 mph. Nada. I can't do that when I'm driving, of course.

Although... that chick JJ I was writing you about? She's if anything even more into the auto mechanics school of physics. She set up a thermistor on the internet in her apartment, so she could bill the landlord (well, withhold rent) for the proper number of days without having to be there, freezing, to testify. Maybe she could come up with a contact microphone for the wheel bearing.

And speaking of JJ, even though it's no longer the coldest week in living memory, she still seems to prefer hanging out at my house to her own apartment. I'm not sure I'd admit this in public, but that suits me just fine. She also helps with the finding motivation for getting out of bed and to the office in the morning.

"We should have a party or something," JJ said one day over lunch. That girl is so organized in the morning she manages to put food into the bag for us to eat. And then she comes and finds me and makes me eat it.

"Or something," seemed to be the thing to say. So we invited both of our research groups, post-docs, grad students, and so forth. I reached out to some of the university lesbian community who had known me as part of the R&R couple. I don't think any of them came. But Andrea did. She brought Ben, her boything, lover, whatever. So mostly it was the Atomic and Molecular lab folks, plus a few x-ray spectroscopists. We bought a whole lotta liquor, a fridge full of beer ("At least you don't have a lot of food that'll be in the way," JJ said). Wedges of cheese, eight different kinds of crackers.

People seemed to enjoy it. I spent too much of my time bringing stuff out from the kitchen and trying to get people to eat it.

Oh, and cake. I think JJ said it was her birthday. I guess I should remember these things.

It was great having some life around here, other than a bitey cat in my lap in the recliner, waiting for bedtime.

Oh, and the reason for having a party just then. JJ had a paper coming out in a journal that cares more for flashy than correct, and so had embargoes on everything until... midnight, as it happens.

"Your attention, please," I said, clanking cheese knife against wine glass. "No physics department party would be complete without physics. As it happens, Professor Jong has a paper coming out in That Other Journal that's been embargoed until... tomorrow."

"JayJay," said JJ. "And I can hardly believe they'll finally let me talk about it. It's so silly, really."

And so the grad students counted down the seconds, looking over JJ's shoulder at the desktop computer. At zero, she pressed the 'submit' button to the online archive where everybody actually goes to read things nowadays. There was a smattering of applause, and various people not in her immediate field tried to read the title aloud. Which is complicated by all the symbols, identifying quantum states in her favorite molecule.

"A molecule is just an atom with too many nuclei," escaped my lips at some point. JJ laughed and went back to sketching out the novelty of her paper.

"I like atoms with just two electrons left," said Andrea.

"One is even simpler," I said.

"It's a solved problem," she said.

"Unlike keeping the cheese tray supplied," I said, excusing myself.

JJ thought of everything, and got the cat some catnip toys, and shut him in the bedroom we weren't using for coat storage. At some point in the evening, I saw him zoom down the stairs and out the cat door. He'll be back, I'm sure, when he runs out of easily caught mice in his neighborhood. Because it is, you know, his neighborhood.

And sure enough, he was right there waiting when we fed him after everybody left.

"Did we have fun?" I asked JJ. We had poured each other into bed without bothering with much picking up.

"Is that a royal we, or an editorial one?" JJ asked. "This wee one enjoyed herself."

"We were amused," I said. I think I said that. I was a little distracted.

Anyway. It was a pretty civilized party. It's fun seeing the people we work with having a good time together.

til next time,
  love always,
  Ravyn

CHAPTER SEVENTEEN

Interesting Shade of Purple

I walked down the hall and around and into that other hallway, found JJ's office door, which was open, and leaned against the door jamb with our lunch bag dangling from my elbow until she looked up from whatever she was doing.

"Eep," she squeaked. "How long have you been there? I could at least have stopped humming to myself..."

"Squeet," I said.

"What?"

"Let's. Go. Eat. Squeet."

"Ah. Um, sure. Bathroom first?"

Down the hall, the other side of which has windows into the second story of the high-bay lab. "They're using the overhead crane," I said, just to have something to say.

"There are geekboys down there, looking up at us," said JJ.

"Yes," I said. One of those situations that doesn't require words. All the things that occurred to me to say were wrong in one way or another. "Bathroom," I reminded her.

"Right."

"Which way?" she asked, as she emerged.

"The Botany department garden is nice," I said. It's right next door to the physics department; I think their actual labs and stuff are in the building just up the hill. The one with the greenhouse, duh. They have nice plantings with grassy paths in between and a few benches, and they don't seem to mind if people come there to sit.

JJ packed our lunch, so I let her unzip the bag (it was swag from some conference and had their logo on the side, slowly rubbing off) and dispense my sandwich and a bag of chips. "Did you put in pickles?"

"Are you having cravings?" JJ asked, without skipping a beat.

This called for folding my nice linen napkin and bopping her in the nose with it.

"Girls, girls, no fighting," said Andi, who was standing opposite our bench shading her eyes.

"Are you the policeman?" JJ asked.

"Somehow everything you say today sounds obscene," I said.

"I notice you're eating out of the same lunch bag," said Andi. "And, wait, what? How's being a policeman obs... oh, I get it." And she blushed.

"Interesting shade of purple," said JJ, as if she were commenting on the weather.

"Join us?" I said, scooting over to make room.

"I did bring my lunch," said Andi, holding it up as evidence.

"Allrighty then," said JJ.

"Who waters all this?" Andi asked, trying desperately to change the subject.

"Botanists," said JJ.

"Have you ever actually known a botanist?" Andi asked.

"Well...," said JJ.

"Never mind," said Andi, quickly.

"All it takes is an hour and a five-gallon bucket," I said.

They both turned to look at me. "There's a story there," said JJ.

"I overheard that once, and it's been waiting to drop into a conversation ever since."

"Yeah, hard to imagine what the story is," said Andi. "And you guys have been stretching my imagination in directions it usually doesn't go."

"See?" said JJ. "I'm not the only one with suggestive language today."

And Andi blushed again.

"Nearly the same shade of purple, I think," my lips said. "Sorry," I said to Andi.

"I don't know why I hang out with you guys," said Andi.

"It's either us or the men," I said.

"Or a botanist," said JJ, faking a full-body shudder.

"I kinda like my guy," said Andi.

"Kinda..." I echoed, in case she wanted to elaborate.

"Back to work, I guess," said Andi, gathering up her stuff.

I put my packaging back in JJ's lunchbag. "Dance with the one that..." I murmured.

"See ya," said Andi, and she left quickly.

"Methinks the Lady doth protest too much," said JJ.

"She does have a way of bringing Ben into the conversation whenever it strays a little," I said.

"Would anybody blush that purple if she wasn't..."

"If she didn't..."

"...wanna dance with someone new?" said JJ.

"Dunno," I said. With a shrug and a hair-toss.

JJ grinned. "Hold that thought," she said. "It's time for work again."

"What thought?" I asked. It was an innocent question when it started. I think. If one were the blushy type, one would be turning colors as the echoes rattled around in one's head. "Dammit, JJ."

"Dammit, Ravyn. I got stuff to do this afternoon."

"Yeah, me too."

"Gimme that," she said, grabbing the lunch bag. She stomped quietly off toward her office.

CHAPTER EIGHTEEN

Paying Rent

It was like the third time that week that JJ and I had dinner together in my dining room.

"So, um," she said.

"I was about to say the same thing," I said.

"You'll have noticed it's not exactly the deeps of winter any more," said JJ. "And my landlord fixed the heat a month ago. I kinda wore out that excuse for bumming a bedroom."

"And yet, here you are. I'm glad you're here," I said. "It's so... empty, this house with just me in it."

"I'm happy we could sit together. Being alone together is better," she said.

"Alone together..." I echoed, smiling.

"You know what I mean, even if I misused the actual words."

"Yeah," I said. "Even though things really should end sometimes, the after part is a pestilence I could do without."

"So say we all," said JJ.

"Tis better to have loved and lost..." I quoted.

"Yeah, bullshit on that," said JJ. And we just had to laugh.

"Now that we're friends again, the landlord wants me to renew my lease," said JJ.

There was an odd sinking feeling in my stomach. "I like having you here," I said.

"And I like being here," said JJ. "What I'm trying to say is, how about if I pay rent and move in and stuff?"

"And stuff..." I said, smiling. It was how Rachael and I used to talk about... Yeah, not going there.

"We can come up with a working document or something, so there are no misunderstandings," said JJ. "Stuff gets weird when money changes hands between friends."

"Is that what we are? Friends?" I asked. We were standing in the front hallway. From here she could either move away from me, retrieve her jacket and go home, or she could move toward me and we could go upstairs.

"I have a recipe for crepes I could try in the morning," I said.

She... smiled. And moved closer.

The crepes were... indifferent. "I wonder if..." said JJ, and made a few suggestions. Beat the eggs before making the batter, for example.

I was more inclined to do a massive internet search and integrate the results.

"A meta-study of the literature," JJ put it.

We walked to the train. Sometimes I drove; I had a pricey parking permit from the college. It was just far enough along in the springtime to have a morning rain shower, and so we huddled as far from the drip as possible at the outdoor platform, instead of walking all the way to the end to wait for the last car out in the weather. Anyway, we got wet.

"I should have left my hair under my coat," I said.

"It's almost as straight as mine when it's wet," said JJ.

"Come find me at lunchtime and I'll show you how not-straight I can be."

"I bet you say that to all the girls," she said, giggling.

"There was this one time, before we moved in together, that I was going over to visit Rachael at the house she shared with like 4 other people. And of course I got rained on, and it was summer and it was hot and I dressed as lightly as possible and so it soaked through... Did I mention some of her housemates were guys?"

"JJ, you're grinning," I said. "Not so very unlike Tiny when he let me in and handed me a towel. I think he was hoping I'd disrobe before dripping on the floor, but I declined."

"I'm sure Rachael loved having you drip all over her little room."

"It was right next to the laundry room, so she put my wet stuff in the dryer," I said.

"And we're going to work, again, while you tell me racy stories, again," said JJ. "I was kinda doing okay, being a good girl. Well, except it was kind of abusive, I guess, if only because he's so much bigger than I am, and didn't seem to have a gentle side. So I kicked the bum out. And you came in like a..."

"Like somebody with a house whose heating works in the winter," I said, smiling.

"So literal. Like a fire-breathing dragon or something. It's enough to melt a frozen heart."

"Or burn the house down. I guess I've tried that experiment too," I said. "Maybe the dragon can live peaceably in the basement or something."

"You are full of metaphors today," said JJ. "I'm impressed."

"And you're laughing at me." Which she was. She laughs a lot, and it's contagious. I like somebody who makes me laugh. Rachael was so serious there toward the end. And then I was so, so sad, after the end.

"So when's your lease up?" I asked.

"End of the month."

"What day is it now?"

"Twentieth," said JJ.

"Ten days to... like..."

"Move and clean everything and change addresses. Ravyn?"

"JJ?" I asked.

"Is this too soon, moving in together, do you think?" She was biting her lip, looking at me.

"In my house there are many... bedrooms," I misquoted. "We can work something out. But I hear what you're asking, and we should pay attention to it."

CHAPTER NINETEEN

Second Thoughts

I don't remember second thoughts when I moved in with Rachael. I mean, sure, we fretted making the decision, but once we did that, I think we were both excited more than apprehensive.

You sleep with a girl a number of times, you think you know most of her quirks. You're wrong, of course, but we did spend a lot of time together, and ultimately decided it would save us both time in our busy grad school schedules, if we just lived together. Not to mention money, which was also scarce.

Now, though, money is not really a problem. I'm still busy, but not like when I was a grad student. We do all-nighters now and then, but mostly that's because of the equipment needing to be run around the clock til the experiment is done or some problem happens that requires venting it and starting over.

And of course I never actually moved in with Renee. When the family moved once, Dad wanted to know if we'd like separate rooms. We both did the head-tilt of confusion, that "your lips are moving but you're not making sense" gesture, and he dropped it. I think it probably saved a big chunk of money on the new place, needing one less bedroom. We roomed together all our lives, up until we left for college. It was the way of things.

But now, though, there were a few more days of solitude, here in my house alone. Times when I could be naked anywhere I wanted. I could sing or scream or cry or just stare at the ceiling wondering who I am, without making excuses to anyone. Eat junk food in front of the television. I could pick up the clerk at the drugstore if I felt like it. That never actually happened. Gay bars, sure, now and then. Oh, and I could sleep with my ex if I felt like it.

There was the time I got a message from Rachael, and I met her at the vet. Bo had taken a turn for the worse, and it was his time to go. We skritched his ears, rubbed his belly, carefully avoiding the sore parts, and wept. Together. We loved that dog, and he loved us. I offered Rachael space next to the other critters, behind the bush in the yard. She said she'd think about it; it would take a week to get his ashes. It was hard, letting her go, but she still had Gus to feed, so she left. I… needed her to stay.

There was no guessing how JJ might feel about any of that. We exchanged a lot of words about giving each other total permission to have different lives, comma, but. But should I believe she actually meant it? It's easy enough to say the words, and even to mean what you say, but somehow there are always second thoughts and somewhat hard feelings later when the other person does something a little off.

And in the wee hours of staring up at the ceiling it occurred to me that I've developed a habit of being unhappy, alone, and bitter about it. Being the lesbian who was categorically excluded from her own life and marriage. I like Rachael, really I do. But I couldn't imagine trying to live the promises we made knowing she needed things I'm unable to give her.

Would I miss the misery? If I painted it over with lusty abandon, would it leak out somewhere else? Not that there's anything wrong with lusty abandon, mind you. It just... has a way of being totally absorbing, for a while, but then it's not.

It was... odd... contemplating moving in with somebody. Past contemplation, just preparing myself for having her around. I mean, odd, because it's not like we were madly in love and couldn't keep our hands off each other.

Well, okay, it's not like we were madly in love. That much is true.

And yet there was this serene kind of a feeling that this is somebody I'd like to see at the breakfast table for the rest of my life. And sleep with her sometimes, sure, when we wanted that. But mostly just the together thing, having each other's backs. Somebody to talk to, smooch occasionally, go shopping with, learn things from (and with). Somebody to wash my hair and massage my back. Somebody who'll appreciate having those things done for her.

Fight with, probably. Because you don't get to where we were: full professors, women in a man's world, without being feisty and opinionated and able to make stuff happen, each with ideas of her very own.

Like Rachael and me. Yes, I know that JJ is not Rachael, and Rachael is not JJ. I'm sure JJ and I will have very different kinds of frictions between us (oh myyyyy), based in part on just how similar our professional lives are. Sometimes her lab and mine are actually running at vacuum at the same time, and I run into her in the bathroom at 3 in the morning. Rachael also did all-nighters sometimes, but usually it was grading, or writing a paper for a conference, or something. Not, you know, actual work. Which didn't win me points when I put it that way.

CHAPTER TWENTY

The Calm Before

Dear Renee,

We have to stop meeting like this. It's not meeting if I never send any of these letters to you, right?

So, right. The thing this week is that my colleague and fellow third of the female faculty of the physics department, JJ Jong, is moving in. To my house. She, uh, stays here sometimes anyway, starting last winter when her heat was out. That's our excuse and we're sticking to it. And I have lots of room now that Rachael's gone, and JJ has a very small expensive apartment near the U. Besides, having a different woman living here will boggle the little straight whitebread suburban wives' club. Not that I actually meet up with them that often, since I'm not walking a dog any more. Come inside; it's warm, there's room for you, where you can spread out your stuff. The place is very empty once Rachael's stuff is gone.

It was... different, with Rachael. I don't remember any dread; just being super in love with her and the nesting hormones banging their drum and sure why not and how long do we have to wait.

Or with you. Not that we consciously moved in together; we grew up in the same room, in the same closet, practically in each others' clothes. I remember being so confused when Dad offered us separate bedrooms once when we were moving. We looked at each other and did the same head-tilt the dog would do when he didn't understand what was going on. Dad laughed and shrugged and we got to continue living together.

These last couple nights alone, though... This is a considered, mostly rational, decision of two adult women who are old enough to know better. I'm not sure what you do exactly, but if it's anything like me, now and then there's an intense, round the clock, operation. For us, after you pump the system down, the experiment should just run until the vacuum system fails or you're sure you have enough data.

So I was laughing when I answered the 2am phone call from my peeps. What's JJ gonna think if I have to climb over her in the night to get to a ringing phone? Oh, right, for public consumption (Do you count as public?), we're sleeping in separate bedrooms. As it happens, in this case, once I woke up enough to understand the question, the matter was easily set right. But then of course I couldn't sleep.

Anyway, we've been rounding up help with the heavy lifting. Most physics people are pencil-neck geeks, not much stronger than the little people (that'd be us). But some of them compensate by owning big trucks. Andrea's, uh, toy? Ben is such a guy. So we invited them along, and some post-docs and a few of the larger grad students. These are the guys you want around when you have to pull the head off the vacuum chamber. There's an overhead crane, but it really helps to have some muscle handy.

So Andi, as she insists we call her (you remember Andy? Yeah, I thought so. I think of him every time she says that) is blonde, and uses it for an excuse so often that I wouldn't be at all surprised to find bleach-stained towels at her place. I guess some people are naturally blonde, but we wouldn't know about that, who came from the 90% of the world where people have pigments all their own. Her eyes are green, for whatever that's worth.

They're coming this weekend. I should get some pizzas and some beer. Says Ravyn, chuckling over a bottle of chocolate stout with peanut butter. According to the label. I can hear Rachael going "EEUW NOOO GET IT AWAY FROM ME" in my head. I'm intrigued, and no longer need to be governed by the ex-wife's tastes. It's... interesting. With the raised eyebrows that we used to signal Mom that whatever she had put before us was disgusting.

JJ's place was not large enough for me to help, and besides, she's the living index to all her stuff, so she spent several days alone, throwing things out. And packing printer paper box after wine box with academic books. And figuring out how to take the futon frame apart so it'd fit through the door.

Thus rejected, I spent my time going through some of my own useless tripe, discarding it to make room. Not that we needed the room, really, and besides Rachael had gone through everything a year or two ago and separated it into hers and hers and ours piles. And then put mine and part of ours back on the shelves.

It was murder, trying to cook. "Oh, the perfect tool for this job is... and I have one that was last seen in this cupboard..." Guess I'll have to ask Rachael if she took that. If I should happen, you know, to run into her in the coffee shop or someplace when I'm feeling really lonely and it's either talk to her or just go home alone and cry. There was... rather more time for conversation than you might be imagining. Shall we say.

Anyway. It's exciting, in a mildly terrifying kind of a way. A new live-in companion. Somebody new to learn how to avoid annoying. To learn her pleasures and dislikes. And to teach her my own. I probably should have been more assertive when Rachael and I moved in together about stuff like that.

So. I'll let you go. Get back to... culling my memories. I promised myself I wouldn't cry over every little thing and the memories it triggers. I'm not keeping that promise.

love always,
    or at least as long as
    there's only imaginary contact,

Ravyn

CHAPTER TWENTY-ONE

Unpacking in Suburbia

And so she moved in. Everything went according to her carefully made plans on moving day, and she insisted the place was too small for me to help with the after-cleaning, so I popped in as she was finishing and took her out for a beer. And my default fast food place, which was Chinese.

There's a little row of store-fronts near the train station. One was empty for a year or so when Rachael was a fixture in my household. Eventually a hand-written sign appeared in the window: "Chinese food come soon," it said. That was our name for the place ever after.

It occurred to me while I was busily regretting the hot egg roll I had bitten into that taking an Asian woman to a Chinese restaurant (not in Chinatown) might be problematic. There's just so much you don't know about somebody new, even if you've hung out together for a while.

"What's that?" I asked, gesturing with poorly-held chopsticks at her food. "Chickens with some kind of glaze?"

"Duckses," said JJ. "Since we need plurals, apparently."

And we laughed. And I told her about word play with a linguist, which is what Rachael was, and that it was like bringing a knife to a gunfight.

"Smooth," she said. "And I'm sorry, but I just can't eat this."

"We'll take it home. I'll eat it for lunch or something."

"Maybe some hot sauce would help," said JJ. She examined all the condiment bottles on the table and found some hot mustard. "Usually for egg rolls," she said, waving a hand at what was left of mine.

So I traded our plates. She ate my egg rolls and stuff with hot mustard. I ate her glazed duckses. I thought it was pretty tasty, but I didn't tell her that.

"Well, the mustard is hot enough to curl your hair," she said.

We looked at each others' hair for maybe twenty seconds: Mine massively curly, hers utterly straight. And then we laughed together and whatever it was we were worried about was gone, like the afterburn from wasabi.

"I'm sorry you don't like their food," I said.

"I'm sure there are other places we can go," said JJ.

One of the first things she set up when moving her kitchen stuff into my space was her rice maker. It seemed there was a bottomless container of leftover rice in the fridge. Left to her own devices, I think she'd eat it for every meal, with this and that depending on the time of day.

"What do JJs eat?" I asked once. And then we had to try to remember the "Wonderful thing about Tiggers" jingle, which doesn't even occur in the Milne book. It's a Disney add-on.

"I dunno... food?" JJ said, when we returned to the topic. "How about you?"

"Food is good," I ventured. "Rachael was the creative one in the kitchen. After she moved out, I spent a month eating everything in the freezer. There's a bag of frozen Vindaloo sauce left; no idea what to do with it."

"Ooooo," said JJ. "What else is in there?"

"A couple chunks of pineapple... one more piece of that chicken I bought at the store already cooked... Celery. A dried out ginger root."

"Onion?"

"Of course. Not in the fridge," I said, showing her which cupboard I had moved the room-temperature veggies to after the cat started counter-surfing.

"This will do, I think," she said. "Now for tools..."

"I have... some stuff? Some of what I think I have is in Rachael's apartment now."

"And I have some stuff... in a box here someplace," said JJ. "We'll be creative."

I felt a little violated, having her rummaging through the drawers and cupboards in my kitchen, muttering and cackling with glee. "And what's this?" she said, pulling that... thing... out of the back of the Et Cetera drawer.

"Finger slicer," I said. "I have the scars to prove it. I told Rachael to take it with her."

"It needs a bath before we can use it," said JJ. "Aaaand a chisel and mallet," she said, exhibiting them as if I would not believe her without evidence.

"Splits frozen food," I said.

"I imagine it would. Now stuff to put in the sauce..."

"There's this," I said, offering her a big plastic jar that had come to us with rice in it, but was now a third full of dried red peppers Rachael had grown in the garden five years ago.

"Mortar and pestle? No? Food processor? Score!"

"And a respirator," I said, eyes streaming, trying not to cough convulsively into the food. "Which I do not have."

"Wash your hands. I'll get a tissue and dry your eyes," said JJ, food preparation forgotten for the moment. "Yeah, that stuff's wicked when you inhale it."

"Thai funny peppers in my snuff," I said.

"Corn starch?" JJ asked.

"I do have some tapioca..." I offered.

"I, uh, huh," said JJ. "How can you run a kitchen without corn starch?"

"I'm impressed," I said to her back as she whipped the sauce together out of this and that, stir-fried everything with a spatula in one hand and a wooden spoon in the other, and dispensed it into bowls. "I had no idea..."

"Given the stuff in your kitchen, it seemed obvious enough..." JJ suggested.

"I'm reading that look on your face as *What kind of an alien are you?*" I said.

And she laughed. "Yes, exactly. This is very strange for both of us, isn't it?" said JJ. "And the rice isn't sticky enough to be chop stickable." She waved her chop sticks around, and traded them for a spoon. "And if my mother ever saw this, I'd deny having anything to do with cooking it."

CHAPTER TWENTY-TWO

May I Wear Your...

Dear Renee,

Again with the write but no send letter. I guess imagining I'm explaining stuff to you helps me put it together or something. Imaginary friends are a poor substitute for the real thing, but, I hope, I'm working on fixing that.

If not a friend, at least of the Best Friend Forever type, at least a roommate. Well, a housemate, certainly. Whether to share a room... You... haven't seen my house, of course; you haven't seen me since I came of real-estate age. There are easily 3 bedrooms on the second floor, two more in the attic, and another on the second floor that would do in a pinch.

And it's not winter. When JJ first came around, it was at least partly because her apartment was cold. And somehow we didn't have enough winter blankets for two beds, so.

You remember a book they gave us when we were kids, about marriage, called *Bed and Board?* We negotiated the board part of it, by the simple expedient of letting her cook the first dinner together using my kitchen stuff, since all of hers was in boxes stacked in the corner. There was only a little bit of muttered *Noooo don't use that thing for this* kinds of stuff.

And she claimed to be tired after moving stuff all day and collapsed into the bed in her room that first night, thus putting off the dread negotiation.

I got up first, wrestled my hair for order, having still not figured out that sleeping alone means I can put it up at night and be spared the disaster in the morning. We needed coffee, so I made some, with a couple extra cups in case JJ is a coffee person. Which she is, so there's that in common. I put out an assortment of what seem to me to be morning foods, plus a few other things... her cooked rice container; a bottle of ketchup; the Rooster sauce.

"Mmmkaaay?" she said, helping herself to granola and milk. "I mean, if you like..."

"Actually granola is fine," I said. "Some of that was intended as a joke; part of it was a *What do JJs eat?* question."

"I grew up in, like, California," she reminded me. "Or whatever," she added, in her best imitation of an undergraduate.

I laughed.

"Oh good, I was hoping you would laugh," she said. "While I have you in a good mood, is it okay if I borrow some of your clothes? We're pretty much the same size..."

"Anything in particular?"

"The little blue dress?" she suggested. "It looks great on you. I have a meeting today where appearances might be important. Most of mine are a little rumpled from being in boxes and stuff."

"Sure," I said, shrugging. "If I'm not actually in it..."

"OoooOOoooo," said JJ. "Now there's an invitation."

I... smiled. And then we got ready for work. I packed us a lunch for two people in one bag. I used to do that for Rachael sometimes, but it stopped working when she started eating out more often. I swear, you pay that girl, she spends it. Anyway, we had leftovers from JJ's stir-fry. It was just hot enough without curling my hair any more than it is already.

"How was the meeting?" I asked. We had spread out the food on the table in the little conference room off my lab.

"It was good." There was some silence as she ate. "Silly committee with a bunch of humanities people. I thought I should let them know that some physics people are under five feet five, have high voices, long hair, and legs."

"I like what you do to that dress," I said. "Or is that sexual harassment?"

"Only if it's repeated and unwelcome. I know you mean it."

"We can continue that conversation tonight, Little Miss Physics. There's one more hour before my lecture, and I mustn't get too distracted."

"Only a little bit distracted?" JJ asked. She put a hand flat on her lap, fingertips at the hem. It was not possible to ignore the twitchiness of those fingers.

"Don't you have work to do?" I asked.

"Yeah, I guess," said JJ. "Funny how one hour's meeting kinda dominated my to-do list today. I forget what else I wanted to do."

"You could get a wet paper towel and wipe down the table," I suggested.

"You just want to see me leaning over in this dress," she said, laughing. But she did it. And then she politely excused herself so I could write my lecture.

Oh. I guess I should sign off if this is a letter.

Love always,
   (yeah right)
   Ravyn

CHAPTER TWENTY-THREE

Friday Jollying

"Hey," said JJ one day, not that long after she moved in.

"What's up?" I asked.

"You remember Christy." said JJ.

"Of course," I said. She was the barista JJ picked up while I watched.

"So I... have a therapist," she said.

"I think sometimes I should have snagged one when I was crying over Rachael," I admitted.

"She's pretty good. Anyway, I mentioned moving in," said JJ. "And I was talking about a long-ago ex, a Hawaiian girl I met when I was in grad school. There's this thing I noticed about bi people, like us." She paused. "Actually she, the therapist, said *lesbians* and I protested that my last... partner... was a guy. There's this kind of an urge to merge or something. She had a fancy word for it, but I thought it was astonishing that I had noticed it in Hawaii all those years ago."

I um-hmmed to encourage her to continue. This was heady stuff.

"I don't want you getting upset," said JJ, "and I told you I'm not very monogamous."

"You did, yeah," I said. "And I said the same, though perhaps we meant it in different ways. My eye certainly finds women interesting from time to time."

"I guess I need us to have an agreement or something, that it really is okay to have other people around sometimes," said JJ. "Without, like, getting sand in our undies or whatever."

"Sand," I repeated. "So what you're saying is wear my nightgown when you have somebody over." We laughed together.

"I dunno what I'm saying," said JJ. "I'm still figuring it out. But maybe having somebody else now and then helps avoid the merging thing?"

"Maybe so," I said.

~

Friday. There's this colloquium at 4 on Friday afternoons. The physics department claim it's a great way to unwind, but if the speaker happens to be in your field, you then have to take him (it's almost always a him) out to dinner, spend an evening at a buffet, aware of him looking down your neck, wondering if he even has a conscience. That's not part of the training to be a physics professor, so probably not. Cynical? Me? Some of them do have cool ideas, so there's that.

We sat in the second row in our usual spot, short legs crossed right over left. The tall long-legged colleagues stretched out in the front row. The talk was about some kind of medical imaging, not our subfield, so none of us had to see him any further.

"You look upset," said JJ to Andrea, who had carefully not been looking at Ben a few seats over and a row ahead of us.

Andrea nodded.

"Can we buy you a beer?" I asked.

Andrea nodded again.

It was getting on towards the end of the spring term. There's a nice quiet little spot at the other end of the campus that seems to like the color of our money; JJ and I go there from time to time to unwind. It seemed a perfect place for the next installment of the departmental girls' night out.

Briefcases in the corner of the booth, something fried; fish or crab cakes or something like that. It's easy to overlook the menu when a friend is in distress.

And she was. She didn't say much about Ben but from her previous tales one began to suspect that he was not nearly as nice at home as he is in, say, faculty meetings. I'd heard from the grad student grape vine that his students were writing a users' manual, to pass on their strategies for managing his moods and surviving his oversight.

"You wanna talk about it?" I asked.

The answer seemed to be maybe. Or yes and no. Or yes, but if I do I'll cry in my beer. There was a stream of consciousness there someplace, and we refilled her beer at least once.

It was about trying (she really had) but becoming convinced that he wasn't the one. And then there was us, dropped into her proverbial lap. Perhaps the lapsed lesbian could renew her membership in the club or whatever it is?

"Or whatever it is," said JJ, smiling.

There was a pinball machine in the corner, and Andrea said she was much better at it when lubricated, which she was by this time of the evening. And she was right. There's a mindless kind of a groove to get into, or something. Except this one reminded her of being out with Ben, and after more streams of consciousness, she broke down sobbing. She went out into the alley where the smokers go, not because she smoked but because she needed the cool air and the feel of her feet crunching on the gravel.

When we returned to the bar, JJ bought herself and Andrea one more round. I stopped because I was the driver. JJ and I exchanged a long searching gaze. Head tilt, might mean, hey, you okay with putting her up tonight? Twitch of the corner of my mouth might mean sure, whatever you need.

"You," JJ announced, "are totally coming home with us."

"I... totally," said Andrea.

Apparently that was that. We'd been kind of out there, letting her know we were here, were queer, and letting her get used to it, a little at a time, for months of girls' nights out. And she was getting more and more frustrated with her guy. Maybe that's all it takes.

That, and some Irish coffee, which is what the nightcap round turned out to be. That stuff is wicked if you depend on the lightness of your head to know when to stop.

By the time we got home, she was crying on JJ's shirt. And then on mine, while JJ checked to make sure we had the beds put together. I gave her a big glass of water to drink, showed her the bathroom, pointed out the night light, and the water hazard that doubles as a drinking bowl for the cat. Who, I told her, would probably be curious about her in the night.

"I hope you're not allergic," I said.

She shook her head no, begged a box of tissues, and blew the tears and snot out of her sinuses. "All better," she said, with a firm nod.

We took her upstairs. "We're just going to borrow..." JJ was saying, as she tugged at the tie of Andrea's skirt. They went into the room where JJ and I had been sleeping since she moved in. I got The Look from JJ over Andrea's shoulder, so I retired to the other room, which was JJ's, kinda sorta. I knew how this worked; if you need comfort, JJ is the person to turn to. She's not possessive, unless someone she cares about is hurting. Maybe she's the emotional, touchy-feely part of the "we're here if you need us" thing. I seem to be the landlady.

The bed is mine, but the girl in the bed is JJ. Should the guest be requiring someone to hold her. If I was a little jealous, I was also generous, and Andrea needed JJ's attentions much more than I did that night.

And I woke several times in the night, worrying. If Ben was as awful as Andrea said, he might be kind of nasty if she moved out. Or even if she poured out her woes into sympathetic ears. I hear tell people like that isolate their victims.

But he didn't storm the house in the night, or the next day, or the next. Andrea and JJ were spooned together, sleeping soundly, when I got up. So I went and made coffee and filled the thermos. I started the first load of Saturday laundry, tiptoeing quietly into their room to retrieve the basket. I ran backups on the computers.

And at last they crept down the stairs. Holding hands. It was cute.

"Coffee," said Andrea, and that was the only word we got out of her for some time. I poured her a mug. She ignored the milk and sugar I offered, folded herself into kitchen chair in a way that wasn't compatible with the little robe JJ had given her, mug on knees under her nose, and stared at nothing, waiting for the caffeine to wake her up.

I got out the bottle of Irish whiskey and some whipped cream we had made because it's rhubarb season in Rachael's legacy garden. I gestured toward JJ's cup. She laughed.

"Save your whiskey," she said. "There's really no need to be jealous. It's not like there's a limited resource to compete for."

"Girl has a point," I said. "How am I going to remember you had a point?" I wasn't even thinking of being jealous, not just then, and here JJ had gone and smoothed my feelings over with a casual, if profound, comment.

Andi stirred, and put one foot down out of her chair.

JJ stood me up and kissed me, right in front of Andrea. "I think our friend might need some... further attention," she said, turning so we both faced Andi. "I'm going to the store. You want anything?"

"Coffee," said Andrea, again.

We laughed, all three of us. JJ collected the grocery list and the shopping bags and let herself out. I collected the girl and took her upstairs.

"That robe..." I said, taking her out of it.

"I know, right?" said Andrea. She tugged upwards on my shirt, so I slid out of it, tossing hair everywhere.

We... looked at each other from as close as we could focus our eyes. "Except for JJ, I haven't slept with a colleague since grad school," I said.

"Except for JJ... and Ben," said Andrea. "Is it okay if I'm bi?"

"Here you can be anything you are," I said. "Especially if I'm in one of your preferred demographics."

"Also, OhMyGod," said Andrea. "I'd forgotten what it can be like with a woman."

"Totally," I said.

"If we're, ahem, an item, you hafta call me Andi," said Andrea.

"Andi," I managed to say, carefully not thinking too much about a guy named Andy from my misspent youth.

"Are we gonna talk, or fuck?" said Andi. "Pardon my French."

"You want French, I'll show you French," I said, kissing her. She squealed when I pushed my tongue into her mouth.

* * *

We rolled over to see JJ standing in the doorway, leaning with her arms crossed under her boobs, grinning at us. "Your undies are wet," I said. "Shorts, too."

"Sooooo gooood," Andi was cooing.

"Yeah, well, I see you've thrilled our colleague," said JJ.

"We could... um..." I said, with a gesture that got the rest of my obscene thought across.

"I'm all sweaty and gross and disgusting," said Andi.

"We can fix that," said JJ, grinning. "We're a full-service outfit."

"Servicing the target," said my stream of consciousness.

"Come with me," said JJ, looking at me with side eyes.

"I'm, uh, naked," said Andi as JJ led her down the stairs toward the bathroom.

"Ain't nobody here but us girls," said JJ.

I let myself in to the bathroom while they were in the shower, stole JJ's wet clothes, and put them in the next load of laundry.

And then it occurred to me, Wicked Wench of the West though I may be, that my two showergirls might be interested in more civilized interaction, so I picked out a selection of things about Andi's size that don't require an exact fit, plus some shorts and a t-shirt of JJ's that were like the ones she'd been wearing. Some folks are squeamish about borrowing undies, so I decided to let Andi weigh in on that subject instead of choosing for her.

In due course they emerged, wearing what I'd given them, laughing about, as it turns out, who got the one pair of underwear. I guess she's not squeamish. JJ went upstairs, wet hair in a towel, to fetch another pair.

I made coffee.

"I... uh... dunno what to say," said Andi.

"You don't have to talk about it," I said.

"I kinda do, I think," said Andi. "And it's tricky because sex seems to come from some primal part of me that's preverbal. Non-verbal. Something."

JJ nodded. "Yeah. Hafta talk about it, can't talk about it. There are no words."

"So Ben likes holding hands in public. I thought it was romantic, but now... I dunno, it's about possession or something. He knows I kinda like it rough, but it goes too far. It's nice enough, I guess, when he can be bothered to remember to play with it. And sometimes he hits all my buttons and, like, wow, or whatever."

Silence, while we sipped coffee.

"I think I hadn't ever seriously considered sleeping with you guys--girls--until you asked," said Andi. "And this is a time for wishing I had hair like yours, to hide behind."

I was, in fact, not looking at her, through a curtain of curls.

"I forgot what it's like, making love with somebody who cares, who knows how things work, where your buttons are hidden, and can figure out what to do by watching your reactions.

JJ was smiling. Serenely.

"And then there's more," she said, pushing a hand across the table to take mine. Apparently she's right handed, so her thumb wanted to be on top, which is what my left hand wanted. Rachael... was not.

"And more," said Andi, reaching across the table to take JJ's other hand. "You guys really are a full-service household. A girl could get used to this."

"Even though..." I started, but got ambushed by a blush before I could describe the moment of confusion when she groped for her guy only to find it was me. I mean, I remember? From the dark ages? After the guy eats you out, you kinda guide him in. I guess Andi does that with Ben, and... Well... I'm not Ben. And the toybox was under the bed, out of reach.

So much for spontaneity. Gee, I wonder if that word has anything to do with the Latin *Sponsa*, spouse. That's the kind of thing Rachael and I would talk about after...

Dammit, Rachael wasn't even there, and she was still in my head.

"Even though," Andi was saying when all that had flitted through my head. "Maybe especially because."

"You gonna tell me what you're talking about?" JJ asked, grinning.

"There's this thing..." said Andi.

"Where he eats you out and..." I said.

"You drag him up by the ears to..." said Andi.

"Uh, fuck," JJ filled in, when there was a pause.

"And you grope for his... uh..." I said.

"Only to remember that your lover is Ravyn and not Ben," said Andi.

JJ's head snapped back and forth watching this. She laughed. "Uh, yeah, I remember. His name was Benny, but yeah, all that."

"Apparently you eat like a guy," said JJ to me.

"I hope that's a good thing?" I said.

"Everybody's different," said JJ. "That's a good thing."

"Lesbian heterosexuality," I said, grinning. It's a Rachael kind of a thing to say. Rachael is still not here at the table. Neither are Ben or Benny, or any of the rest of our exes.

"We have toys like that if it's important to you," I added. Something that, in principle, Andi knew, having browsed in our toybox, but it's rather overwhelming in its diversity. Especially if you're in the moment.

Andi was not to be drawn on the subject. "I mean, I don't, like, sleep with random people," she said.

"We're not random," said JJ. "I am an Officially Certified Quantum Mechanic, and so are both of you, and we know a thing or two about randomness."

"My quantum is busted. You wanna have a look at it?" That seemed to be the thing to say, since she'd claimed to be a mechanic.

"I'm more than happy to look at anything you want to show me," said JJ, looking at me.

"I bet you say that to all the girls," I said.

So she turned to Andi. "I'm happy to look..." she started, but Andi guffawed in her face.

CHAPTER TWENTY-FOUR

Andi Unstacks

"We should think about dinner," I suggested. "In case something needs to be thawed."

"You wanna cook?" JJ asked Andi.

"Um, sure?" said Andi. "Chip in a little something? Since you've been so kind to me."

"I can hardly wait for more kindness," my mouth said. She's going to get me into trouble someday, that mouth of mine.

"What do you have? Besides the coffee I ordered this morning when you were going to the store, I mean," said Andi.

So we rifled through the pantry and the fridge and the freezer, and found that most of the stuff we had was sized for two portions, since, after all, there were two of us actually living here.

"Hmm... Risotto," said Andi.

"I never knew what Rachael intended to do with that," I said.

""Chicken broth? And a chicken breast? Yeah, start that thawing. Or I can do something else if it brings back memories," said Andi.

"Everything brings back memories," I said. "Maybe I shoulda moved, too."

I got a group hug that evolved into a light group grope and some tickling.

"It's hard to mope and laugh at the same time," said JJ. Smiling. Serenely.

When it had thawed, Andi shredded the chicken, added the broth, and soon she was stirring a thick gooey sauce with risotto kernels in it. "At my house, the cook stirs for one standard grope," she said.

So I obliged, and came up with a reasonable approximation of the time period. And handfuls of boobage, to make lesbian lusts dance through dinnertime.

"I never really understood why people are so uptight about sex," said JJ. "There are things you have to be wary of, but if you learn that stuff..." She looked at us, looking at her. "What??" she said.

"You either need to write a book, or just sign up to manage my sex life for me," I said.

"We can put the this into the freezer for a bit, roll it into balls when it sets up and then deep fry them for later," said Andi. She picked up the bottle of cooking oil to be sure there would be enough.

"How long is a bit?" I asked, wondering if the time interval was also measured in gropes.

She looked at me. "Oh, no no no," she laughed. "We did that once, Ben and I. It all froze solid before we came back to it.

So we sat down with glasses of a nice crisp white wine.

"I mean, sure," JJ said. "Tread carefully, but the flowers are there to be trampled."

"What are you talking about?" I asked her.

"Oh good," said Andi. "I was hoping I wasn't the only one who was lost."

"Sex," said JJ. "Carefully only sleeping with one person you don't actually like all that much. We've all been there, done that. I kinda like this arrangement," she said, waving a hand to include all three of us. "I mean I'm presuming, I guess? But having some lovers who all know about each other seems pretty much ideal to me."

"If they're sane," said Andi.

"And don't suddenly change orientations and preferences," I said.

"I did," said JJ. "And you seemed okay with that. Andi's doing it too."

"A little different, I think?" said Andi. "I haven't totally given up on men in general, or Ben in particular. If he's okay with you guys being part of my life."

"We all have tenure. We're stuck with each other," JJ pointed out.

"Don't hafta sleep together," I said. "Unless we want to."

"I hope we want to," said JJ.

"Could get ugly if Ben's the jealous type," I said.

"The few times it's come up, he seems fascinated by you being a lesbian. Maybe he can deal with me being bi," said Andi.

"Fraught," I said, remembering Rachael.

"Risotto balls," said Andi, so we went back to the kitchen, where we got our hands chilled and gooey, but put together a very nice dish.

"I love this," I said, crunching into another one.

"It works well for pot lucks," said Andi. "Fancy and, as you saw, easily made. A bit much for a weeknight dinner, but perfect for a lazy Saturday."

"A lazy Saturday filled with love," I said.

"The best kind," said JJ. "We're so happy you're here," she said, giving a hand to Andi.

"I'm glad," said Andi. "Things were... ungood at home."

"If you need to stay longer, there's room for you here," I said. "You don't even have to sleep with us."

"That's no problem," said Andi, laughing. "But thank you. I guess I'll call Ben tomorrow and we'll see."

"Mañana," said JJ.

"Exactly," I said.

"Exactly," said Andi. "Now about the sleeping with you part..."

"Love to," JJ and I both said at once.

"It's... kinda been growing on me since you two moved in together," said Andi. "I made no promises to Ben, except to give it a try, and we did that. And here you are, loving each other (and me!) without even bothering to be discreet about it. It's... breathtaking."

"I'm glad you think so," I said. "I'm not going into any closets, any more."

"I hear you," said JJ. "And I thought we were being a little bit discreet?"

"Maybe to everybody but me. It worked, didn't it?" said Andi.

~

Andi unstacked herself from the spot in the middle, found one of the robes I'd left out, and went downstairs to the bathroom. After being climbed over, I took the other one down to the kitchen, and started putting together some coffee while I waited my turn.

"Nine cups of water," I said, pushing the pot into Andi's hands in passing.

JJ had swiped my bathrobe just before I was ready to put it on again. We have two of them in the closet, because, well, there are two of us most mornings.

"Uh, nine? What am I doing?" Andi was asking JJ. "Calling Ben at nine."

"You're holding a coffee pot," JJ pointed out. "How about putting some water in it and pouring it into the machine?"

"Oh right, that," said Andi.

"I can set my phone to ring at nine..." I suggested, and then realized it was in the pocket of the robe I wasn't wearing. So I did the only sensible thing, walking up behind JJ and undoing her robe, to get at the phone. She slid out of it with a certain grace, and I felt the phone in its pocket hit my foot on the way to being wrapped around me again.

"Coffee pot, plus water, equals... coffee," Andi said slowly as she removed her attention from JJ and paid it to the coffee maker.

"And turn it on," said JJ, slipping past Andi to hit the button. "I'm chilly. We're going back to bed, since you won't let me have a robe."

I looked around the kitchen for breakfast stuff, and managed to find the fixings for a cheese omelette, which would do nicely. I guess one of the qualifications for running a house like mine is feeding whoever's around on whatever a person can find.

Breakfast was finished before my phone let us know it was nine o'clock. "We can... find something out of earshot if you want some privacy," I suggested, pulling JJ toward the shower by the hand. We... made some noise. Besides the water sound, which was probably enough to prevent overhearing. We hadn't, like, made love, JJ and I, since Andi arrived, and it was good to take the time to do it. We looked into each others' eyes, through the stream of shower droplets, and I thought how wonderful it was, being there with her, and how much more wonderful it was that we could share the wealth with a willing third person. The cat helpfully pushed open the bathroom door partway through, and sat down to groom himself in the middle of the floor. Not stepping on him when we were drying off was quite a trick.

"So, Ben's going in to the lab this afternoon," said Andi. Her eyes were puffy. "If you'd like to help me get some of my stuff, I'd appreciate it. Also, is it okay if I move in for a while? I didn't ask."

"Of course," I said. "Anything you need, just ask."

"How does that poem go? Grief is the thing with long tail feathers?" said JJ.

Andi turned in my arms to face her, inhaling sharply.

"Hope is the thing with feathers," I quoted. "Emily Dickinson, I think."

"The peacock of despair," said Andi.

"Ben's been spreading his feathers again, has he?" said JJ.

And the tension was broken, while Andi laughed until she was weak in the knees.

"Do we know anybody with boxes?" I asked JJ. "Usually somebody we know is moving."

We called around and found one or two carloads of boxes. After lunch we did a search and rescue of Andi's most important stuff. She sensibly keeps her professional books at work, so it was only 20 boxes of novels and such, plus a suitcase, plus a big box or two of other clothes, and another book box for shoes. And the laundry basket. "It's the weekend. I didn't get around to washing."

But it fit in our cars, and by suppertime we at least had her boxes in the house and her clothes in the wash.

"This sleeping together thing?" Andi yawned, "Will it eventually involve actual sleep? I'm really tired."

"A fraught day," said JJ.

"Peak fraughtness. Fraughtiness. Fraughtitude," I said, not being smart enough to keep my mouth shut when too tired to make sense.

"Freight, might be the word," JJ suggested.

"Where's Rachael when we need her vocabulary?" I said, also impervious to the consequences.

"Not moving in here," said JJ.

"Thankfully no," I said. "That would be fraught."

"Capital G capital H fraught," said JJ.

"I have no idea what you guys are talking about," said Andi, yawning again.

"Neither do we," I said. "I think we used up today's helping of Deep Meaningfulness when we invited you to move in with us."

"Is there more tomorrow?" JJ asked.

"I guess we'll be finding out," said Andi. "I'm going to bed."

"I'll stay up and get your stuff out of the dryer," I said.

CHAPTER TWENTY-FIVE

An Odd Number

Dear Renee,

Three, as they say, is a crowd. Somehow Andi found it so much less annoying, being here with us, that she kinda never went home after JJ and I took her out to a bar to let her blow off a little extra steam about her living situation. Her quasi-husband was apparently something else. I mean, he seems nice enough around the department, but one hears through the grad student grape vine that he's a bitch to work for, pardon my sexist French, and I can imagine that might extend to his home life.

So we were happy to help Andi dismantle his little narcissist ego a bit. Give him a taste of an earth where not all goes the way he wants it to. Crossing one minion off his list. A minion with credentials every bit as impressive as his own, including funding, tenure, a tribe of students. All that and blonde hair to excuse the absent-minded professor thing. She is always making blonde jokes.

And there are actually times now that calling her Andi doesn't bring to mind Andy Kreicek. Here let us both pause for a collective shudder. You remember him, I'm sure. Whatever was I thinking?

Three is a good number for this house, I think, because there are three bedrooms (more in a pinch). More than that and bathroom space becomes a real problem. If you've been reading these letters (and of course you haven't, since I haven't ever mailed any of them), you'll be utterly unsurprised that while we have three people living here, and three bedrooms, they are sufficient but not exactly necessary. Conditionally. Necessary and sufficient are conditions. Kind of like rheumatism, I think.

"So, um," said Andi one evening. We were sitting around the living room sipping rum. She'd been here long enough to know just exactly how volatile this particular spirit is, and she didn't choke on it. Yet.

"So, um," said JJ, smiling. She danced a curtain of straight black hair behind one shoulder.

"Three is... an odd number," said Andi.

"Three is indeed an odd number," said JJ. Her smile transmogrified into something more mystical. Or at least mysterious. Her knees did not twitch; I was watching them. Andi's did.

"I... don't want to... uh...," said Andi. "Breakupahappyfamily," she added, as if it were all one word.

I... smiled. That particular smile has gotten me into really sticky situations all my life. As I'm sure you remember, Renee, since I would use it on you sometimes.

JJ and Andi looked at me smiling at Andi.

"Yeah, you know what? I don't think that's going to be a problem," said JJ. "Tomorrow is tomorrow and tomorrow and tomorrow."

"How... poetic," said Andi. "And how opaque."

"Saying all without saying anything," said JJ.

I literally hadn't said anything.

Anyway. It turns out Andi had a good deal of weeping yet to do, over her situation, her questionable judgement about Ben, whether it was possible to think of herself as a good girl and live like we are living.

My house seems to be a good place for women to weep out our existential angst or whatever. Late additions have the advantage that there are other people's shirts around to soak with their tears. At least nobody (so far) is fond of mascara. Tears just dry. That shit is forever.

So as physicists will, we got into some pretty detailed conversations over dinner. My napkins are actual fabric, washable and all, so JJ donated a pad of yellow paper to the table furnishings, so people could draw diagrams and scribble equations. One of my grad students has a folder in which she carefully preserves the drawings and scribblings I put on paper napkins when we have lunch together.

Andi was interested in what we do, in our antipodal spot in the department, and so I was showing her some of the cool stuff we'd thought up, my post-doc and I.

"That's really complicated, and you can't actually solve the equations," she pointed out.

"True," I admitted. "But we have an abiding faith that it's electromagnetic, and the left hand knoweth not whether it be left hand or right."

"I'm guessing you're misquoting scripture or something," said JJ.

"Smart girl," I said. "Is it okay to call you a girl?"

JJ has a very eloquent way of shrugging, which she demonstrated.

"Anyway, this transition here, between these two states?" I said, pointing at the energy level diagram I'd drawn. "If it actually does know left from right, we've seen the Weak Interaction in... ter... action. As it were."

"Woh. Clever," said Andi. "And it just depends on... a few dozen things you don't know."

"That's the tricky bit, yes," I said. "Why it takes arguably smart people years to measure it."

"Arguably smart," JJ snorted.

Anyway. Enough for now. If it's really a letter, I'll sign off with

love,
   Ravyn

CHAPTER TWENTY-SIX

Alone in the Woods

Dear Renee,

It's kinda silly to pretend I'm writing this stuff for you to read someday... I'm not. So there. And now I need to know how to spell the raspberry sound we used to make after the "So there" in that dialog.

It's coming up on Labor Day, a time for remembering that other day when Rachael moved out. Which... Well, I have strong and mixed feelings about.

There's a park-like thing near the house; it must be a square mile of forest, with a lake and some stuff, with just a few roads going through. Rachael and I used to take the canine part of the menagerie we lived with up there and they would have a blast. They'd start out running three times as far as we walked, and then tucker out and walk at someone's heel, no farther than absolutely necessary. And they'd come home and, when we washed their paws, sleep the rest of the day in a puppy pile. It always looked so peaceful.

There are people, living in my house, nowadays, so I decided to take my sad elsewhere. Not to rain on their parade or whatever. Rachael had the map, but I remember hunting for yellow-colored markings, so how hard could it be to follow the trail? A good six miles with no destination but midnight. I slipped out after a perfunctory breakfast, with a sippy cup of coffee and a bottle of water, and a granola bar in the littlest backpack, whose surface was covered in cat hair. It was warm already at seven. On with the boots, lock the door quietly, and I'm off. J and A can... enjoy each others' company, unhindered by memories they don't share.

I left them a note. GONE WALKABOUT STOP IF NOT BACK BY TUESDAY SEND HELP STOP

Hey, it seemed amusing at the time.

I found the trail no problem. I walked til I was tired, came around a corner into the sun, braided my hair, and waited for Rachael to do her part, which was to give me one of the elastic bands she always seemed to have around her wrist, even after she cut her hair. "Can't keep track of basic supplies," she would sniff. I found a rock to sit on because my eyes were glazed over. The braid will stay for a while without a tie, but then it comes apart again. In a way that Rachael always found fetching. You know the deal; it's been doing that since we were kids. I'm imagining you nodding your head because that man of yours also appreciates that particular view.

Speaking of basic supplies, a hankie or some tissues would have been useful. But hey, I'm alone in the woods. I can wash the ookey stuff off the back of my hand when I find the stream, or when I get home or something.

I don't remember the observation tower being part of this trail, but there it was. Maybe there was something to be seen from up there. With... binoculars... if only I'd thought to bring them along. But there was a guy up there with a pair, which he loaned to me. "I wonder if the airport..." I was saying aloud when I found it, and an airplane taking off headed straight for me. "Woh," I said, and like Frodo taking off the Ring, I pulled my attention out of the binocs and it passed me by, unnoticed.

Which was a very Rachael-like thing to be thinking, and there were tears in my eyes when I handed them back to their owner.

"You want to talk about it?" he asked.

"Girlfriend left me," I said. There. If he doesn't run away screaming he can stay.

"Matt," he said. "I'm kind of between... guys... right now, myself."

We found a spot in the shade, shared my granola bar and coffee and water, sniffled at each others' woes, and about coming here with Significant Others, now yet more significantly past.

"Two years tomorrow," I said, sniffling. Bless him, Matt had a handkerchief which he gave me.

"You gonna be okay?" Matt asked. He was about to drive back to town, and I was like miles to go before I sleep, perchance to dream, aye there's the rub.

"No," I said. "I'm done with okay."

He chuckled sadly.

"Thanks for the hankie," I said, using it to dry my eyes again.

Coffee, water, wilderness, girl... bad combination. I found a suitable spot just off the trail. It's pretty much the only time nowadays that I could wish the fantasy Rachael and I loved to act out was actually true. And now I was leaking out of the eyes again. But Matt's hankie was good for that.

But come to think of it, maybe that was exactly the problem, from Rachael's point of view. She wants a man. I'm not that. End of... fairytale, nobody living happily ever after.

It reminds me... of you, Renee, to tell the truth. The parentals, who surely must have known everything about us, right? They pretty much insisted we go to different colleges, meet boys, fall in love, get married, bear them grandchildren. Stop living out of the same closet, inside each others' minds, sharing... everything... and become our own women.

They had a point. It was wrong, surely, everything about it, but oh so good. And then we got booted out of our own lives, because... not suitable for a dozen different reasons, most of which we could do nothing about.

Over the winter holidays that first year, sleeping on opposite sides of our shared bedroom... "Is there more?" you asked, after we said good night. Yes. Oh yes, indeed. But it only made jetting off to different states all the harder the next day.

Come sunset, I found myself near another parking area, and there were JJ and Andi and... unexpectedly, Rachael, waiting to take me home.

"I came out here to get away from you," I told Rachael. I know, ouch.

"JJ contacted me for help finding you. You're welcome," she said. But she was smiling. There was a rubber band on her wrist, which she offered me.

"Thank you," I told them both. "For rescuing me from my memories. I guess I was out here longer than I thought I would be."

"Not to mention lions and tigers and bears," said Andi.

And Matt, who's arguably gay, I didn't say.

Anyway. Enough.

love,
    i think?
    Ravyn

CHAPTER TWENTY-SEVEN

You Wanna Talk About It?

"You wanna talk about it?" said JJ, when we got home.

"Not really," I said. "Right now I want to pee and then have a shower."

So I did all that. My lovely housemates even put a towel in the dryer to warm it up for me, and brought me different clothes. It was a purple t-shirt with a dragon on the front, and a purple and gold tie-dye wrap skirt. No way they could know this, but Rachael picked it out for me when we were in Provincetown for our wedding. It's striking, it's also something that hangs in my closet unused for a year at a time.

Deep breath, in the steam, put it on. Smile, say thank you. For rescuing me from my demons, even if they had summoned one of them to help. For dressing me in striking purple duds, picked out by my ex. For... I could go on.

"You need to talk about it?" said JJ. It wasn't exactly a question.

"Probly," I admitted.

So they sat me down, me in the cushy chair, them on the couch, side by side. Wearing the usual summer duds around here, tank tops and shorts. Watching my knees behave themselves under a skirt that seems shorter every time I wear it.

"What's up?" said JJ.

I opened my mouth, but only a whimper came out. Andi went and found a tissue box and a waste paper basket. Then she opened a beer for each of us. She held hers against her neck for a while, trading body heat for refrigerated coolness. So I did that too, under the fluff cloud that had replaced my hair. It wasn't really time yet to wash my hair, but I did it anyway. Maybe to wash a certain somebody out, down the drain, with the shampoo, which was not the brand we used when we were a thing.

"Tell me about Rachael," said Andi. "JJ may have heard the stories, but I haven't."

"All those girls' nights out..." I said. "That's not enough stories?"

"That's just the whiney parts," said Andi.

"True enough," I said. "Where to start? She bought this outfit. Do you know Provincetown at all? When we were over there getting married, she herded me into this funky Tibetan shop right by the dock where the ferry lands. Aaaaand then what with all the purple, she rustled up some bleach and some purple hair die. I spent at least one night out dancing with her in this, with purple pubes. Ah, love."

Andi laughed.

JJ looked distraught, and said, "I'm sorry, I didn't know."

"Of course you didn't," I said. "It's all good unless you start dyeing my crotch."

"I have to say it had never occurred to me," said JJ, smiling.

"So many things we still have to learn about each other," I said. "What else? I'm still working in the same office where Rachael used to drop by to ask me out to lunch. I'm still sleeping in the same bed where... Uh, yeah."

"Probably time for a new mattress anyway," said JJ.

"I guess it feels sometimes like my life is a minefield. Things everywhere remind me of her, of us, of the girl I was when she was around. All gone now. And they remind me of how very sad it was when she decided after all the flirting with genders and swapping identities, it just wasn't going to work. Because there are actual men in the world, and I'm not one of them. Or something. I don't know." I stopped to sniffle some more.

"I mean, when the cat is trying to decide whether to go out, I often say, *I am not a cat, I do not understand these things.* This one's more like I'm not Rachael. Or straight. Or whatever the fuck she is this week. I do not understand these things."

"You are not Rachael, and you are not straight. I love both of those things about you," said JJ. "And you're generous with what you have, scraping up the rest of the women in the department whenever we managed to faceplant, letting us move in, loving us as we find our feet again."

"You guys seem to be gay. Unlike, it seems, the love of my life?" I said. "Somehow it seems like the work of a lifetime, coming up with a way to live as a gay person with a relationship or two."

"Bi," said Andi. "Not so very unlike Rachael, actually."

"You don't get to break my heart," I said.

"Okay," said Andi. "I'll try to remember that." She glanced quickly at JJ.

"Thank you," I said. "I'm sorry I'm such a mess today. The thing is, I'm not at all sure I could say no if she asked me. Again. I mean, I see her around sometimes." I dropped a hand into my lap.

"I hear ya," said Andi, looking at her hands.

"Even though I know from experience how it makes me feel," I said.

"Yeah," said Andi. "That."

"I guess I'm lucky my ex moved back to Hawaii, and was big and gross and repulsive by the time I dumped him," said JJ. "I don't feel lucky. Except that we found each other. That was the one good thing in my life the last few years."

"Work..." I suggested. She's a very successful scientist, and published some well-regarded results recently.

"Besides that," said JJ.

Andi laughed. "*Besides that*, she says. Like it was nothing. Young girls doing... uh... molecular beam physics, is that what you do? Girls doing that all over the world look up to you."

"Both of them," said JJ, but she was laughing.

CHAPTER TWENTY-EIGHT

Wonderful Tale, Spun

Every now and then, there comes a day I just want to unwind. Before I asked everybody to move in with me, what we would do with this kind of a feeling was to round up all the women in the physics department (the faculty, at least; it's a very manageable size table in a restaurant that way) and go out drinking. And eating. I suppose it reduces the hassle, but the co-housing raises the possibility of never going out at all. Just go home, crack open the decent liquor, make something spicy for dinner.

Somehow when it was an every other month kind of a thing, we got into heart to heart conversations. When it's just a housemate, it's like, eh, whatever. We'll talk when we have something to say. For me, that's likely to be 3AM. JJ's really not coherent at that hour, and Andi is... spacey any time of the day or night. Did I say that out loud?

Anyway. Train, check. Turns out JJ and Andi were in another car on the same train, and got out of the station before they saw me. So I followed them home, got delayed by traffic crossing the one busy street, lost sight of them, and was really looking forward to having the thermostat turned up and a welcoming party to take off my gloves and my boots and my coat, run fingers though my hair, and take our sweet time deciding what, if anything, to do about dinner.

Maybe this is part of what JJ was on about, though. Not assuming too much about who's going to be up for what, just because they might be up for doing somebody else. And despite what it sounds like, it's really not competitive, because there's much more wherever that came from. It's just... Sitting home on a Friday night, going through all the coming home stuff, including feeding the cat... those meanies didn't even do that when they got home... Picking up boots and coats and stuff from the stairway and the bannister, hanging them up. Figuring out what to do about food, that would be smelly enough to roust out the army.

It's... just not a situation I figured I'd ever be in, especially during those long years of living alone.

I remember once when Rachael and I were a thing... Becca was in town. We had her over to dinner; I think maybe Stephan had taken the kid home to go to school or something. We got to talking about the great unwinding at the end of a stressful day. She spun this wonderful story about coming home, swinging the door shut with a foot, stacking all of her luggage in its place, waiting for Stephan to look up from his papers or his book and, ahem, just kinda not stopping after her coat, let me say?

That can't have been particularly recent, even when she was telling us about it, what with the kid. It's one thing with just the two of you, but quite something else with little people around. They have eyes and they learn stuff by watching. I remember watching our folks do something strange, and turning to commune telepathically with Renee while we figured out what we'd just seen.

Anyway. Lights were on, only just, but nobody was home, at least on the ground floor. I was not going upstairs to see what they were doing. Which means no changing clothes until... later. Aw hell, I was saying as a tear dripped into the half-empty glass of wine. I should just call Rachael.

Beeecause, as JJ taught me, making assumptions about what other people might or might not be doing, and what they might or might not be wanting to do if only they'd thought of it, of me, of us... Not a good thing. Rachael chose to live her life apart, and I need to let her, she needs me to let her, just get on with it, without nostalgic whatevers once a season, whether we need it or not. Them. Plural. Whether we need *them* or not.

And Kat... is probably nearby. She's also very young, has really remarkably prehensile thumbs and... I had to stop to writhe a bit, remembering... She prolly has all the attention she wants, thank you very much, without that old lady who lives with her choirgirl friend. Maybe I should join Andi's choir. I used to do that, back in the day... not that choir but another one. I could not keep track of which day of the week it was, missed too many rehearsals, and spared the director the embarrassment of asking me to leave. I do remember the little lecture about showing up for rehearsals. "But I'm preaching to the choir," he said at the end.

I kicked off the slippers I'd put on to replace my boots, put my feet under me, figured out my balance against the sofa pillow and arm, with the added complication of trying to stay inside a dress. All without spilling the last couple fingers of wine in my glass. There was a curl that wanted in, but it's easy enough to lick the wine out of your hair. Crude, but effective.

So I was sitting in the half light, pondering my misspent life, wondering how it is that I got there, to that particular Friday night, sniffling tears in a solo glass of wine, while my altogether wonderful life partners (at least for a season) were... ahem. Otherwise involved. One presumes. Shall we say.

And I had to wonder if I picked up Kat, oh and Rachael (of course), and if JJ did her barista Christy... Was that just to get a reaction from each other? And now of course we had Andi actually living here. Despite all the blushing and insisting that she really wasn't interested, she's interested.

I'm a little slow, figuring out how I feel about stuff. I don't think that's it? But I could be wrong. I mean, JJ has this thing about balancing... stuff... so we don't, like, go all u-haul on each other, promising forever when we mean the next hour and then we'll see. Or something. I dunno what she's talking about, but it sounds profound.

CHAPTER TWENTY-NINE
Picking Up Chicks

Right. There were three of us most nights for, what, a year or so. Three amigas or something. When it came out (she said "come out") that all three of the women on the physics faculty were living together, there was a lot of idle teasing about Three Amigos, but we had to correct the gender, at least twice, for every one of our colleagues, I think. And I'm the only one that speaks any Spanish.

Three is an odd number. An odd number of very odd people, none of whom had ever met anybody quite like us before. It was, fun, sometimes, just kinda going with whatever, but I felt the need to keep score, make sure everybody was getting what she wanted or needed.

There was this hot summer day, which reminded me of my sojourn in the South, we decided going home to a house with no air conditioning wouldn't be that much fun, at least until sunset, after which the window fans might be able to keep up.

"The Six?" JJ suggested, naming a bar near the campus.

"They don't serve food there, do they? I'm for eating something before I get into a compromising situation," I said. Ever the practical one, keeping score, generally being everybody's mom.

So we ended up at a honky-tonk kind of a place farther away, but they had a juke box, aqua upholstery to make you sweat, and a wide open space with black and white floor tiles. I remember trying to get Janet to dance with Renee and me at the after-school place we used to frequent as kids. She was sooooo scandalized. But of course she had no idea.

Anyway. They had fish and chips wrapped in stained newspapers, lending a kind of old-world poetry synthesis to the traditional Fish Fry. Fusion, I think they call it. I am not a foodie, I do not know these things. And a juke box. Did I mention the juke box?

Of course nobody has figured out how to dance with three people... well, two, three counting myself... at once, so we took turns.

"You choose," I said, coming up with an astonishing fistful of quarters from the lower reaches of my purse.

So Andi picked out some disco stuff with a beat that I dimly remembered. Quite possibly including the one we picked out for Janet. The seventies... what *were* we thinking? Well, they. And why on earth would anybody have a seventies throwback bar?

The answer, it seems, is so we could, just by chance, meet Joy.

Who was sitting at the end of the bar, alone, with one of those *wish I had an eyeshade because the glare is killing my headache* grimaces. She's somebody I've seen across the room at, um, faculty senate meetings maybe? She dipped into her bag and extracted a textbook, still shrink-wrapped, broke open the seal, and left the resulting trash for the bartender. I went back to Andi. She could make even me aware of the beat. Come to think of it, maybe that's why Janet was so scandalized: Renee and I can't either one of us dance.

I glanced at Joy once or twice. Sometimes she was watching us, which is interesting in itself. Once she was inhaling deeply from the middle of her new book. I wonder if it's like the solvents they used to make copies back in the dark ages when we were kids.

But eventually the book went back in the bag, and apparently the spectacle of two women dancing made her sad. JJ is a dear, and not only noticed, but took her to the bathroom to fix her face and stuff.

The music ended, and we went back to another round of beer. With a nod, JJ added a fourth to the order. Which, jumping the gun only a little bit, added a Fourth to the Order as well.

"Hey everybody," JJ was saying. "Meet Joy. She's the girl I just picked up at the bar."

And we all laughed, because we'd seen it done, but not exactly like what the words might imply.

"Joy, meet the rest of the physics department," said JJ.

"The interesting part of it, at least," I said, lifting an eyebrow at Joy.

She laughed. Laughing is good, isn't it? It was a weird situation in a year or two of weird social situations that had become my life. I stopped worrying a while ago, and it has worked out so far.

"Have you eaten?" JJ asked. For once, she was being the mom.

Joy shook her head no.

"We could chip in..." Andi suggested.

"And fish in..." popped out of my mouth. "Seriously, the fish and chips are wonderful."

"I am gainfully employed," Joy said, but again, she had the grace to laugh at our inane banter.

There being four of us now, we got a table and drank beer while we watched her eat. You can learn a lot about a woman by watching how she... ahem. Eats.

"So tell us about Joy," we said, waiting for a time when most of the food was gone and her mouth wasn't full.

Vital statistics... History department, living alone, waaaaay too single...

"I know that one," I said.

"Valent," said JJ. "What?" she added when everybody looked at her. "Chemistry. Easy to form bonds."

Tears formed in Joy's eyes, but she nodded.

"We," JJ announced, "are totally taking you home with us tonight. I mean, if you want to."

Joy nodded again, tears overflowing, trying to look into JJ's eyes with the resulting impaired vision.

Andi and I settled with the bartender while Joy got another sample of JJ's excellent attention in the bathroom.

"Don't you have something better to do?" she asked when we were together again. "I mean, three of you... and you're out picking up chicks."

"Pff," I pffed. "We met you, didn't we? Besides, the house is probably hot, until... right about now, what with the sun going down."

"Oh good. The sun was giving me a headache," Joy said.

"Yeah," I said.

"That obvious?"

"Yeah," I said again.

Meet Joy, who completes the household.

CHAPTER THIRTY

Regrettables

Into every life (mine, at least) come some happenings that should arguably not have happened. At least not with my willing participation.

Now four of us living in my house. It's a bit much, I guess? But each of the roomies is her own woman, all very different, each of us kind of thrilled by the prospect of living in a place where there are fewer beds than people. And, to tell the truth, where being gay is not even unusual, let alone a problem.

Afternoon was kind of wearing on with no immediate appointments in prospect, and there was this odd thing in the equations pulling at the corners of my mind. So I took myself out for a date with some coffee and a couple napkins to scribble on. That was the plan. Apparently Rachael had exactly the same idea at the same time, because there we were, sharing a table, knees pointed at each other but firmly pressed together. Staring our unrequited feelings at each other. Did I say unrequited? Unresolved, perhaps. I'm sure we both had better things to do.

"How are you, really?" Rachael asked.

Back when... yeah. Back when, we had this thing where she'd ask how I was, and having established that things were okay, the usual run of pains and inconveniences was on schedule, etc. I would answer, "Fine." She would look at me and ask, "Should I believe you?"

So I answered, "Would you believe me if I said Fine?"

She chuckled. The frown lines smoothed a little; the kerf between her eyebrows was a little less deep and craggy. "No," she answered.

"Okay, then," I said. "A bit overwhelming."

"You're seeing someone?" Rachael asked.

"Um... you could say that. You could say too many of them. Like, living in my house."

It's been a while since I did it, but the coffee shop seems to bring out this particular posture: leaning forward, elbows on the low table, backs of my hands together dangling off my side of the table toward my lap. Which is visible between the various cups and saucers on the table, since it's glass.

And just as they did back when, unbeknownst to either of us, Raitch and I were romancing each other right here, the tips of my hair stole around a shoulder and dunked themselves in my drink.

Rachael's hair was long like mine Back When, but being a sensible person, she cut it not long after we moved in. She laughed, retrieved the errant lock, ran it through her lips to do a first cleaning of milk foam from hair, and tucked it behind my shoulder. Her face was suddenly very close to mine. And, um, there were battles fought along those roads; if you listen you can hear the sighs of despair from the casualties.

The next task, having given this much consent, was explaining to my housemates, especially JJ who takes a certain proprietary interest in my emotional wellbeing, why it was that my very-ex wife was drinking good rum with us in the parlor.

Joy has a way of cutting right through all the conversational ruses I dreamed up to spare my modesty and save face. "Beeeeecauuuuse," she drawled, "fuck." She likes the F-word. It seems to drip from her lips anytime it's in anybody's head. Which is rather often around here.

"Yeahthat," Rachael said, eyeing me. At the same moment, my mouth opened to say "Exactly."

"Carry on then," said Andi, lifting her glass to us.

"That was the plan, apparently," said JJ, grinning. "Carrying on."

I was going to ask if they were okay with three people sharing two beds. I was going to ask if they would throw me out in the morning for... I dunno, something untoward I was about to do. I was going to ask... so many things. Joy smiled, put a finger to my lips, and swatted us up the stairs together.

The frown lines in Rachael's face were gone by morning. I hadn't seen that smile in years, come to think of it. The space between her eyebrows was smooth as well. If I looked very closely, on the way in to kiss her hairline, don't you know, I could just see the mark left by the otherwise perpetual crease, hidden by her uni-brow, gloriously untrimmed.

"How are you, really?" she asked, in a kitchen full of sleepy lesbians.

Oh Raitch. You so don't get to ask me that.

I was doing fine til you left me for a man? Should I say that?

I was in mortal dread of losing you til you actually moved out, and then I couldn't remember being with you. The facts, yes, but what it was like, how it felt, no.

I'm not sure the rerun helped with that. I'm not sure if I slept with Rachael hoping JJ would get jealous. Are my motives mixed if I'm not even aware of them? JJ's not that kind of a person, but I was a little afraid I'd strained the relationship, finding out.

It's good to see you feeling good about things, I could say. And it is.

It's just... sooo muuuch sadness gone under the bridge, while I stand at the upstream rail waiting for the Poohsticks to come out again. They never will.

What's then is then, I could tell you. What's now is now. And what's tomorrow is tomorrow. Probably without you.

I'm so sorry it came to this. Whatever this is. Nobody's dead; we never even filed papers or anything. But that thing we had, whatever it was then, is so over. So very over.

The person I was then, shattered on the hard floor. I miss that person.

I found most of the broken pieces and put them together into something that sort of looks like a life. It almost functions, some weeks. JJ helps hold me together, and now I've gone and done something that has her looking across the table at me, concerned, while I blush for what I've become, between Rachael-that-was (and now briefly is again), and JJ who is tomorrow and tomorrow and tomorrow.

CHAPTER THIRTY-ONE

Serenity

Stuff happens, sometimes because I make it happen, and I wonder what, and if, I was thinking. But JJ watches me, looks me in the eyes going "Really?" and then somehow helps me forget all that by the time we wake up together. I'm keeping her, if I have anything to say about it.

Which me, is the question, does the saying? She seems to like the more or less rational me, and she's into what we've created here, with a tight core group of women who are all in this together. There's something... I dunno, I was going to say alien, and maybe that's exactly the right word... imported, maybe, from her Chinese culture. Where my reaction to the stupid stuff I do is shame, hers is serenity. Which... she tries to teach me. When the word drifted across my conscious scribblings, I looked up the Serenity Prayer from the AA movement, and she goes, "Yeah, pretty much. Where did you find that?"

And so I told her that in Western culture, our native meanness herds the serenity off into recovery programs for addicts. She's almost as Western as we are, but of course with a generous dollop of Chinese stuff mixed in.

"Meh," she says. "It's just kinda there? You know?"

"Not really," I said.

"All my life. Not knowing if I'm Chinese or American. Not being either one, really, while at the same time being both."

"I admire your serenity, all the same," I said. "And I guess it's probably racist or something. Sorry."

Somehow everybody else in the household was out that night. Dancing or some damn thing. I'm sure it's marginally transgressive for a group of women to be out dancing in what is not an actual gay bar. With each other, I mean.

So JJ and I went to the local Mexican joint for dinner. The one where the wait staff speak English, but with a Spanish accent, and many of the kitchen staff and bus girls don't do English much at all. There are cute, brightly painted wood carvings in the booth seat backs, on Mexican themes.

"Authentic, is what you're trying to say," JJ said.

"I guess." And it is. Not like our grandmama's cooking, but Mexico is large and there's quite a lot of variation in the food.

"Buenos dias, Ravyn," said the waiter.

"Have I told you my family name is Menendez?" I asked him.

"No, señorita," he said, but looked at me with more respect. "I will warn the staff to be careful what they say around you."

And we laughed together, but I could hear him doing just that, around the corner in the kitchen.

"I guess I come here a little often," I said to JJ.

"I hope their Mexican is better than that Chinese Food Come Soon place."

"It's pretty good," I said to JJ. "The chiles rellenos are really something."

"I'm not really into stuffed peppers that much," said JJ.

The waiter brought us our food, and being in the corner near the kitchen, mostly left us alone, together. Which was why we were there, after all. The half-Mexican chica and her Chinese girlfriend, making eyes at each other.

"We could... ask José for a box for the leftovers," I suggested, waving hair aside and lifting one eyebrow.

"A girl after my own..." said JJ, leaving the noun unspoken.

"Tell me some lies," I murmured in her ear as she hustled me out of the restaurant.

"I only have eyes for you? That kind of lies?" said JJ, laughing. She pulled me around the corner into the alley instead of walking me to the car. She pushed me up against the wall.

"Mmm, hot tamales," she said, letting me go.

"And I have ivy in my hair," I told her.

"I can wash that out," she said. "Later."

Anyway, that's what we were doing when the rest of the household came home, a tad inebriated, letting themselves in to the bathroom to use the facilities. And then of course there's that "Huh. I should know by now that my hair takes hours to dry, and not wash it at bedtime" thing.

"There were actual twigs in it," JJ pointed out. She had filtered the drain water through her toes to keep them from getting stuck.

CHAPTER THIRTY-TWO

An Evening at Ravynscroft

Sometime after Joy moved in... I dunno, the days and seasons merge and swirl together and I can't keep track, so eventually I stopped trying. Just hang out underwater watching whatever my hair wants to do, coming up for air when I need to. The years go by, whether swiftly or slowly, I cannot say.

"We used to do a Physics Department girls' night out thing," said JJ. "Mostly when Andi didn't want to go home all that much. We should do a night in sometimes. Heart to heart talks. That kind of thing."

"Thanks, so much, for jollying me, for showing me I had options," said Andi.

"It was our pleasure," I said, somewhat to my own surprise. "A gift that keeps on giving. Tell us about Joy," I said, turning to the one non-Physics person in the room.

"Joy Wainright," said Joy. "Oh, Joy. Lessee. Vital statistics. I grew up, married my college sweetheart, went to grad school, and we both figured out I was smarter than he was. I wrote a thesis. I wrote a book. I wrote him out of my life. He was, kinda, um, how do I say this... *male*, maybe. And yeah, I do social history, and I can't put words to it. Populations I can write about all day. It's people who are mysterious. There was this woman I met, actually at an adult education class at the Women's Center about how to divorce your bum of a husband. We both needed roommates for practical reasons. We both needed lovers for emotional reasons. It was... crazy, in a word. Jin was crazy, she was angry, she was a lover, she submerged into my emotional life with mad abandon, throwing any consequences to the wind. I'm sure you know the story."

"Nesting hormones for the win," I said.

"It's an affective disorder lesbians seem to have. She's either nothing, or she's inside your underwear," said JJ. "My therapist told me about it when I first mentioned, uh, seeing Ravyn."

"And you fuck like crazed weasels for a year and then... nothing," said Joy.

We nodded solemnly.

"Soooo I started pushing her boundaries," said Joy. She stopped for a larger than average sip of rum, and the choking and snorting that causes. She handed the snifter to Andi, flopped back against the cushions of the couch, knees a little farther apart. "And, how to say this, Jin and I discovered that I have a kinky side that just won't quit. She would think of leaving, wanting something, anything really, that was exciting, and I would take her to bed, watch while her eyes bugged out, while her little-o orgasms became OMFG huge ones, going out with the rip current, sure she was going to drown, and then tumbling up the beach in a sensual tsunami. Or something. Figured out what she wanted, as opposed to what she said she wanted, where her boundaries were, and how to flirt shamelessly with them until she forgot she had any."

"Andi, I believe you're drooling," said JJ, with a serene smile.

"Huh?" said Andi, wiping her mouth on the back of her hand. "I... uh..."

"How very *interesting*," said Joy, her full attention on Andi. Somehow she managed to italicize the word while speaking out loud.

Joy and Andi looked into each others' eyes.

And then Joy smiled, to herself mostly. Andi's expression had turned to puppy-like adoration, which was both very cute and kind of disturbing on an adult woman's face.

"Tell me about JJ," said Joy, "and how she ended up being, uh, cruise director, or whatever it is you do here in this little... whatever this is." She waved her hand at the assemblage.

"Harem," I suggested.

"Religious order," Andi said.

"Little sisters of the..." I suggested. We are small people, after all.

"Holy... because religious order?" said Andi.

"Fuck!" said Joy.

"Little Sisters of the Holy Fuck," said JJ. "It has potential. Each word right where it belongs."

"I am not fucking my sister," said Andi.

I... blushed. Subtly, I hoped?

JJ glanced at me and changed the subject. "Tell you about JJ, you asked," she said. "I grew up in an immigrant household in California, complete with the proverbial Chinese mother who was never satisfied. We don't really speak the same language, so it's convenient for both of us, sometimes, to pretend we didn't understand what the other one said. I went off to grad school in Hawaii in a time when long-distance telephone was a thing and pricey. Worked hard, to satisfy the insatiable ambition of my mother. Eventually I discovered I was living in paradise, and started playing as hard as I worked. Learned scuba and underwater photography. Some of my fish photos are in a book that's here someplace."

So we went and found the book, found the pictures, and puzzled through her signature in Chinese characters etched into the corners.

"It doesn't say *JJ Jong*," Andi pointed out, reading the English version from the caption.

"No," said JJ.

"It's weird, having a lover whose name I fundamentally don't know," I said.

"I do try to teach you now and then," said JJ, who was laughing.

"And I have a fancy diploma that says I'm educable," I said.

"But only in physics," said JJ. "Anyway. I took a hula class. There was this girl there, Mua, and yadda yadda yadda. We, uh, how to say this? We experimented at length with all the failure modes of grass skirts, how to get each other out of them, willing or not. The merging thing was pretty frightening, and I kinda freaked. Benny was also in the hula class, and hula for men seems to involve alternately spreading and... unspreading... drawing attention to... He knew where there was a nude beach on Maui. He was over twice my size and totally ripped. He taught me to fly, kinda sorta. It was love at first... twirl... naked around the beach under the full moon."

"JJ the romantic," I said.

"The dynamics were really fascinating," said JJ.

"Spoken like a physicist," I said. "But I bet you weren't thinking about that."

"Meh," said JJ. "It was overwhelmingly wonderful the first... I dunno, dozen times. After that, the bruises in weird places and the scrapes from landing unexpectedly in the sand kind of got old. I probably should have listened to my practical objections instead of my cunt."

"I hate that word," Andi said.

"Quim," I suggested. "A word I learned from Rachael."

"Who probably got it from Erica Jong. No relation. Anyway," said JJ. "I graduated, got a job, moved here, got tenure, got my hip dislocated trying to do, uh, dynamical things in a small Boston bedroom. Once was an accident. Twice was unfortunate. Third time, I dumped his fucking ass."

"And I happened to be there to bring you home when your apartment didn't have heat," I said. "On the coldest night in living memory."

"I remember that week," said Andi. "So that's when you..."

"Shacked up," Joy suggested, grinning.

"Sharing body heat," I said.

"And body fluids," said Joy.

"And remembering Mua in Hawaii, trying to come up with something sustainable, and somehow avoid the affective merging thing. Which is where it was handy, having another woman around in the department who was friendly and soooo not straight, despite what she was telling herself," said JJ, looking at Andi.

"Yeah, well, it was you who drew a bell curve on a napkin and labeled it *Kinsey Scale*," said Andi. "Kinsey probably thought people were mostly either straight or gay with not all that many in the desert between."

"We live in the desert between," said JJ. "In so many ways. Between indifference and merging. Balancing multiple lovers helps with that, but it's tricky."

"Learning, again and again, not to keep score," I said. "There's plenty of love here, to go with the abundance of available womenfolk. No need for jealousy, there'll be more where all that came from."

"A sharing economy of overwhelming abundance," said JJ.

"Fuck," said Joy.

"Exactly," said JJ. "And if now and then somebody has a fling with..."

"Christy," I said, naming the barista JJ picked up once.

"Ben," said Andi, reminding us that she's bi, and still sleeping now and then with her ex.

"Rachael," I said. Andi's not the only one who sleeps with her ex.

"Or Kat," said Andi. She was a choirgirl friend of Andi's who... had... double-jointed thumbs. And, uh, I had her double-jointed thumbs after that one concert...

"As I was saying," said JJ, "if somebody has a fling, we make sweet love to her afterwards, to help remind her how the balanced life works."

"The urge to fall in love with Rachael again was neatly averted by an equally strong urge to fall in love with you that same weekend," I said, looking into JJ's eyes.

She... smiled. Serenely. She's so fucking serene sometimes. "Seriously? You'll fall for the latest girl to eat you out. It's a thing I know about you, and it's a thing we can live with if we know."

"Managing Ravyn's..." said Andi.

"...fucking..." said Joy.

"...affective disorder," said JJ.

"So calculated," I said, with a sniffle.

"But the results are sooooo goooood," said JJ, smiling. For once, lustier than she was serene.

"Yes," I admitted. "I guess somebody has to keep score. And it really needs to not be me."

"Exactly," said JJ.

"Exactly," said Andi.

"Exactly," said Joy. "Your turn now, Andi."

"Uh, I," said Andi. She turned to look Joy full in the face, and then me, and lastly JJ. "There's not much to tell, really? I mean, quintessentially American girl, Andrea Smith, goes to college, discovers men, as opposed to the boys in high school. Discovers women, not all of whom are straight. Most of whom are not, actually, now that I come to think of it. There might be a sampling bias in my experience."

"Ya think?" laughed JJ.

"I carefully pulled up my roots in the women's groups I'd become part of, went to grad school, found Ben, we got jobs together, we got a house together, we went through pregnancy scares together, and unlike our serene sister here, I found it impossible to manage his... I guess you'd have to call it narcissistic streak. He's fine, he's witty and charming even, in public. But it's all an act. Having you guys around to keep him civil has really helped."

"Huh. I wonder if it's the flip side of our affective thingie," I said.

"I dunno, maybe," said Andi. "Anyway, what, maybe fifteen years later, offices next to each other, co-authors on each others' papers, it was a little too much togetherness. Thanks for taking me in." She turned to me. "Eventually I figured out that, even though it was a mutual lust for JJ that brought me home, what you-all have going here is really special, and it's okay to love you all. Each," she added, looking at us in turn, "in her own unique way."

"So everybody else knows most of it already, but tell the new girl about Ravyn," said Joy.

"Oh my. I was afraid my turn was coming," I said. "Where to start. I've always known I was into girls, I think. Since we... since I was, like, ten. About the time of my last haircut, then. Except hey, there are boys in the world and they're soooo available aaaand, gosh, I fucked a lot of people. Roommate

Annie and the girls down the hall. And Annie's... I was gonna say boyfriends but they were toys more than friends. Grad school. A lot of the dorm girls were going straight once we graduated, so, like, why not. Except, well, there's a lot of men out there and they all wanted to be exclusive. And the women are there, but they're quieter on the whole and it's hard to see them through the crowd of tall smelly cockpeople."

"Tall smelly cockpeople," JJ laughed.

"I found myself in a coffee shop making eyes at the barista with a certain Jewish woman, bitching about relationships, bitching about hair care, bitching about life. Bitching, in private at least, about Rachael's researches into linguistics and how our native language influences our gender identities. *Assigned Female*, is how the trans people put it. You're born, they look at your crotch, tick the F box on the paperwork, and your life is forever changed."

Nods around the room while I refilled my rum.

"Raitch--Rachael Cohen--daughter of generations of rabbis, schooled in the finer points of social justice movements, had other ideas. We probably had a frequent buyer card at the sex toy shop, trying stuff together that broke the gender binary. She felt badly writing about it, I think, but it did inform some of her research, I'm pretty sure. We took turns being the boy, and we found some toys that were anything but a simulation of straight sex. Rachael was endlessly fascinated, trying to catalog the various gender and sexual identities, preferences, and practices, and associate them with the stuff in the box of unmentionables that lived under our bed. As for the being in each others' underwear, I wore her boxers sometimes. So, uh, yeah."

"So, uh, yeah," Joy prompted when I fell silent.

"I hafta wonder who Ravyn would have been if I'd made other choices. Maybe listened less to where my clit was leading me," I said.

But I was very carefully not thinking about Renee, who, starting from exactly the same place, did make different choices.

"Whatcha thinkin'?" JJ asked gently.

I looked into her eyes, but didn't answer. She smiled. Serenely. I really wanna fuck the serenity right off that girl's face. As often as possible.

"Anyway, being a linguist, Rachael eventually got interested in a bunch of languages in the Caucasus that don't have any grammatical gender at all. Native speakers have a lot of trouble trying to figure out how pronouns work in English, just because assigning genders to people is... foreign. And as she had done in her previous research project, she sort of became asexual, or ungendered, or non-binary or some such shit. Which left me... on the other side of the bed, watching. But the urge to mate is strong, and she found John online, a returning memory from her days as a bubble-headed schoolgirl. She decided the toybox wasn't enough and went to, like..."

"Fuck," said Joy.

"Right. Fuck actual cockpeople," I said. "Well, one. That I know of. It was very very sad."

"'Tis better to have loved and lost..." Joy suggested.

"Bullshit," the other three of us interrupted.

We all laughed together.

CHAPTER THIRTY-THREE

Rachael's Birthday

Dear Renee,

What a week.

It's complicated. Like, what isn't, when you have a house full of lesbians?

Back in the day, Rachael and I had this friend...

Rachael had this friend...

Rachael's ex. There we go. Becca was her name. Before I ever met Rachael, she, ahem, found herself in a relationship (ain't it the way) with Becca and her husband Stephan. Becca's husband. It was... intense, to hear the tales. And then Bec and Steph got Actual Jobs and moved away, leaving Raitch in grad school, bitching about relationships in general and hers in particular, which is where I came in, joined in the bitching games, and zapwhampow, we ended up married. Like, woh.

Anyway, Rachael still had a thing for Becca, kinda sorta. Everything in our love lives is kinda sorta, isn't it? Anyway again, Becca is a person who can't walk by somebody in need, especially if they're queer and female, and so once after she was visiting Boston we ended up with a trans houseguest for a few days whom Becca had rescued off the street. And then, much later, there was Lia. Who was having... problems... and lived next door to Bec, so when she had to leave her wife behind, Bec thought of us, and even though Raitch and I were not really an item (well, we were, but only kinda sorta), I was the one with extra bedrooms, and here she was. A lesbian who's not polyamorous. Apparently there exist such people, because there was one living in my house. (I know there are lots of them. At least in the kinda sorta sense.)

And we made her uncomfortable and she made us uncomfortable, and she saw Rachael making eyes at me (and I at her, kinda sorta maybe?) and proposed she swap places with Rachael. Lia got a solitary apartment, and Rachael moved into my house. Which already had four people living in it. But she was inspired by Andi's business model, importing the occasional person of the male persuasion when the need struck. Raitch apparently figured that would be enough to skritch the itch.

My house has many... bedrooms, and it all worked remarkably well.

All this to explain how it was that Rachael was living in my house again, when it came to be her birthday, again. As it does, every year for the rest of her life, I suppose.

When we were romantic love birds living together behind enemy lines in Suburbia, the thing about birthdays was that the celebrant got to pick a restaurant or a getaway or something, and the partner would fund it and go along for the fun. We still do that, at what the Order has taken to calling Ravynscroft. Apparently it's an old-fashioned word for a birdhouse for a murder of ravens. It's crows that come in murders. And I'm glad there's only one of me. Even if there are two of us, kinda sorta, but you're not Ravyn and I am. (Nyeah, nyeah. However you spell that.)

And what Rachael decided to do with her birthday was go out with John for a nice dinner, just the two of them, a movie, just the two of them, and going home, just the two of them, to John's apartment.

It made me, well, a little weepy, remembering doing all that with her myself in years past. I'm not jealous, really? Except some of my emotions take time to catch up to that. Or something.

~

"What's up?" JJ wanted to know, around the dinner table. Intimate, just the four of us. We hadn't, any of us, thought of candle light, though someone might have if Rachael had been around...

"Raitch," I said, before tearing up. I pulled my sleeve down over my hand and pushed the back of my wrist into my eye to stop the leak.

"I'm listening," said JJ, pushing her sleeves halfway up to her elbows.

"We're also watching how pulling your sleeves down like that stretches the rest of your shirt," said Joy.

So I crossed my arms, hid my hands in opposite armpits, leaned back in my chair with a thud, and emitted a sigh unlike anything I remember doing since we were exasperated teenagers. Fine. Let the tears run down my face then.

"It's Rachael's birthday," said Andi. "She gets to do whatever she wants to celebrate."

"It used to be..." I said, and stopped.

"Allow me to fill in the blanks," said Joy.

JJ shot her a look that would have shut anybody else up.

"It used to be," continued Joy, unfazed, "that she would go out with you, have a nice dinner, a movie or a concert, and come home to the room upstairs." Joy paused to shrug an elaborate reference to the bedroom.

I was expecting... something graphic. And I got it.

"We all remember what you wanted for your birthday," said JJ.

"Speaking of eating out," said Joy.

"That's what she said," said Andi.

"Nice birthday suit," said Joy.

"To each, according to her needs; from each, according to her abilities," said JJ.

"So say we all," said Andi.

"So say we all," Joy confirmed.

"Like any sensible... whatever it is we are," said JJ.

"Little Sisters of the Holy Fuck," said Andi.

"Yeah, that," said JJ. "It beats trying to come up with another phrase for lesbian polyamorous sex-positive wenches."

"As for the Mother Superior of our little Order..." said Joy.

"I still think that sounds like a sex position," said Andi.

"...we could arrange for your half of that wish to come true," said Joy.

"Dry your tears," said JJ. "Unless, of course, weeping is part of the experience for you."

"Interesting kink," said Joy. I'm sure she was already pondering how to use that notion to push me over the edge somehow. But only a little over the edge. Unlike somebody else at the table, who seemed to thrive on being thrown over the edge with great force, ending up in places she had never imagined existed. Joy could provide that service as well, if one wanted it.

It's... a little horrifying, in a thrilling kind of a way, seeing somebody else's kink acted out. Come to think of it, I suppose my little birthday adventure was a kind of a kink, if the vanilla person in the commune can have kinks. I mean, besides that knot in my shoulder muscles, that Rachael used to call a kink in my neck. I would call her a pain in my neck, and we would laugh, and she would massage that, and... other things.

And now, she was out with *him*. "Ordinarily I don't mind," I explained, "maybe because she does it here, and I know she's staying, even though, eeuw, she seems to like boys, what's up with that?"

"I like boys," said Andi, who's very much into reminding the rest of us about bisexual visibility issues in the queer community.

"Yes," I said. "And I'm fine with that, too."

"But you're not all *In Love* with me," said Andi, the capitals and italics audible in her tone of voice. "And stuff."

"But I do love you," I said, offering a tear-dampened hand.

"I know you do," she said. "And that works remarkably well, considering."

"And you," I said to JJ, who smiled serenely. She's too serene, that one. And I promised myself, and her, that I'd stop using that adjective to describe her.

"And you," I said to Joy. In part so she wouldn't be left out. "Though sometimes I wonder why," I said, recalling to mind some of the places she's taken me. I kind of wanted to curl up in my chair into a fetal position, but the skirt… would show Joy everything, and, um, no.

"Beeecause," drawled Joy in what became her trademark, "... fuck."

"Exactly," said JJ.

"Exactly," said Andi.

It's hard not to laugh, being dissected with such confidence.

"Are we gonna talk this to death?" Andi asked.

The door banged open and Rachael appeared. "We're going dancing," she announced. "And me with PMS boobs and no sports bra."

John had the grace to blush while she hurried upstairs to change. "Don't let me interrupt anything," he said.

"Fuck," said Joy, just because.

"Later," said JJ.

"That was the plan," said Andi.

John had the grace to blush, again. Rachael thundered down the stairs, a little less bouncy. "Rescue me," said John.

"Are the scary lesbians annoying you?" said Rachael, grinning like the birthday girl she was.

He looked at her, and then us, and then her again. He closed his mouth. Good boy. We have him well trained.

"Dancing," said Rachael. She patted Gus on the head and skritched his ears.

"Right," said John. "See ya."

Gus put his front paws up on the windowsill and watched his person go away. He sat down with a big sigh. He adapted to being everybody's dog, but he really loved Rachael the best.

"Have fun... uh... dancing... or whatever." I said, with my overly fertile imagination filling in all manner of entendres where the dots are.

"Where were we?" said JJ.

"Fuck," said Joy, just because.

And the rest, as we say, was herstory.

thanks for letting me natter on like this,
    love,
    Ravyn

CHAPTER THIRTY-FOUR

Green Hair

I got invited to visit another university, give a talk, meet with folks doing similar kinds of things there. As usual, in a big department, almost nobody knows or cares all that much about atoms and stuff you can actually measure to a gnat's eyelash, so it's tricky getting them excited. But the notion of looking for the Weak Interaction, which normally only the particle physics people care about, in atomic structure, that's kinda sexy. OK, dangerous word in a room full of male scientists.

They had me scheduled to chat with people most of the day. They even assigned me a minder, a grad student, to make sure I could find my way from Professor A to Professor B, and kept to the schedule.

The talk was in mid-afternoon, and I did it up right, tying in this and that from all over the various bits of physics. Well, except I couldn't think of a reason the plasma people should care. Can't have everything. In the questions after, a green-haired student in the back row asked really detailed, really insightful questions. So when one of the appointments after the talk fell through, I asked my guide who she was.

"Alice? She, like, lives in the basement with the mushrooms."

"They keep you in the dark and feed you bullshit?" I quoted, from my own time in basement labs in grad school.

He laughed. "You wanna talk to her?"

So we had a chat, Alice and I. She was nearing completion on a thesis that was really quite interesting. They'd picked out a different system than I had, but she could articulate the reasons for that choice, and it made the effect they were looking for bigger than ours.

"Neat," I said.

"I know, right?" said Alice. "Like, totally rad."

We grinned at each other for a while.

She uncrossed her legs. "Can I ask you something, unrelated?" she asked.

"I think you just did," I said.

"There's one more prof who wanted to talk to you," said my minder, knocking at the open door.

"Are you coming to dinner? They're taking me out to dinner," I asked Alice.

"I, uh..." said Alice.

"How about I make them pay your way?" I said, grinning, remembering how poor I was as a grad student. Not as poor as some others, because Rachael was around, and two can certainly live more cheaply together than apart.

"Sold," she said.

"Uh... that Chinese place over on Pleasant Street," said my minder, consulting his printout. "They're leaving from the lobby at five."

"Totes cool," said Alice, crossing her legs again.

And then I had a chat with another particle physics guy who couldn't wrap his mind around what we were trying to do, and why quantum interference between electron states had anything to do with his pet Weak Interaction. He's a neutrino guy, totally bought into the Big Science paradigm where you collaborate with hundreds of people in huge underground labs somewhere. And find the one woman in the collaboration and make her the spokesperson, in hopes of skewing the perception of the gender balance of their project and procuring more funding.

Anyway. During dinner, Alice and I were in the bathroom together and she wanted to know if it's true what the rumors say, that I'm gay. Apparently there's a queer physics grapevine the younger folks are tuned in to nowadays.

"Ayup," I said. "Wife just moved out last year, in fact." It was longer than that, but I can't keep track.

"Oh right, you're from Massachusetts," she said.

We... made eyes at each other across the big round table for the rest of the meal.

She was the last one to leave the restaurant, so she walked me to the hotel. "I think being gay and out about it in academia is really fucking cool," she said. "Pardon my language. Especially for lesbians in physics."

"Well, it just kinda happened?" I said, with rising intonation like an undergrad.

She was grinning, and she made no move to leave after she helped me find my room.

CHAPTER THIRTY-FIVE

We've Met

Dear Renee,

So there comes a time that everybody who's anybody, in physics, goes to the American Physical Society meeting. It's a huge conference, as you know; I imagine you go yourself sometimes. I get there every five years or so. The hotel and conference center folks have discovered that academics tip poorly, so we end up in out of the way places like Albuquerque on Labor Day weekend or something.

It's tough, getting there. Thunderstorms, somewhere we weren't going, seem to have fouled up the airline schedules. JJ and I had to run to make a connection in... Chicago, I think it was. It was supposed to be Denver, but that didn't happen. Unsurprisingly, only one of our suitcases made the change. I should pack lighter and put everything in a backpack. Really. This is me, writing *buy backpack* on my to-do list.

So we collected what the airlines hadn't lost, told them about what they had, and hopped a shuttle to the hotel. Checked in, no problem. A hotel room is a hotel room. Generic carpet that won't show spills; industrial bathroom, view of... nothing much, out the window.

"There's two queen-sized beds in here," I said.

"Just the thing for two queens," said JJ.

I went down several floors to the hotel lobby to vegetate and let the airplane noise out of my head. There's a nice chair in a corner, and I recognized a bunch of old grey bald men checking in... physicists. Some astrophysics people come, and they're something like half of them women, so that's something.

And there was a couple checking in at the desk that I vaguely recognized. It was taking them a while, and JJ reappeared while they were doing it.

"Hey, I recognize you," I said at the woman's elbow. "Becca."

"Ravyn," she said. "They seem to have lost our reservation, and there's no room in the inn."

I summoned JJ, got the clerk's attention, and said, "So there are two queen-sized beds in our room, and we're only going to use one of them." I put an arm around JJ.

Tired clerk looked at me, wild curly hair down to the waist, and her, Asian with straight hair even longer, both in dresses, and he figured it out. No confession necessary.

"Could they share our room?" I asked him. It would be kind of a twisted situation, but it was a way of paying Becca back for the charity she had given to other folks without a place to stay.

"There'll be an extra charge," he said.

"Which is less than the cost of the room you don't have to rent them," I said, with a smile.

"True," he said, and cut them two extra keys.

"Thank you," said Becca.

"No problem," I said.

"Not yet," said JJ, laughing.

You may know Becca... Um, Grossman, is her last name. What you probably don't know is that she—they—she's a package deal with Stephan Larkin—are kinda sorta Rachael's exes. Did I tell you all that? Maybe in another letter.

We helped them upstairs with a few extra boxes, and while they were unpacking their luggage, mine arrived. There are never enough hangers; we should have talked the clerk out of more as part of the deal.

JJ kinda nuzzled up behind my ear and murmured that we'd have to behave ourselves, since we had straight people in our room.

And I laughed and turned and kissed her while Stephan watched. "Behave? Me??" And during the embrace for watchful eyes, I told her Becca's not exactly straight.

"Have you met JJ?" I asked Stephan and Becca. "This is JJ Jong."

"Oh," said Stephan. "I've read some of your papers. You're nothing like what I was imagining."

JJ offered a hand, which he kissed.

"When we're settled in here, there's a reception in the ballroom," said Becca.

"The best food Albuquerque Hoteldom has to offer on a holiday weekend, I'm sure," said Stephan.

"And house wine, I imagine," I was saying as we got off the elevator.

These meetings are huge; well over a thousand people were milling around the great open space. I'm not tall, as you know, and it's easy to get lost in the crowd. But I found several people I hadn't seen in years, and we managed to make ourselves heard. The others wandered off in different directions, mingling, sampling the finger food, and the beer. In these days of craft beers, some of the locals were pretty decent.

In due course, I found my way to the far corner of the hall, where there was an actual table with people I recognized sitting at it.

"Oh, here she is," said JJ, coming over to me, and pulling me by the elbow. "Let me introduce you to..."

And there you were, big glasses hiding much of your face, twisted mouth not quite smiling and yet not quite frowning.

"We've met," we both said.

"Oh," said JJ. "I thought she looked a lot like you."

"Identical twins," I said.

"She's my evil twin," you said.

And we both took off our glasses, swept mountains of curly black hair out of our eyes, and curtseyed together. Not that anybody does that any more, but it was a thing when we were teenagers.

"I've known her since before we were born," you said.

"Snuggling naked with underage girls," I said, and JJ laughed.

We looked at each other. "Oh, God," we both said, with deep sighs.

"How long has it been, Renee?" I asked you.

"Too long. Not long enough," you said. "I dunno, twenty years?"

"More, I think," I said.

"You may be right."

"I'm buying you both beer and you're going to tell me everything," said JJ.

We both looked at her like, yeah, that's not happening.

"If you want to," said JJ.

"Beer sounds good," you said.

"Alllrighty, then," I said.

The expedition attracted Becca, who stayed for one beer and went out to eat with somebody else.

"Food?" JJ said. "What do Renees eat?"

"Food sounds good," you said. "And just what's your relationship with Ravyn?"

JJ and I looked at each other. "Colleagues," she said.

"Lovers," I said. "She picked me up and put me back together when my wife left because she's straight."

"Ouch," you said. "I married late," you added. "With a man, I should say, because not everybody lives in Massachusetts."

"Aaaand thirteen-year-old Ravyn just had an urge to put out her tongue at you," I admitted.

JJ laughed, and we demonstrated for her.

We... looked into each others' eyes, you and I, Ravyn and Renee from of old, remembering. A little too long, it might be. It's always a little too something, with us, isn't it?

It was... interesting... And is there any point in signing off after you became a character in the letter I was writing to you?

love,
    really, this time I mean it,
    now that we've met as adults.
    Ravyn

P.S. My boobs really are bigger than yours. And that's not a good thing. I think JJ was duly scandalized. There's so much adolescent bad-girl water under that bridge, how is it we picked that particular thing to bring back? And of course we waited til the elevator door was open. You step off the elevator, look around, turn towards us, and there they are. And my reflexes take over and I'm going "Nuh-uh!" and presenting the evidence.

"Jesus," said JJ. "Are you guys fifteen? Or forty-five?" She hustled me into our room while I was still getting the passengers strapped in again. Where, if you recall, there were two other people, one of whom is male. Both of whom enjoy ogling women.

CHAPTER THIRTY-SIX

Incendiary

So, um, never mind pretending to be a letter I'm not sending.

"I'm not hungry," said JJ, when I proposed breakfast. She wasn't looking at me, but at Becca, who was returning the favor. So I let myself out and found Renee at the hotel's breakfast buffet. We sat together, with our hair the same, mostly loose but kinda glued out of our eyes. Because while we'd been apart for 20 years or more, we still thought alike, apparently.

"So, yeah," she said. "After I was miserable and alone for years, Max sent me to her brother Eric for counseling."

"Max?" I said. Max... she... color me intrigued.

"Elizabeth Maxwell. She was my lover and my mentor in grad school," said Renee. "She let me house sit for her while she was away on sabbatical, and I wrote my thesis in her spare bedroom. Fell in love with her all over again every time she happened through town, and then was devastated whenever she left again. I guess it was kind of abusive."

"Kinda," I said.

"Anyway. She had a complicated data analysis project, like five years ago, I think? And she looked me up and... she decided I needed to be less sad and lonely. I can't say she's wrong. Turns out her brother is an Episcopal priest in Denver, just 25 miles from me, so I put on my best little black dress and went to see him. He let me cry all over his shirt, and I kept going back until we were no longer counselor and client. I still live in Boulder close to the campus, but he's in the rectory in Denver. We see each other once or twice a week. I guess that's enough?"

"Sounds hard," I suggested.

"Everything in my life is hard," said Renee. "How's by you?"

"Well, where to start. I walked into a coffee shop and found a very cute grad student from the linguistics department. Rachael and I made eyes at the barrista together. We bitched together about how hard it is to form relationships. We failed to notice we were in fact forming a relationship over our mutual disclosure of foibles and flaws. When it came the day for leases to expire, we moved in together. When we finished our degrees, we got married in Provincetown and bought a house. In the Straight Whitebread Suburbs. It had a picket fence. The way Rachael tells it, we got down to the 2.3 kids part and discovered we were both women, both gay, and there was a little something missing."

Renee laughed.

"Five years or so later she decided she's more on the straight side of bi, and that was that. All the... Can I talk about this here?" I asked, looking around. Nobody seemed to be listening in. "All the sex toys and genderswapping and stuff... not enough. She fed me really really strong coffee, in the stated hope it would put hair on my chest. She moved out. I moped. My labbies didn't know what to do so they recruited the other two female physics department faculty members to hold me together, at least long enough for them to graduate."

"JJ seems sweet on you," said Renee. "And let me state for the record I'm sorry we flashed her. What are we? Fifteen?"

"Yeah, I'm sorry too. You'd think... Well, apparently whatever you'd think about us would be wrong. We really are still fifteen. My housemates tell me that pretty much every week."

"Plural," said Renee.

"Well, yeah. JJ's guy was... big. And clumsy. And he dislocated her hip several times. She dumped him. Andrea... thinks her guy is really fucking annoying (her words), and while she reminds us often that she's bi, she likes living with a houseful of women. And Joy... We kinda picked her up in a bar and she never went home. She's in history."

"Seems an embarrassment of..." said Renee, and I laughed.

"An embarrassment of lesbians," I crowed, a little too loud for a family hotel breakfast bar.

"Riches, dammit," said Renee, but she was grinning.

"Damn," said Stephan. "There are two of you. May I join you?"

"Renee, Stephan. Stephan, Renee," I said.

Renee and I glanced at each other, and said together, "She's my evil twin." Stephan laughed.

"Where's Becca?" I asked.

"Um, upstairs. With JJ," said Stephan. "Who seems a little bashful, so here I am."

"Rachael lived with Stephan and Becca before she met me," I explained to Renee.

"This is complicated," said Renee. "I mean, that's what people say online about their relationships nowadays, but this is the real deal."

"Thanks, by the way," said Stephan, "for sharing. Becca is happy being married to me, but she has needs I can't meet."

"Welcome," I said. "JJ's a grown-up, and we're not monogamous, and..."

And I was looking at Renee, who's also bisexual (I happen to know, having lived with her until we left for college) and now married to a man.

"Did I say it was complicated?" said Renee, mostly looking at her hands, but stealing glances at Stephan. "That would be so much more complicated."

I suppressed the urge to start my next statement with "you should" or "we could" or "would you?" Instead I said, "Don't be a stranger. Look us up if you're ever in Boston."

Renee looked up and we stared into each others' eyes. It's... kind of incendiary.

But there was a conference to attend, and my talk was that afternoon, so it was time to go upstairs and put on girl clothes, at least if JJ and Becca were... presentable. "See you around the conference hall," I said, waving fingers over one shoulder.

Turning as I left the room, I could see Renee in conversation with Stephan. I hoped she could learn something she wants to know from the way Becca and Stephan do their lives.

Which seems to involve Becca in the shower with my lover, while Stephan is chatting up my sister at the breakfast table.

CHAPTER THIRTY-SEVEN

Kinda... Like...

There's that semi-conscious state when you wake up and all is not quite as you had expected. It happens all the time in hotel rooms, but having reassured myself about that, I went back to sleep. One never gets enough rest at these things.

But there was still something rattling around in my unconscious mind... Not the same room as last night, it could be. Private room, for another, with just the one bed. A mop of black curls on the pillow, only some of which were my own.

The silly little black dress with the open lacework band around, a few inches above the hem? Yeah, that would not be good in daylight hours outside the hotel room we were sharing. It was fun to play with. That was gone, but something of JJ's was draped over the chair. So I took that and did the elevator ride of shame, showered alone, thank you very much, got dressed, and kinda sat shaking my head at what I had done.

I mean, really. We. Are. Not. Fifteen. Any. More. You'd think the consenting adults thing might involve actually thinking about what we're doing. But that's not the way it works, at least for me. I honestly don't know nuthin about nuthin. This from the woman who could marry in good faith, and be all hurt and bothered when her wife left a few years later.

Lemme just say this, Renee: I am so sorry. You said it would be complicated and it is, and I'm at least partly responsible.

JJ was likewise morose. "Happy Labor Day," she said, without any enthusiasm, looking at her phone. "The rest of the household sent us e-mail."

"Yeah," I said, not quite looking at JJ, who was not quite looking at me.

"Yeah. We should..." said JJ.

"We should," I agreed. So many things we should. Like getting it through my thick skull that other people don't live like we do. Like that my sister is every bit as fragile as I am, and has braced herself against different kinds of storms. Like maybe we should grow up, and start acting like it. "We really should," I said aloud.

"What actually happened?" I asked JJ on the elevator, going down to breakfast.

"Renee and I... kinda... Like..." JJ stammered. And then quickly, as if it were all one word, added, "got all kissy in the elevator and went to her room and…"

"And you didn't actually ask *Do you really want to*, not right out loud."

"Prolly not," said JJ. "And you'll notice I didn't turn up in our room at bedtime."

"Which would be why I put on that silly dress you brought for us to play with, and came to find you in the wee hours," I said. "Equal opportunity whatever, that's what we are."

"What. Evar," JJ said, just like our undergrad students, as the door was opening. "And I went back upstairs wearing the silly dress, leaving you two alone."

Renee was breakfasting alone, and she beckoned us over, with, remarkably, a smile. "Thank you, both of you, so much," was the first thing she said when we sat down.

JJ and I looked at each other, and then at Renee, and then at each other again. The mouth opens, hangs fire for a long moment, and then closes again.

"What??" said Renee. "The sun's out, for the first time I remember seeing it in... eons."

"We're in Alkaburkey," I said, purposely mispronouncing the city, the way Renee and I did when we were kids and found it on a map. "The skies are not cloudy all day."

"It's a metaphor," JJ explained.

"Duh," said Renee, and laughed. "You guys are cute when you're all remorseful and stuff."

She's my sister, all right. Every bit as much fifteen and forty-five, both at once. We dug this hole for her; we should at least help her out of it again.

CHAPTER THIRTY-EIGHT

October O'Clock and All's Well

To: ravyn@ravynscroft.org
  From: renee@physics.etc

dear ravyn,

i like your e-mail address. can you fix me up with one like that?

love,
  renee

"JJ?" I said. "Can you fix Renee up with an e-mail address on your server?"

"Suuuure," she said. She pulled both feet up onto the couch with her, pushed her sleeves up past her elbows, flipped hair over her shoulder and started muttering. "I can do that. How am I gonna do that?" The keyboard rattled for some time.

To: renee@physics.etc
   From: jj@ravynscroft.org

Now try it.

--JJ

"Thanks, Jay, you're a dear," I said.

"You're just saying that because you want to sleep with me," said JJ, grinning.

"True," I admitted.

To: ravyn@ravynscroft.org
   From: renee@ravynscroft.org

woo. apparently it works. thanks be to jj who giveth us the e-mail account.

and i'll spare you details and stuff, but after what i figured would be a grim conversation with no idea where it would end up, a couple things.

one, i'm still married. i'm kinda amazed. eric's... amazing. and also every bit as gay as i am. or bi or whatever. it's... complicated. thank heavens that one of his wealthy parishioners has a cabin in the mountains we could borrow for a day or two. heart to heart over a spectacular view. a crazy hour later, i asked him, "are we still married?"

"i am if you are," he answered. which is both obvious and profound.

so it's october o'clock and all's surprisingly well.

two, now he knows i have a sister. who's very very gay. not unlike his sister, who was my intro to the family. it's... complicated. he wants to invite max and you for christmas. and an, um, friend. i didn't ask if plus twos and plus threes would be a happening. so prolly not, but i will ask if you want me to.

i objected that all the lesbians would scandalize the little old church ladies, but he said they're pretty tough old birds, not easily perturbed.

and so there were visions of perturbation theory dancing in my head. physics nerd humor. gotta love it.

and i made him promise not to divorce me for a year after you come to visit. he laughed and agreed.

so there we are... ravyn, please come to denver for christmas. bring a friend. pleeeease bring a friend. hahahaha snort (nervous laughter).

we invited max and laurie too. it'll be five lesbians and eric. what could go wrong?

lemme know,
    love,

renee

"Heeeeeyyy," I said, over dinner.

Everybody sort of rolled their eyes and turned to look at me.

"What's up?" Joy asked.

"It's Renee," I said. "She sent me e-mail."

"Aaaaand?" JJ prompted. "Should I be nervous?"

"Apparently not," I said, with a shrug. "She says..." and I paused dramatically to extract the phone from the thigh pocket of my cargo pants. "She says she's still married."

"Oh good," said JJ.

"And she wants, Eric wants, somebody wants, to invite me and an 'um, friend', as she puts it, to visit for Christmas."

"What could go wrong?" JJ asked.

"I know, right? Renee asked exactly the same thing," I said. "Eric promises not to divorce her for a year after we visit."

"That's probably a good thing?" said JJ. "And you're looking at me."

"What plans does anybody have for Christmas?" I asked.

"Zip," said JJ. "Nada. Christmas is not a thing in Chinese culture."

"My brother might want me to visit, I suppose?" said Rachael. "Or there's John."

"Or there's John," said JJ, looking at me for a reaction. Yes, my ex sleeps with men. I know this, and it's mostly okay with me. Not that it's my call. She also lives in my house, which is likewise okay with me. And she sleeps with me sometimes.

Andi and Joy and possibly Ben had something elaborate cooked up, which I'm sure would boggle my imagination if I knew the details, so they didn't supply any. Who knows, it might be perfectly innocent for once, like family obligations.

"So you wanna go with me?" I asked JJ.

"Ummmm, suuuure," said JJ. "Maybe I can keep things from going too wrong?"

"Thanks, Jay," I said. "Tell me a story about queer people getting together again after years and not hating each other before the end of the visit."

"I'll be making it up as we go along, I'm sure," said JJ.

To: renee@ravynscroft.org
     From: ravyn@ravynscroft.org

Dear Renee,

JJ says she'll do it. See you in the After-Finals timeframe. I hope we behave ourselves to Eric's satisfaction.

love,
    Ravyn.

To: ravyn@ravynscroft.org
    From: renee@ravynscroft.org

yay! i think...

renee

CHAPTER THIRTY-NINE

Christmas Invitation

To: renee@ravynscroft.org
  From: Ravyn@ravynscroft.org

Dear Renee,

I guess I can just send this stuff now. I've been writing you letters for months, no, years, trying to sort stuff out in my own head, and then not sending them.

It's November. You've invited us to visit over Christmas. And I'm remembering the American Physical Society meeting in Alkaburkey, wondering. You seemed to roll with it, though, so I hope everything really is okay. I didn't want to get you into trouble with your guy. Not an excuse, but it is a reason, you just needed to be touched so much. I recognize the feeling myself.

JJ seems to be intrigued by the fact that I have a twin and didn't tell her all about it before. I... kinda suppressed... telling people in my life about you, after practically living in your underwear all through high school. I figured they didn't need to know, and it would help me become my own person if they didn't. Or something.

Anyway, well met, I think, and thanks for inviting me. Us. You kinda got to know JJ a little yourself. She's a dear, isn't she? She kinda held me together when Rachael left and my life imploded. Well, there was a year or two (wherever did my intuitive sense of the passage of time go?) where I was not together, and JJ was trying to hold her own relationship (and her hip) together. Benny separated that once too many times, and she dumped him.

Right about the same time as the chronic weeping in my office got to be such a problem that my disciples made me start doing girls' nights out with the rest of the female physics faculty (JJ and Andrea, who wants to be called Andi, which reminds me, every time, of Andy Kreicek the pimplefaced geek that... gah. You remember him, I'm sure.

Go ahead, laugh at me, I deserve it.

Anyway, see you in a month.

love,
    Ravyn

hitting send in 3... 2... 1...

From: renee@ravynscroft.org
    To: ravyn@ravynscroft.org

hey, you. just relax. it'll be fine. really it will. if i keep telling myself that it'll be true, right?

aaaaand jj's a dear, as you say. and that huuuuge sucking sound you hear (you remember ross perot? what a cartoon character he was.) would be my skinhunger absorbing any moisturizer that might be available. i really need some female just-friends in my life. the whole department is male, pretty much. my partner is male. my office teddy bear is even male. d'you have stuffed animals?

all the things i could ask after 30 years and that's what pops into my head.

seriously, sometime we should talk about physics. i bet we've both learned a thing or two it'd be useful to share. jj can help if she wants to. oh, and, who's your third? andrea something? i don't think i've read her papers.

it sounds like you-all have way too much fun. so much it's dangerous.

anyway.
   see ya xmas.
   love (can i write that out loud?),
   renee

From: jj@ravynscroft.org
   To: renee@ravynscroft.org, ravyn@ravynscroft.org

Renee,

So Herself suggested that since I did the arranging and stuff I should just send you the itinerary myself. It's stapled onto these few bits of ether, someplace.

We'll be arriving on Monday before the holiday itself (herself? It seems like it should be herself.) at, um, 5:23pm. I presume they have a cell phone lot, so if you-all (R&R) would be good girls and exchange phone numbers, we can let you know when we get there.

cheers,
    JJ

From: jj@ravynscroft.org
    To: renee@ravynscroft.org, ravyn@ravynscroft.org
    cc: LSHF@ravynscroft.org

Now with the attachment actually attached...

And copying the Order.

J

<attachment>

To: jj@ravynscroft.org
    From: renee@ravynscroft.org

got it, thx.

also i think 'ravynscroft' is very cute. i imagine everybody there is more than happy there's only one ravyn living in the croft. she's... quite...

just, quite.

also, comma, LSHF?

renee

To: jj@ravynscroft.org
   From: renee@ravynscroft.org

> just, quite.

Quite.

> LSHF?

The whole gang. I'll tell you the story in person.

JJ

CHAPTER FORTY

Sharing is Good, Right?

to: ravyn@ravynscroft.org
   from: renee@ravynscroft.org

dear ravyn,

yeah i know i said i'd spare you the details but i gotta talk to somebody, and you said that writing to me, whether you actually sent the results or not, was helpful. so mebbe i'll try it, shall i?

of course i came back from alkaburkey, back to whatever was left of my regular life, my real life, after that... fantasyland, let's call it. except part of the trouble is i can't really tell what's real and what's fantasy.

thank you, ravyn, for swamping my little canoe.

eric picked me up at the airport. we'd missed our regular weekend together, so. and i find that while i can't figure out how to say anything to him, my commitment is still there. i want to love, cherish, etc. etc. as long as we both shall live.

but there was jj tugging at the corners of my eyes. that sounded bad; she's asian. tugging at the corners of my attention, how bout? and i looked at her, unscrunched myself from the corner of the elevator we were sharing, accepted her smoochies, shared my hotel room with her.

sharing is good, right? it's what we tell the kids. i even tell my lab students that. work together, you might get ideas from each other.

and somehow dressing in the morning it was you and not her. i guess she shares, too. and somehow after all these years, you're just like me: shirt either covers the hands or is pushed up to the elbows, nothing near the wrists.

are you *sure* we're two people?

so i went back to boulder to my condo, alone, after ...

and tried to focus my mind on the stuff i learned at the conference (the physics, silly) but kept getting distracted by the stuff i learned at the conference (the, um, well, ..., since i used that in the last paragraph).

and somehow the ellipsis kept growing, crowding out everything else. so here we are wednesday, and he's smart and he's figured out that, um, i dunno what he figured out, but we need to talk. a phrase to strike terror into the stomachs of guilty people everywhere. i have thursdays off this term, and he does too.

"you remember hank and gracie?" he asked me when i got into his car. he drove, not toward denver as usual but to my condo. "pack a bag," he said. "we're going to the high country."

turns out hank and gracie own this cabin up near the tree line west of boulder. it sits empty most of the time. eric borrows it sometimes for retreats with his youth group. "the utes" he calls them, after the local indian tribe. hank gave him the keys for our thursday.

it's a cool place. there's a drawbridge between the driveway and the cabin. there's a wood stove. there's an outhouse, built over the top of an old mine shaft. i guess it won't ever be filling up. and here i am in overalls, so i practically hafta get naked to pee. i guess i should ask more questions. oh, and it's cold, since the wood stove is the only heat and it's in the cabin, like, duh.

anyway, thanks be to hank, who giveth us the cabin keys. and a place with spectacular scenery and zero background noise except wind in pine and spruce trees, to talk.

perchance to ...

but i'm sure you'd filled in that blank already.

anyway, some of the ... is neither here nor there, but there's stuff we won't be trying again.

so we ended up sitting side by side on the balcony with our boots on the bottom rail, not looking at the spectacular scenery between our feet, and talking about, i was gonna put in three dots and i guess that'd fit, but more than that, about that long lost sister i somehow kinda never told him about. and meeting up with her in alkaburkey. and her lover, well, one of them, how many are there i dunno i didn't ask but there's more where she came from? and, um, ...

because it was relevant.

"i figured there'd be shouting or tears or something," i said into the silence.

"yeah, it rarely helps, in my experience," said eric, with a sigh. "i guess i should prolly tell you" (you can tell i'm paraphrasing, just from the use of "prolly") "that i'm not that straight either. there was this guy andrew i knew in seminary. seedy part of milwaukee, bar, too much to drink, not enough sense or caution, we got beat up. he died. i still dunno how i feel about that."

well, at least the silence was symmetrical.

the sun started going down. the shadows in the mountains are really something. we weren't looking at them.

"are we still married?" i asked him after a while.

"i am if you are," said eric, with a sad kind of a grin.

i mean, duh, but still it's profound somehow.

"and what happened to that couple who just this morning, like, ..." i asked him.

"we're still here," he said. "a little more real. a little more grit in the love, i think."

i guess pretending we're not gay isn't gonna be part of wherever we go from here.

i kinda can't imagine where that will be.

thanks for listening... i think i'm all writ out for now.

love,
   i think?
   maybe?

renee

p.s. hitting "send" in 3, 2, 1, now.

CHAPTER FORTY-ONE

Growth and Standards

I wish growth didn't hurt so much.

Who knows, maybe if I'd been a housewife, birthed a few kids and raised them while keeping my man happy, that would have been a life. But noooo, I had to be gay. Or maybe bi or something. And ever so... yeah. Unsure of myself, maybe?

Rachael almost had me thinking I was somewhere on the trans spectrum. Blow in my ear and I'll follow you anywhere. Honestly? I wonder sometimes if maybe she's something like what she had me believing I am. Though at least since she moved in again she seems to be enjoying the female thing.

It's so freaking loud, that desire, sometimes.

Even when I don't feed the gremlin after midnight, she's whining about that. She's like a snake wrapped around my spine, coiled up somewhere resting on my abdominal floor. Or that tingling sensation up and down my spine could be her, crawling into the unused places in my mind, waving forked tongue, prospecting for another warm body.

Dammit, I'm picky nowadays. A warm body is not enough.

They hafta be female. Well, except Stephan, who I... kinda ogled a little? When they were staying in our room in Alkaburkey.

They hafta be gay. Well, bi. I mean, Andi. And, for that matter, Rachael.

They hafta be somebody I trust. Well, there was Kat. Andi's choirgirl friend who, um, fell into a mutual attraction one night after a concert when our household and some part of the alto section were having ice cream. Her thumbs... bend in really interesting ways. Neither of us could wait to get her out of that whimsical dress.

I think someone told me Kat's shacked up with JJ's barrista Christy. We teased JJ about sleeping with twelve year olds, even though Christy really is in her late 20s. You expected bubblegum. Which was deemed unprofessional by the coffee shop where she worked.

They hafta not be my sister. That shoooooould go without saying... dammit.

They hafta be vanilla. Except for Joy, for whom everything is kinky. Actual vanilla beans are a little kinky, right? Gnarled seed pods with kinks in them. She knows just where my limits are and flirts with them outrageously.

They hafta not be my students or other folks who depend on me to be professional. I'd prefer, you might think, women my own age... I have a house full of them.

What are you doing to me, sister libido?

"What are you fretting about?" JJ murmured in my ear.

"Renee," I said, not really wanting to get into the apparently infinite well of Ravyn's Slutitude.

"She can take care of herself," said JJ. "Without our help. Maybe better if we don't help."

"Maybe so."

A few minutes passed.

"Seriously, girl, you're squirming," said JJ. "What's roasting your ass tonight?"

"Thinking over all the mistakes that are my life," I admitted.

"Like getting a great job. Or figuring out how the weak interaction manifests in atomic structure. Or inviting me to live here. All huge mistakes," said JJ. She pulled free of me, turned on the bedside lamp, and leaned up against the headboard.

"Oh, hush," I said.

"You're actually blushing," said JJ. "I thought it was only Andi who did that."

"Now I really am blushing," I said.

"I thought it was only me who did that," said Andi, who just happened to be walking through the bedroom on her way to the closet. One thing about sharing beds and lovers is that your stuff is usually hanging in a closet in another room. Nobody seems to mind, much. The doors don't really stay latched very well. I suppose we could fix that, but as I said, nobody seems to mind, much.

"I'm just thinking about Renee, and regretting the folks I've left behind," I said. "And, um, hoping I'll be worthy of knowing her again."

"In the Biblical sense?" Rachael snorted from where she was standing in the doorway. Sometimes I swear my bedroom, whichever one I'm in, is conversation central. She even adopted the standard posture, leaning one shoulder on the door jamb, arms folded, the extra leg kinda waving around, coming to rest gently crossed over to the other side of the foot she was standing on.

"Where does that come from?" I asked, hoping to pivot away from my sex life to any other topic of conversation.

"It's a Hebrew metaphor," said Rachael. "Now spill."

So much for conversational gambitry.

So much for dignity, such as it is.

"Just trying to convince myself I have standards," I admitted, with a sigh. "Everything I come up with has exceptions."

"Exceptions that prove the rules," said Andi, who was very cute sitting cross legged on the foot of the bed.

"There are rules?" JJ asked. "Anglos are weird, all tied up in knots over who's sleeping with whom."

"Who wants to be tied up in knots?" Joy wanted to know. Rachael briefly lost her balance as Joy pushed past her into the room.

There was one of those silences that speak louder than words. Watching who was looking at whom with drooly expressions on their faces. Consulting Sister Libido who despite the snake metaphor from my dreams has no desire to meet up with a rope.

"Right," I said, laughing nervously. "I don't wanna know the answers to that."

The droolers adjourned to another bedroom, I lay down again, and JJ turned out the light and snuggled in. "Now lie still," she said, as I drifted off to sleep.

CHAPTER FORTY-TWO

Travels with JJ

The time came at last. Finals were finished. I dropped by the department office to chat with Madeleine, the admin person in charge of posting the grades to the computer, to let her know mine were in.

"Thank you," she said, looking up from her screen. "You always do it right. So many of the very smart people who work here can't figure out a simple computer interface." She typed for a while. "Oh, and do have some spiced cider. I think I outdid myself this year."

"This really is good," I said, having blown on the mug until it was cool enough to stuff between my boobs. Good thermal contact, is what JJ calls this maneuver. I extracted it again when the chairman bumbled through. This space is after all his outer office.

"Any plans for the holidays?" Madeleine asked, in a lull between grade submissions.

"Well, JJ and I..."

"Oh right, I forget all the women in this department are living together." She smiled.

"...recently re-discovered my sister. So she invited us to visit over the holidays." Along with another of her exes, I didn't say.

"Re-discovered?" asked Madeleine.

"So many queer people are estranged from their families of origin," I said. Which is true in general, and even true in detail for this case. But it's not even half the story. It wasn't that she wanted nothing to do with me being a lesbian. It's that she wanted everything to do with it, and that was not a recipe for becoming separate people. "When I was in kindergarten, they asked me what I wanted to be when I grew up. *Together*, I answered. I've missed her for always, but I'm a little afraid of how different we've become over the years."

"You'll have to tell me all about it when you get back. Here's another batch of grades to post."

For what values of 'all', I wondered to myself as I went to find JJ. And then Andi, who had already made arrangements to meet up with the Humanities half of the household for a holiday meal (and more spiced cider, this time with nog).

"Aren't we a sight?" JJ asked. I hadn't noticed it in the morning when we were getting ready, but we all seemed to be wearing bright colors, with hose that matched somebody else's dress.

"We represent... the Lollypop Guild," Andi sang, a little too loud even for a noisy restaurant.

There was one of those lulls in the conversation in the big dining room.

"Oopsie," said Andi, under her breath.

"The waters of the Red Sea have flowed together again," said Rachael over the following din, "and no actual Egyptians were harmed in the making of this scene."

"You're very strange," said Joy to Rachael. "I like that in a lover." It's a line I've heard from each of these women in various circumstances. It's part of the liturgy of the Order, I think.

A couple days later, we had a date with an airplane. One cool thing about having four other licensed drivers in the household is that somebody's bound to be able to get us at least as far as the train. Driving to the airport is a bit much, so we settled for the subway.

"Mmm, breakfast on the concourse, my favorite," I said, just to have something to break up the silence zombies while we waited for the caffeine to take effect. Not too much because we were about to agree to sit for four hours. It's easier if you don't need the bathroom.

"Are we having fun yet?" JJ asked. "I kinda like sausage for breakfast. I should remember that."

"Duly noted. A sleepy JJ is a carnivorous JJ," I said, pretending to punch said fact into my phone.

"Are you nervous?" JJ asked.

"After Alkaburkey? Yes, lots! None at all!"

"And now we're quoting Bilbo Baggins," said JJ. "And I feel about the same way, though of course she's not my sister. Maybe we should have..."

And we both waited for Joy to say something unprintable, but of course she was at home and not waiting for an airplane.

"Maybe so," I admitted. "Danced with the one that brung ya," I added.

JJ laughed. "Zackly, as Andi might put it."

In due course we boarded, texted the home crowd that we were underway, turned off our phones, and launched into the air with a hundred some odd of our closest strangers. JJ put her head on my shoulder and drifted off to sleep. I sort of propped my face on her head, and dozed some, dreaming of her shampoo. And all the free associations a semi-conscious mind could make.

When the plane turned south to land in Denver, the sun was in my eye, so I woke JJ up, we put on our shoes like good girls, put our seat backs and tray tables in the upright and locked position, stowed any electronics we'd been using, and waited until the plane was done with the roll out before turning our phones on again.

Joy had texted several times with identical content: "Are you there yet? Are you there yet? Are you there yet?"

I showed JJ, and said, "I'm not the only one who's twelve."

"I guess we take turns being the adult in the room," said JJ. "Or something. Whatever we're doing, it seems to work."

"It really kinda does. Who knew?"

"Landed," I texted back.

And then I sent the same word to Renee. There was no response. "Maybe she figured it'd take us half an hour to get out and so she's driving or whatever."

"Maybe she hates telephones," JJ suggested. "I'm not sure she had one in Albuquerque."

"She did give me a cell number," I said. "Which I think she read off the screen in Alkaburkey." Somehow I had to wedge Renee's and my childhood pronunciation of that city's name into the conversation.

When the plane let us out at last, we found a quiet place and I called the number.

"Hey, it's Ravyn," said Renee. "At least that's what the phone tells me."

"Hiya," I said. "We're in the concourse, uh C I think."

"So there's a train connecting each concourse to the main terminal. It's downstairs. Like a subway."

"Subway, got it," I said.

"Find your luggage, and call me with an outside door number. I'm parked in the cell phone lot, and it'll take me five minutes or so to get there when you call."

"Luggage, bathroom, coffee, call with door number. Got it."

"Bathroom," JJ said, crossing her legs.

So we did all that. "Five Oh Four," was the first thing I said into the phone when she answered.

"Right. Passenger pickup is on the fourth level, so go down one floor and I'll get you at 404 in five minutes."

"Four Oh Four, page not found," said JJ, just to have something mindless to say, I think. We did find it. And it was breathtakingly cold, being outdoors for the first time in hours.

We were still struggling with zippers and gloves when a van pulled up, Renee popped out, shouted "Brrr!", and helped us hustle our luggage into the back of the van. JJ got in the right front door, and Renee and I shared the middle seat.

"Eric," said Eric, as he scanned the traffic.

"JJ," said JJ. "And one of those guys in the back is Ravyn."

"It's amazingly hard to tell which, and I happen to know what coat Renee is wearing," said Eric. "We'll just find the cell phone lot again and wait for Max and Laurie to arrive."

"Your ex?" I asked Renee.

"Why did I sign up to have every chapter of my sordid past in the same house for a week?" Renee said.

"Because I wanted to meet my out-laws," said Eric.

"Outlaws. I like it," said JJ.

Renee's phone tweetled. "Max, the phone tells me." She put it on speaker.

"It's Laurie. Herself is in the bathroom. What's the plan?"

"Read me the number off the nearest outside door," said Renee.

"Five thirteen," said Laurie. "And it's the same on the outside as in."

"When you find Max, go down one flight and wait outside 413. We'll be there in about 5 minutes. It's cold out, zip up your coats."

"Yes, mother," Laurie laughed, and disconnected.

"Four thirteen would be on the other side of the terminal," Eric said aloud. "So, uh, that way," he added when we came to the split in the access road. The terminal is kind of stunning from that viewpoint, like a campground of huge teepees on the plains. They didn't bother with the detail of smoke holes in the roof, or lodge poles sticking out.

"Four oh nine...," said Eric.

"There they are," said Renee, leaning across me. She handed me her glasses, which I put on.

We swooped in and acquired two more women and their luggage.

"Renee!" said Max, and hugged me. So I hugged her back before correcting her. It was like being fifteen again, in so many ways.

"Sorry," said Max. "I recognized the glasses."

"Which are giving me a headache already," I said.

"It's colder than a witch's tit," said Max when the door slid shut with all of us inside.

"My tits are warm, thanks," said Laurie.

"Mine, too," said JJ.

"Oookay then," said Eric, before Renee and I could start the bidding for who was the raunchier twin today.

He drove in silence for some time, sometimes distracted by traffic, other times glancing at us in the mirror. "Seventy is... over there," he murmured. "I always get confused by this interchange."

"How are you doing, Liz?" Eric asked, when he had a moment's attention for his sister.

"This is going to be confusing," she laughed. "Everybody else calls me Max, but you're as much The Maxwell here as I am, so of course you'll call me Liz."

"We never did figure that out, did we?" said Eric.

I glanced at Renee, who was looking at me.

"It's good to see you," she said. "I wasn't sure it would be, but it's good to be in contact again."

I snuggled my leg up closer to hers.

"Ever the literal one," she laughed. She ran the fingers of both hands through her hair. I stopped myself before I did exactly the same thing. I guess it's a nervous tic I've had since we were kids. How... odd... to feel the butterflies in her stomach.

CHAPTER FORTY-THREE

We're Home

"And we're home," said Eric. He pulled into the driveway at the house next door to the church.

"Come in, come in," Renee said as soon as she had unlocked the door. "There are two spare bedrooms upstairs. Max and Laurie get the one on the right, as always, and we cleaned all the stuff out of the front room on the left for Ravyn and JJ."

So we wrestled all the luggage upstairs into the indicated rooms. In the moment we had alone, JJ pulled me in for a kiss. I groped her boob. She laughed, thank heavens.

"It really is colder outside than a witch's tit," I announced

JJ laughed again, with an edge of panic to her voice. Embarrassment, perhaps. She's never embarrassed. But I guess the situation was even more awkward for her than it was for me: a not quite partner witnessing the long awaited reunion of sisters, wondering what she could do to prevent spontaneous combustion.

"So, there's stew in the slow cooker, and some rice. And a very nice bottle of wine," Renee announced from the hallway, while she distributed towels and sheets. "Sorry I didn't have the beds put together, but I haven't actually been here in a week."

"I dunno if I could live apart from my, uh..." I blurted out.

"Lover," JJ suggested.

"Um, friend," said Max.

"Seemed the thing to do at the time," Renee said breezily. But I could see her lower lip quiver.

"Sorry," I murmured in her ear on the way downstairs. "I touched a nerve."

"Meh," she said. "It's okay. At least mostly."

"Merry Christmas, everybody!" said Eric, as we sat down to dinner.

"This is... perfect," said Laurie. "I need to get the recipe."

"Moroccan spice mixes are unique to each household," said Eric.

"We're all sorta related here," said Laurie.

"Eric and Renee, their respective sisters, and their..." I said, again waiting for Joy to say "fuckers".

"Lovers," said JJ.

"Um, friends," said Max.

"Wives," said Laurie. "Kinda sorta."

"Well, Ravyn has a wife who is not me," said JJ. "It's... complicated."

"We're not allowed to have wives in Wisconsin," said Max.

"Thanks for not remarking you're both my exes," said Renee. "Sisterhood is powerful enough."

"Um, oopsie," I said, looking at Renee.

"Pff," she pffed. "I told Eric all about it."

"All..." Max prompted.

"We've been snuggling together naked since before we were born," said Renee.

"True," I said. "And... um..." Joy, who was not even there, said *fuuuuuck* in my head.

"And, um," said Renee, looking into my eyes. She... smiled.

"Dang," said JJ, recognizing the smile, but on the wrong face.

"Yeah," I said, and decided not to look at either Renee or JJ.

"It's snowing," Eric said, to fill the ensuing silence. "And it's Christmas. And we're all on vacation. Well, except I have a service to run Christmas Eve. And the community dinner for the homeless folk on Christmas Day.

"Can we help with that?" Max asked.

"The service? You're not ordained," said Eric, grinning.

"The community dinner, silly," said Max.

"It'd be great if you wanted to do that," said Eric. "Doris from the parish is a retired chef, and she does amazing things with the budget we have. More hands are always welcome. And I imagine some of the usual volunteers might be doing family things that day."

"This will be our family thing." I looked around to see who had said that, and apparently it was me. I guess our experience with Becca and inviting her homeless friends to stay for a few days or a few weeks had gotten under my skin.

"Otherwise we'd be cooking over here while Doris is cooking next door," said Renee. "It makes sense to join them. Other otherwise, we could do stuff like the museum with the dinosaur bones, or visit Boulder, my lab, and my humble abode. Or go outdoors and let Eric dump trees full of snow on our heads."

Eric was grinning. "You're always so trusting."

"And then you vanish from my side, just in time to avoid the avalanche you've caused," said Renee. She was also smiling.

"And then you just have to wait while my hair dries. Poetic justice or something."

"More wine?" Renee said, dividing what was left among several glasses.

"It's delicious," I said.

"I don't think I've heard you use that word un-ironically," said JJ.

"Rachael used to use it when she was trying to get me to try something disgusting like slimy okra or fried eggplant," I said. "I rooted it out of my vocabulary."

"Until now," said Renee. "Huh."

"Until now," said JJ. "Huh."

"Alright, so I'll admit I'm not exactly sure if I'm fifteen or... forty-something, here with you. Is that a bad thing?" I was looking at Renee.

"Ravyn has been fifteen for decades," said JJ. "We tease her about it all the time at home."

"That might... explain..." said Renee. "It's very strange, having you suddenly there again, feeling my feelings, saying what I was about to say. Flipping your hair in just the same way."

"For me, too," I said. "But you knew that."

Renee nodded. "So there's this story our mom used to tell us..."

"The one where..." I asked.

"Yes!" Renee interrupted, almost before my thought came together in my own head.

"Spill," said JJ.

"We asked her which of us was older..." said Renee.

"Because being identical, any difference was something to be grasped at," I said. Carefully not saying anything more about...

"And she said they never knew, that they got us mixed up as infants and that which baby got which name was a random thing anyway..."

"Which is true, of course, but." I said. "So maybe I'm you and you're me."

"Or the other way around," said Renee.

"Wait..." said JJ. "I've had too much of this very good wine. Whichever of you is the real Ravyn, please join me upstairs at your convenience."

"Now is convenient," I said. "Good night everybody. Good to meet you both, Max and Laurie. And Eric. Thanks for putting up with us."

JJ was about to say something polite, but it got stomped on by a yawn. She was... sleepy by the time we got snuggled into bed together. As I lay awake listening to her breathing, it occurred to me that it's not at all a given that I'd be permitted to sleep with my lover under the roof of the church rectory. I mean, it made sense from a logistical point of view; fewer beds are needed if people are chummy with the folks they sleep with back home. I couldn't help but wonder if former occupants of this house were rolling over in their respective graves. Not that we did anything, at least not that first night, since JJ was sleepy.

I should really find out what she uses for shampoo sometime. I'm sure the bottle is in the cabinet at the end of the shower at home, but I haven't ever looked at it. There are such pleasant associations with that scent.

CHAPTER FORTY-FOUR

One Mug or Two?

"Huh," I said, idly fussing with my hair, half-heartedly trying to impose order on the turbulent chaos. It's morning; it's a thing I do in the morning.

"Mmphrmph," said JJ, or words to that effect. Her face was against the mattress somewhere near my hip. Being a person of very straight hair, she's spared the daily battle, for the most part.

I looked around the room, wondering how many other couples like us had slept there, awakened there, made love there. "When did sex in the morning become a lesbian thing?" I asked, aloud. "Did we learn it from male lovers, or our bi sisters or something?"

Apparently going back to sleep was also a thing. "What?" JJ wanted to know when she finally figured out which way was up and turned her face that way.

"Just thinking aloud," I said. "I bet I can find us some coffee."

"Coooofffffeeee," JJ moaned.

So I slipped out of bed, checked my jammies, and flitted downstairs barefoot.

"Hey," said Renee, when I found the kitchen.

"Hey, yourself," I said. "My beloved wants coffee."

"Mine, too," said Renee. "Hang on a bit."

"Long enough to go get slippers?" I asked.

"Just stand here on the heating grate," said Renee.

The grate is only so big, and in order for it to be effective, you have to leave some room between your feet. So I got an up-close view of the chaos that is Renee's hair in the morning.

"Your hair is just like mine. Kind of a disaster in the morning."

"Think of it as a diagram of the dynamo effect," said Renee, grinning. "All the currents and eddys in the earth's outer core, transporting heat but getting folded over on themselves and generating a magnetic field in the process."

"Or in the sun," I suggested. "Electrons spiraling around magnetic field lines." I pulled playfully at one of her curls, which snapped back when I released it.

We looked into each others' eyes, close enough to see... everything, it felt like, even without our glasses. The coffee maker snorted.

"Time to resuscitate the spouse equivalents," said Renee.

"Thanks," I said, meaning for the coffee, but I was rewarded with another soul-searching, lingering gaze.

"Oh," said Renee. "You'll enjoy this." She got the bag of beans out of the freezer and handed it to me.

"Resurrection blend," I read from the label. "That's cute."

We poured four mugs of coffee. Renee rinsed out a thermos bottle with hot water and put the rest of the coffee into it. I handed her the stopper, which she almost forgot. She smiled and laughed a little.

I put both mugs on the night stand and snuggled in.

JJ squealed when my cold feet found something warm. "Okay, I'm awake now," she said. "And I smell coffee." She climbed over me making a mess of the covers, but she found her drugs. Not having been paid any attention, her hair kept trying to close like curtains around her face and coffee mug, and her usual head-shaking motions weren't helping. I watched her check to see if she had a rubber band on her wrist, which she did not. They were on the top of the dresser, across the room. Nevertheless, she braided her hair, handed me the end of it, and said, "Hold that." And went back to drinking coffee, with apparently no thought for a more permanent hair management solution.

"Hold that," she repeated, giving me her mug. So I had two mugs of coffee in one hand and her braid in the other. "I should just..." and she squirmed just enough to pull her night dress down. "Thanks," she said, offering a hand.

I gave her the braid. She dropped it, took her mug, and by the time her hair came all apart, the coffee was mostly consumed, so it made little difference.

"We live such different lives together," I said, petting the nearest lock of her straight hair.

"Mmm? Nearly everything else is identical," said JJ.

But in this household, identical is a very strong word. "Um," I said. "One identical sister is enough, thanks."

"Oh," said JJ. "Right. I forgot."

"I used to think I was her, she was me, we were two people in one body, or one person in two bodies just alike. The thing about not knowing which baby got which name really rattled my sense of myself for a long time," I said.

"I hear you," said JJ.

"Anyway. I bet there's breakfast." So I got out of bed, shrugged out of my jammies, found my luggage and set about locating clothes for the day.

"I want a shower," said JJ.

"You remember where the bathroom is," I said.

"I was hoping you'd come too," said JJ.

I looked at her, considering. She raised an eyebrow to mirror my own expression. Fuck, why not? So that's what we did. I forget that it's kind of provocative, since we do it all the time at home; it's more efficient cycling five women through the shower in the morning if they do it in pairs. Um, unless. Of course. But JJ was polite, which is to say not sexy at all, and we finished in good time.

Back to getting dressed. Braid hair. Black t-shirt, check. Jeans, kind of pale blue. Big sheepskin slippers, knowing it's cold downstairs. Besides, they flatten nicely in the suitcase.

Renee's consideration of who she was that morning seemed to come to the same conclusion: black t-shirt, braided hair, faded jeans. Her slippers were somewhat more domestic, what with not having to fly through the air for a thousand miles.

For the moment there were three of us in the kitchen. We looked at each other, we both looked at JJ. We apparently both thought of the elevator incident in Alkaburkey. I pulled my shirt up about 3 inches and smirked. A flicker of amusement disturbed her eyebrows. JJ's mouth was open. I pulled my shirt down again and the moment passed.

"Mine really are bigger, I think," I said, "and that's not a good thing." I did not offer evidence.

"Pff," Renee pffed. "I hafta wonder why we thought it was."

"This is gonna be a wild ride," JJ murmured.

Laurie walked into the kitchen followed by Eric. "Coffee?" Laurie asked.

"One mug or two?" Renee said, holding the thermos bottle.

"One for now. The Maxwells value their sleep."

"We do," said Eric, yawning. Renee poured him a mug and set about making more.

"We have the usual approximations of breakfast," Renee said when the coffee maker started to gurgle. "Yogurt, milk, cereal, granola for the nuts and berries people..."

"Is that nuts, comma, and berries-people? Or nuts-and-berries people?" I had to ask.

"Yes," said Renee. She grinned. "Various fruits... Could do eggs and sausage if anybody's up for that."

JJ moved in a way that betokened consent.

"All right, then," said Renee.

"Ravyn and I had breakfast at the airport yesterday. I'd forgotten about sausage for breakfast."

"Anything for my sister's keeper," said Renee.

An odd turn of phrase that left me wondering if she thinks I'm a little on the wild side, in need of a zookeeper. I mean, I am, I suppose, so it's natural enough she would think so.

"Another mug now, if you please," said Laurie. She had apparently detected the sounds of her mate stirring.

And sure enough, there was Max. Liz. Elizabeth Maxwell, who's known as Max everywhere except in her brother's house. Formerly a plasma physics person, but she got interested in dirt, in particular fluid flow through porous solids, so I gather from the literature that she's actually on the Ag School faculty in Madison. Just at the moment she was looking like a former person, scraped off the front of a bus.

She murmured something thankful but otherwise unintelligible, held the steaming mug under her nose, and inhaled deeply. Mug on table. Body in chair, thud. Mug retrieved.

Laurie smiled. "I had to work for years to train her to do that. Mostly it involved denying her coffee until she was sitting at the table, or until she learned to handle it while still mostly asleep."

JJ was loving the sausages. "Our shopping trust should consult you on the subject of buying breakfast sausage," she said to Renee.

Renee shrugged. "Eric bought that. I just work here."

"I hope it's not hard labor," said Eric.

And Joy, who was not even there, ran off somewhere cackling with the double entendres. I raised an eyebrow at JJ, who seemed to be having the same vicarious experience of Joy.

"I think they said it was Bratwurst," said Eric. "Which I gather is a thing unto itself in Wisconsin."

Laurie confirmed this.

"The name just means fried sausage in German, which is remarkably non-specific."

JJ found a pen in what in any other household would have been a bud vase in the middle of the table. She wrote "Bratwurst" on her hand.

"I keep a pad of paper for stuff like that," said Renee, retrieving it from the napkin rack and handing it to JJ.

"If your students are anything like mine, one of them has a folder full of scribblings from that pad, and on restaurant napkins."

Renee laughed. "They totally do. Are we identical or what?"

"Even in non-genetic ways, apparently," I said. "It's kinda freaky."

"In a good way, I hope," said Renee.

And our respective lovers were looking at our reactions very closely. So I nodded. Because while I may be conflicted about which of us is who, there's no reason to expose her to that malady.

"It is kind of uncanny," said Max. "I remember many of Renee's mannerisms very well; how she moved around a room, how she messed with her hair, the expressions on her face. And you're doing many of the same things in very similar ways."

My hand stopped halfway to sinking its fingers into the hair behind my ear.

"Right, I can see that too," said JJ, looking at Renee.

Renee's hand stopped in just the same place, mid-fidget.

"Freaky," Renee and I both said at once, looking at each other.

"Oh, so," said Renee. She opened up the freezer, and dumped a bag of frozen chicken cubes, some cut up vegetables, and an ice cube tray full of chicken stock into the slow cooker, and turned it on. "There's dinner. Remind me to start the rice cooker tonight sometime."

CHAPTER FORTY-FIVE

Options

"So what's up for today?" I asked Renee, if only to change the subject from the empathic connection with my sister. It's not quite telepathic, but if I'm feeling what she's feeling, it's almost eerie how often we come up with the same reactions.

"You're all on vacation, we have options, not plans," said Renee.

"I like that," said Max.

"Well, a few things. One is that there's a choir at the church that's always short-handed. I know several of you are musical..."

"Not I," said JJ.

"Me neither," said Laurie.

"I happen to know both Max and Ravyn can read music and carry a tune," said Renee.

"I'd need to see the music ahead of time, if possible," I said. "I used to be able to sight read, kinda sorta, but it's been a while now." And I was wondering if I would get the screaming heebee jeebees during the service, like PTSD or something, since my own parish was unhelpful when it came to grief support. But I didn't say all that.

"A running start would be good, yes," said Max.

"There's a rehearsal tonight at seven," said Renee.

"I have keys," said Eric.

So we put on our coats and went over to the church. It was warmer than the day before, and we weren't out for very long.

Renee found her folder. "Right where the librarian can stuff it full of music. I should take it home with me, but I don't. Bad girl." We photocopied the sheet music in Eric's outer office. "Fair use," Renee said. "There is a complete set of legal copies in the file here someplace."

"Ah, so what else?" said Renee. "I interrupted myself. There's a botanical garden; I hear they have an exhibit on the Venus Flytrap."

"Could be fun," said JJ.

"And there's midnight Mass. The choir will be singing, and of course I'll be a little busy with it," said Eric. "You're all welcome to come."

JJ and Laurie looked at each other. "I'm not exactly the churchgoing type," said JJ.

"I'll sit with you and turn pages and stuff," said Laurie. "It's not to be missed."

"There are dinosaur bones in the natural history museum," said Renee. "There's a lab and a condo in Boulder some of you might be interested in seeing."

"A museum without dinosaur bones is like a day without sunshine," said JJ.

"And we said we'd help out with the community Christmas dinner for the homeless folk at the church," said Eric.

"I'm actually looking forward to helping out with that," I said.

"I should call the choir director," said Renee. So we got to listen to her side of a contrite conversation in which she agreed to come to more rehearsals in the new year.

"Maybe we can work that out with our day off. Thursdays could work," said Renee to Eric. "I live just a little too far away for regular commuting."

"I like visiting your condo," said Eric. "But it sounds like that could work. And I'm sure Jim would be happier with a regular participant."

"Speaking of days without sunshine, it's snowing again," said Laurie.

"The museum is indoors and not that far away," said Renee.

"Sold," I said.

"You go. I have a service to prepare for," said Eric.

So we piled into the van, and had a grand time at the museum. When we got back, Max and I compared notes with Renee about the music, polished off a few of the tricky bits, and pronounced ourselves ready. "Probably not actually ready," said Max, "but it's not likely to get much better between now and then."

The choirgirls went over to the church in the evening.

"Jim, meet my sister Ravyn," said Renee.

"Woh, there are two of you," said Jim. "And I thought one was enough."

We glanced at each other, pointed at each other, and said, "She's my evil twin," in unison.

"And you know Eric's sister, Liz. Max. What are we calling you?" said Renee.

"I remember meeting you," said Jim.

"Everybody except Eric calls me Max," said Max.

"Sorry I hung up on you," Renee said to Jim. "Did I hang up on you?"

"Meh," said Jim. He was apparently used to being abused by the Rector's wife.

"I copied out the music for Ravyn and Max, and you'll be happy to know we studied it together for a while this afternoon."

Jim somewhat huffily got out legal copies, confiscated the photocopies, but only after letting us transfer whatever markings we'd put in them. "I see your pencils all say 'Stolen from St Bart's Church' on them."

"Well, they wander off. Renee found three of them in her hair once."

"I lose stuff in my hair all the time," I said.

The rehearsal went well, and it was so much easier singing the alto part when it was surrounded by the other voices.

"Tomorrow night," said Jim, dismissing us. "We warm up starting at eleven. Don't be late, or you won't get any mulled cider."

"Can we find robes for the guests?" Renee asked Jim as things broke up.

"Right, come with me. What size?"

"If it fits Renee it'll fit me," I said.

"I'm a little bigger than these little people," Max pointed out.

Jim found some vestments, red with a white overlay. "Officially red is for the Chapel Royal, which we're not."

"It's Christmas," I said.

"Exactly," said Jim.

And we wandered home to a house full of our favorite people. JJ had even thought to start the rice cooker. She takes care of that detail at our house, too.

CHAPTER FORTY-SIX

Ice Maiden

Second day of the visit. Since we hadn't provoked comment the first day, JJ and I showered together again, and went down to breakfast. The conversation was a little confusing, taking place in several rooms with people coming and going. The takeaway here seemed to be that Ravyn should shut the fuck up, especially when a bright idea popped into my head. And especially if it involved my sister, who was doing okay without me in her life, thank you very much.

At some point the light banter turned serious. "How is it one of you turned out to be a lesbian while the other is straight?" Laurie wanted to know.

"Both bi," Renee and I said together.

"I don't talk about it very much," she added.

"Yeah, me neither," I said.

We looked at each other, remembering Alkaburkey, and our misspent youth.

"I'm bi also," said Eric.

JJ was nodding, having had this conversation with him earlier in the kitchen or somewhere.

"You know," said my mouth. Of course she knew. "Here's an option... You should... You could... come visit us sometime, on the way to Provincetown or something."

"Rave," said JJ.

"Jay?" I said.

"Get your coat," said JJ.

"Yes'm," I said. So we got our coats and went outside.

"Yo Dude, what the fuck?" JJ said, as soon as she had closed the door.

Quoting banter from our household might not be the best way to let me know she was actually upset with me. "I just thought..."

"You just didn't think, and that's a problem," said JJ.

"Um," I said, or something equally eloquent.

"I mean, yeah, we're all bi here. That doesn't make people available. As you know, having survived Rachael finding herself."

"Ouch," I said.

"Renee seems to have a pretty good life going here."

"Yeah, she does," I admitted.

"And a... how shall I say... long lost sister who's poly-unsaturated and eager to spread her particular version of the gospel? Could destabilize the boat."

"Rock the boat, I think is how you say that," I said quietly. "You're right, of course. I found something that works for me, for us. People should know about it."

"Excuse me, Renee," said JJ, doing a remarkable job of imitating my voice and mannerisms. "Do you have some time to talk about the Little Sisters of the Holy Fuck?"

"Seems a little heavy handed," I said.

"Ya think?" JJ demanded.

"I think," I answered.

"Speaking of which," said JJ, "Renee wanted to know what the LSHF acronym was for, in our household e-mail distribution list. I guess I should tell her."

"I'm sorry, JJ," I said.

"Tell it to Renee," said JJ. "I can supervise if you want."

"It might be good if you did."

"Tell me what?" Renee asked, joining us on the porch.

"I'm sorry I was so pushy," I said. "I found something that works for me, for us, and of course I want to share it. But I should pay more attention to how other people live their lives, and try to be at least a little sensitive."

"Thanks," said Renee. "You've made an interesting point, in a typically Ravyn-like provocative way. Eric and I have a lot of talking to do, figuring out how to live, together I hope, without burying half of ourselves."

"Y'know," said JJ, "You can think of it as more options, maybe. Being bi means you can fall for anybody. It doesn't mean you hafta go for everybody. Or even one of each."

"Ravyn?" said Renee, looking at JJ and not me.

"Renee?" I said.

"Where did you find this wise woman?"

"In my bed," I said.

"Hey!" said JJ. "We knew each other for years with our clothes on."

"You should totally keep her," said Renee, still looking at JJ. "What you said was profound," she added, to JJ.

And then she turned to me. "Come here, I wanna show you something."

We crunched out into the yard, getting only a little snow in our shoes.

"Right over there," she said, pointing so that I turned my head away from her to look.

There was a little bit of a rumble, and the tree unloaded its snow on top of me.

Renee and JJ were on the sidewalk, laughing at the ice maiden, trying to dig her way out of an avalanche.

"I prolly deserved that," I admitted.

Renee found me a towel, and she hung up my coat to dry.

CHAPTER FORTY-SEVEN

Christmas Eve

The winter afternoon drew to its close, Renee served up something tasty and not too filling (since three of us would be singing, plus possibly Eric... In some cases the priest actually sings much of the service), so it wouldn't do to have our bellies full.

"Save the wine for tomorrow or sometime," I said, "because I can't do music if I'm tipsy."

"Totally," said Renee, and Max was also nodding.

"You guys are fine, if you'd like some," I said to JJ and Laurie.

"I hope it's not too scary," I said to JJ. She is not even formerly a believer, so all the trappings of a festival Mass could be bewildering. Rachael put up with my love for such things, but at least she's Jewish, so is familiar with liturgy even if the ancestral language is different.

"What do I wear?" JJ asked.

"Something nice, something warm," said Renee.

"Something nice and warm," said Max. "I always find churches chilly."

"They're expensive to heat," said Eric.

"Did you bring a dress?" Renee asked.

"I'm wearing the black one," I said. JJ and I smiled at each other for a long moment, mentally playing tug of war or dominance games or something over who got to wear what.

"Um, not really," said JJ. "I'm almost the same size as Ravyn, though," she said, looking at Renee.

When they came downstairs again, Renee was in red and JJ in a dress identical in every detail except it was green.

"At least the twins are not dressed alike," I said.

"Yeeeeah, no," said Renee. "We did that waaaay too much when we were kids."

"After we put our robes on you will be," Max pointed out.

We trooped over to the church for choir warm-ups by 11, with Eric.

"Break a leg," he said, after kissing Renee. "Merry Christmas!"

"When he says that, it's like it means something," I said to Max.

"Yeah, I noticed that, too. And it's sweet, seeing Renee and Eric together," said Max.

We suited up, sang some scales and some exercises, ran through the music once or twice, and adjourned to the still mostly empty church where we repeated that, while listening to the acoustic of the space. Acolytes were coming and going and lighting candles and turning on the electric lights. When I could spare a cycle or two, I noticed Laurie and JJ sitting together on the aisle in the front pew. I remember doing that with Renee when we were kids, and getting choked up watching all the pageantry.

We went back upstairs to drink some (non-alcoholic) spiced cider while the church filled up.

"Wow, there are two of you," someone would say.

And Renee and I would glance at each other, and say, together, "She's my evil twin."

"Oh?" said Anne, who had introduced herself as Jim's wife. "There's a story there." She's a soprano, so there's that.

"Well," said Renee, "When we were kids..."

"We would argue over who got to be good," I added. "Now..."

"It's more about who gets to be the evil one," said Renee, stifling a giggle.

"It's partly the 'bad girl and proud of it' thing," I said.

"'Well behaved women rarely make history,' quoting the bumper sticker," said Renee.

"But partly it's trying to apologize for things we've done to each other," I said.

Anne wandered off, but Renee and I looked into each other's eyes and mouthed "Alkaburkey" together.

"Yeah, exactly," I said.

"Zackly," she said, almost at the same moment.

"You two really are identical," said Max. "It's kind of disconcerting."

"Five minutes," said Jim, gathering up his organ music and sweeping out the door.

So we went downstairs and stood quietly in the hallway outside the actual church, listening through the closed door to the organ music. A minute or two later a small army of acolytes carrying various things formed up in their half of the hallway. Eric, dressed in elaborate gold-colored vestments, stood behind them.

"Let us pray," he said.

And we did. His voice is kind of amazing, flowing through my soul, expressing the inexpressible. Making me wish I could stand doing this more often.

Hold that thought.

An acolyte unlatched the door, Jim started the opening hymn, a Christmas carol Renee and I had known since we were little (we're still little, but we were littler then), and we walked slowly down the aisle with acolytes ahead, one swinging an incense pot over his head, making Frankincense smoke. More acolytes followed us, and then Grace, Eric's assistant, and Eric himself.

I had been away from this long enough that I forgot we were supposed to genuflect together. Max and I stood out like the bad girls we are.

Eric started the service. At some point I caught JJ's eye from where she sat twenty feet away, and there were tears on her face. And on mine.

One's mind wanders. Why do I not do this more often? Somebody, I think it was St Teresa, maybe? As quoted by Dorothy Day, it could be, said that Christ has no hands on this earth but yours. The idea is to inspire people to pray, yes, but then to act in the name of Christ, putting their own hands to work for him. They tell us we are the body of Christ; we are also his hands and his voice in the world.

And yet, when I needed support because my wife left me for being the wrong kind of queer, they let me dangle. I slipped through the enervated hands of Christ.

I know thinking of things that way hurts me; that's why I sat there weeping gently, not only at the beauty of the moment, the excitement, the mystery, but also at the sense of my exclusion from all of that. I'm not sure what to do with that knowledge. Maybe Eric could dispense some sage advice.

And yet, I think that sitting across the same desk from Eric, in the same chair where Renee sat when she came for counseling, wearing the same face, give or take, might be too much for him. As Max said, it's freaky how alike we are, way beyond the genetics. And he fell in love with her, married her, jollied her out of her funks. Which, being identical, are much like my own funks.

It was time to sing. Jim got our attention and held it, and if I say so myself, the music came out very well. I could hear a few mistakes, but it's live, it's sincere, it's the best we could do given the circumstances. There's something to be said for bringing your best. And blending it with other people's voices. Renee sat between Max and me, so we could hear her singing our part in our ears. But I was also in the middle, so I could hear a soprano in my other ear, and a bass and a tenor from behind me. There was a really interesting woman singing tenor, but in the bustle I never got to talk to her.

Renee went to communion when the time came, and it was beautiful, in a way, seeing Eric place the wafer in his wife's hands. We did it together for the first years of our lives. And now, she's there, in communion with these people. I'm here, sitting next to Max, and a couple of the male choir people who are obviously gay, watching how living people interact with their God.

Renee and the others came back from the altar rail, and we sang through a long series of carols and other simple music for the holiday, while the congregation made their communions. There were a lot of them; people sitting in every pew, but it's not til they get out of their seats and line up that you realize just how many 200 people is.

A couple hours after midnight, I suppressed a yawn, and Renee elbowed me in the ribs to let me know it was time to pack up and go back the way we came in. The choir spreads out at the back of the church until the last hymn ends, by which time Eric was where he could shake hands or embrace everybody as they left. There was a guy with a white beard and a red coat who did the "Ho ho ho" thing loudly, and exchanged Merry Christmases with Eric.

In due course, Laurie and JJ found their way to the back of the church. So I gave JJ a hug, and kissed her tears away, as she did with mine. Max and Laurie also exchanged a kiss. "Our sisters are lesbians," Eric said to more than one of his people, Renee standing by his side.

We choirgirls went upstairs, changed vestments for the coats we had come in, turned in our music, and went to find the rest of the people. Renee took us to the rectory, where we were soon joined by Eric.

There were a lot of smiles, a few tears, a lot of laughs, and basically just overflowing with comfort and joy, letting it flow freely like the wine we were drinking.

"Merry Christmas, everybody," Eric said. "It's so good to be together at last, all of us."

"Hear, hear," said Renee, lifting her wine glass.

I stifled another yawn.

"Yeahthat," said JJ. "Lemme help gather wine glasses."

"Nope. We'll do all that tomorrow morning," said Renee. "Later this morning. After sleeping."

"How are you?" I asked JJ when we were alone.

"I, uh, I'm not sure. Overwhelmed might be a good word," she said.

"It can be pretty magical," I said. "I used to do church a lot. I kinda miss it."

JJ murmured something about showing me real magic.

We were mid-snuggles when the car alarm in the driveway went off.

There was nothing for it but to investigate, so we watched Renee returning from the darkened dining room downstairs, just inside the window from the offending vehicle, keys in hand.

"You're, um, naked," said my mouth. Mistress of the obvious, that's me.

"I am aware of that," said Renee. "So are you."

"Your, um, fuckbuddy?" I said. "He's a boy."

"I am aware of that, too," said Renee.

"Nothing to see here, move along," said Laurie, pulling Max back into their room and closing the door.

"Keys go on the nightstand," Renee was saying to Eric. "So you can't step on them."

"What Laurie said," said JJ, pushing me onto the bed, latching the door by leaning against it, and then climbing on top of me.

"Oh, and Merry Christmas," she said, as I drifted off to sleep.

CHAPTER FORTY-EIGHT

Community Feast

"It's Christmas," I whispered in JJ's ear. There was sun at the curtains. There were muffled vocalizations from another room.

"And we'll all be merry and gay," said JJ, who proceeded to demonstrate. There may have been muffled vocalizations from our room also. Just sayin.

An hour or so later, given how far the sunbeam moved across our bed, we put on each others' jammies and flitted to the bathroom.

When we came out again, there was something of a traffic jam in the upstairs hallway.

Renee, hair in full-fright mode, was staring at nothing, wearing one of Eric's clergy shirts. Eric put the white collar around her neck and fastened it down, grinning.

"I remember that girl in my house, long ago," said Max, checking out the still-open buttons on the shirt. Eric is tall and thin. Renee is short, so the shirt reached her knees, but female, so, um, cleavage. And stuff.

"What?" said Renee, refusing to be embarrassed. "They're all women."

"They're all lesbians," said Eric.

"Yup," we all said, one after another.

"The bathroom is empty," Renee said. "Wash me, Father, for I have sinned."

"Is it a sin if..." I was asking as the door closed.

"Hush," said JJ.

We got dressed and met Laurie and Max in the kitchen. "Merry Christmas," I said to Max.

"You two are really a lot alike," said Max.

"I've never seen you in a clerical collar," said JJ.

We were still laughing at that image when Renee and Eric appeared.

"What??" Renee demanded. "I've missed the joke."

"We were giggling over the thought of Ravyn in a clerical collar," said Max. "She's so..."

"Gay," said JJ, in the pause.

"Exactly," said Max.

"Although..." said JJ. "I probly shouldn't share this, but I'm gonna share this."

"Ruh-roh," I said.

"As you know there are five of us living in Ravyn's house."

"Ravynscroft," said Renee. "I like the word coinage. A place where Ravyns live."

"Just the one, thankfully," said JJ. "But somebody... who was it?"

"Christy?" I asked. "Barrista babe JJ picked up once."

"Kat?" said JJ. "Choirgirl who, um, like, yeah, with Ravyn. Just to... kinda set the scene, and, um, somebody mentioned sin earlier."

Renee was having trouble keeping a straight face. In both senses of the word.

"Anyway, whoever it was mentioned over coffee the morning after that we were kind of like a religious order," said JJ. "Well, except for the sex, of course."

"Of course," said Max. "I think I'm following so far."

"So the free association banter around the table started with Little Sisters," said JJ.

"Of the...," I said, "and a bunch of attempts to fill in the blank."

"'Holy,' somebody suggested, because religious," said JJ.

"Aaaand our resident Tourette's person, Joy, filled in the 'Fuck' on the end," I said.

"After nervous laughter and letting it rattle around in our heads, it's, like, who we are," said JJ. "The Little Sisters of the Holy Fuck."

"Which would explain the acronym you used for your everybody e-mail list," said Renee.

"Is it okay if I say Oh My God now?" Laurie asked. "Because, Oh My God."

Eric was trying not to look mortified, with much of his face hidden in a hand.

"As I said, I probly shouldn't have shared that," said JJ.

"I'm okay with it if you are," I told her.

"Not to change the subject," said Eric, "but I'm going to change the subject."

"Thank God," said Renee.

"At our house, somebody would have said," I started.

"Hush," said JJ. And she's right, of course. "Thank fucking God" wouldn't go over as well in this company.

"We have a few gifts," said Eric, trying to ignore the banter.

Renee found the switch for the lights in the Christmas tree, and retrieved a book-sized package from the pile under it. She handed it to Laurie.

"Oh my," said Laurie. "A bound copy of your grammar. I'm looking forward to picking the brain of Renee Menendez, computational linguist, again. She essentially invented the field, blundering through all the objections people who actually do linguistics had encountered. Thank you!"

"For my sister," said Eric, handing Max a package.

Opening several nested individually gift-wrapped boxes, eventually Max found an envelope. "It's a coupon good for room and board here, any time I want to visit. Signed by you both. How thoughtful."

"It's good to have you around," said Renee. "I wasn't sure it would be, but it really is."

"I'm glad," said Max.

"JJ," said Renee. "It's so good getting to know you."

"She said *know*," chuckled JJ. "You, too. Despite the identical thing, you two are really very different people. It's an honor to know you both."

"She said *know*," cackled itself out of my lips. Seriously, girl, wash your mind out with soap sometime.

"I wasn't sure what to get you," said Renee.

"A physics book," said JJ. "Thank you. These things are pricey and I don't have this one yet."

"And for my sister," said Renee. "I *really* didn't know what to get you. So I searched through all the pictures I have and found our prom picture."

"Oh no!" seemed the only thing to say.

"Oh my," said Max.

"Wheeee!" squealed JJ. "There are boys in this picture."

"No idea who they were," I said.

"Yeah, me neither," said Renee.

"We were probably more into each other than either of them," I said.

Renee stared into my eyes for a long moment. There's so much we could say.

"We brought you a bottle of wine," Max was telling Eric, when we returned to the present decade.

"Thanks," said Eric.

"And a bottle of whiskey," said Laurie.

"Oh my, that'll be wonderful," said Eric.

"My turn?" I asked. "I didn't know what to do for you, either," I said to Renee. "I remember you pointing out we got clothes for our birthday and toys for Christmas."

"Uh-oh," said Renee.

"And we talked about it around our kitchen table," said JJ. "Is she kinky? somebody wanted to know."

"Um, no," I said.

"No fun, somebody else said," said JJ.

"Anyway," I said, handing the box to my sister.

"Can I open it here?" Renee asked, almost afraid to even look at the box in her hands.

"Yes," I said, glancing at Eric.

"Another bottle of whiskey," said Renee, visibly relieved. "It's the same brand as yours," she added, to Eric. "We can drink them together while we video chat on the computer."

"We did a little coordinating behind the scenes," JJ said.

"I like the idea of a coupon for room and board," I said. "You can come visit any time you want. You know that, right?"

"I, uh, do, yeah," said Renee. "It's complicated."

"Or it's very simple," I said. "It's hard to tell the difference sometimes."

Renee laughed and nodded her head.

"Anyway. It's nearly time to go help with dinner," said Eric.

"What do I wear to this?" JJ asked. "Do I hafta wear a dress?"

"Something warm, maybe layered. Dresses not required," said Eric. "I might wear a cassock; it helps keep order if I actually look like a priest."

"So," said Max, "the boy wears a dress and the girls don't. Gotcha." She was smiling.

The crowd was well behaved, happy to be out of the weather for a few hours, and well fed. Doris was grateful for all the helping hands to set tables, dish out food, and chat with the guests. "You're very much like your sister, Renee," Doris said to me.

I just nodded politely. It was like being twelve again.

"They really are," said Eric, who was standing at my elbow.

When dinner was served there were a few extra seats at one table, so JJ and I sat down, and Renee joined us.

"Oh my," said one of the guests. "There are two of you."

We glanced at each other, and said, together, "She's my evil twin."

"I'm Emily," said the guest. "You're Renee," she said to me.

"I'm Renee," said Renee. "This is Ravyn. And this is JJ, Ravyn's, um..."

"Lover," I said.

JJ nodded, smiling.

"So..." said Emily. "Huh." She looked at Eric across the room.

"Identical, obviously," said Renee. "Both bi. She ended up with women; I married a man."

"Gotcha," said Emily. "Not that it's my business."

"I guess people need labels," said Renee.

"I guess," said Emily. "Like homeless."

"Here, you're our guest," said Renee.

"Thank you," said Emily, looking down.

"Don't be sad," I said, pushing my hands across the table to Emily. She took them. A tear slid down her cheek.

"Look," I said. "I'm not very good at this. My... Well, a woman I knew, Becca, was always bringing people home, giving them a place to stay for a few days, and if she was visiting in another city, finding somebody local to give. Rachael and I had a houseguest for a while, after Bec visited."

Emily looked up into my eyes.

"And I'm visiting here, but my sister isn't," I said, glancing at Renee. "Soooo," I said, with a more significant look at Renee. "Let's get you a bath and a bed for a few days and some contacts that'll help on a longer term."

Emily dropped one of my hands so she could wipe her eye on her sleeve. "You'd do that for me? Both of you?"

Renee glanced around for Eric, but then straightened up in her chair. "We'll find a way," she said.

"You're good," Renee said to me.

"Nuh-uh," seemed to be the thing to say in reply. It was like being eight again.

"Happy Christmas," Renee said to Emily.

When the other guests had gone, we brought Emily to the rectory. Renee got out towels and put her clothes in the washer. She found a robe Emily could use while her stuff was in the dryer. Both JJ and Renee, while I was almost out of earshot, quietly warned Emily about how pushy I am, and told her she didn't have to do anything she was uncomfortable doing.

Which, duh, I hope is obvious. But I do get carried away sometimes.

CHAPTER FORTY-NINE

Boulder

It wasn't even sunset yet, so after some consideration, JJ and Emily and I piled into Renee's car and she drove us to Boulder.

"I love Boulder," said Emily, as we were coming over the hill looking down on the town. The lights were just beginning to come on.

"Me, too," said Renee. "I could move to Denver and live with Eric, and that does have its attractions, but I like living here. I guess I'd get this view every morning if I moved, though."

Renee parked next to her condo building. "Wow," I said. "Right by the creek, the mountains, it's wonderful."

"I knew you'd like it," said Renee. "I do."

We went upstairs, Renee opened the door, turned on the lights, and we went inside.

"And transparent walls," I said, looking through one of them at her bed. Tastefully made, unlike the rumpled ones at our house. "Who knew you were an exhibitionist?" my mouth said.

Renee inhaled sharply, turned to me, and said, "Well, you are."

We looked into each other's eyes for a longer moment.

"Jay?" I said, still looking into Renee's eyes.

"Rave?" said JJ.

"How about you go out for supper with Emily?"

"Kay," said JJ. "I'll call in an hour or so."

They closed the door and Renee locked it from the inside. Her hand twitched near the light switch.

"I wanna show you the view," said Renee. She kicked off her shoes, led me into her bedroom, and sat down, fully clothed, on the bed, leaning against the headboard.

So I did likewise. We kept our hands to ourselves, except for incidental contact while keeping our hair in order.

"That's quite something, watching the city lights coming on across the creek," I said.

"Yeah, exactly," she said. "I knew you'd understand. You can see it better in the dark." And she jumped out of bed, hit the light switch next to the entrance door, and was back, all in about four seconds.

"I can now truthfully tell JJ that I've been bounced on your bedsprings," I said.

She laughed.

I took her hand in mine in the dark. I put my fingers between hers. I'd say it was like being sixteen again, only we stopped there.

With, to be sure, matching sighs of regret. Not so much at opportunities missed as the complexity of modern life, life apart, during which we'd developed valued attachments to other people.

"It never could have worked, anyway," I said at last.

"No," said Renee. "So how are you really?" she asked at last. She dropped my hand, went into the big room, turned on the light, found two glasses and a bottle of wine, and sat down at the table.

I was about three steps behind.

"Doin' okay, mostly," I said.

"Yeah?" Renee asked.

"Prolly not," I admitted. "Rachael leaving, closing me out of my own marriage because... I don't fit her demographic or something... that was really sad."

"I spent the longest time alone, after moving here to follow the job market," said Renee. "Max was... a really hard act for anybody else to follow. She was so understanding and so right on about what was wrong with me and what I needed to fix it. She was on sabbatical the year I wrote my thesis in her house. Every time she blew through town everything was right again, for a while. And then I'd hafta work extra hard to make up for lost time, and to recover my mood from wherever she left it at the end of her visit."

"But JJ and I found each other. And Andi. And Joy," I said.

"I collaborated with Max later on a project, and seeing how sad I was, she sent me to Eric. He's... pretty amazing. He jollied me out of my funk, out of my solitude, out of wanting Max herself back. And into his bed and a marriage. Which seems to work even though both of us are gay. And there, I said it out loud."

"I had... way too many guys," I said. "They're so available..."

"Ayup," said Renee.

"I guess it's a little easier for me, being obviously gay. but there's a part of me that envies what you've done with your life," I said.

"Yeah, me too," said Renee. "JJ is amazingly wise and amazingly sexy, both at once."

"Totally," I said. "What an odd combination, but it's all true."

"You should keep her," said Renee.

"And you should keep Eric. He's all kinds of wonderful for you."

"He really is. I forget, sometimes," said Renee. "Especially when I'm looking into your eyes, imagining how life is from the other side of my table."

So I stood up, pulled her up, traded places with her, and we sat in each others' chairs for a while.

My phone tweetled, and it was JJ, so I put her on speaker.

"We're hungry," I said. "Did you eat?"

"Uh, yeah," said JJ. "That was kinda the idea. A Jew and an Asian walk into a Chinese restaurant on Christmas Day... Stop me if you've heard this one. It's what we do."

"No wonder Rachael left me. I had no idea," I said.

"We're in front of a bar at, uh, 11th and Pearl," said JJ. "It's even open."

"You know this place?" I asked Renee.

"Yup," she said. "We'll be there in a couple minutes."

"Y'know," I said, when we'd hung up. "JJ is going to think we... did stuff."

"We could at least trade shirts," said Renee. "Give her something to guess about."

"I like the seams on this," I said.

"It's inside out," said Renee.

"All the better," I said. "Tickle JJ's sense of wonder."

"Ooookay then," said Renee.

We went into the bar and I took off my coat. The hostess breezed by and said, "Hello, Renee," and then she was gone. Renee was standing next to me by the time she returned. "Oh," she said. "There are two of you."

So we did the "she's my evil twin" routine for her, and she laughed.

"My Chinese partner is probably here already?" I said.

"I thought you were married to that priest," she said.

"That would be me," said Renee. "JJ and Emily are over there."

So we joined them. "What's good here?" I asked.

"They have buffalo burgers if you're into red meat," said Renee.

"Fine."

"If Andi were here she would explain to the waitress that you want fries with that, because it's not sinful enough," said JJ.

"I guess I want fries with that," I told the waitress. As I had done a couple years earlier, and a thousand miles away.

JJ ordered whiskey for herself and Emily, and beer for Renee and me.

"You're wearing each others' shirts," said JJ.

We smiled and laughed.

"So I guess things went well," JJ suggested.

And we smiled and laughed some more.

"I think you're going to like Emily," JJ told Renee.

"Yeah," said Renee. "Welcome to my town."

"Thanks," said Emily. "You guys are amazing."

"Dammit, girl, spill," said JJ to me.

"Me?" I said.

"You really don't do the innocent ingenue very well at all," said JJ.

"Fuck you?" I said, laughing. Just to change tack.

"Um, sure," said JJ. "Pretty much any time you want."

Putting down her beer, Renee started it. "We kinda..."

"Thought," I said, "that it'd be fun..."

"To swap clothes and pretend..."

"...let you guess..."

"because your imagination..."

"would surely run with..."

"whatever clues we provided."

"Fair enough," said JJ. "And it's like watching a tennis match when you two finish each others', um, I was gonna say sentences, but that was like all one big long sentence."

"And you'll notice," she added to Emily, "that they carefully neither confirmed nor denied any particular activity other then the obvious, which was changing clothes."

"We're girls," said Renee.

"Girls change clothes all the time," I said.

"Some of us more than others," said JJ.

Emily was laughing and nodding along. So we hadn't excluded her yet. It's hard to know.

"Oh," I said, remembering something in my purse. "Here." There was a little vegetation in a zip-loc bag. I figured...

Renee took it, removed the bag, held it over JJ's head, and said "Mistletoe!" and kissed her.

"Mmm," said JJ. "Bacon cheeseburger."

"Sorry," said Renee.

"Let me just..." and quickly so she couldn't chicken out, JJ took the mistletoe, offered it to Emily, who smiled and accepted her kiss.

"You guys are amazing," said Emily. "Thanks so much..."

"Happy to help," said Renee, interrupting. "Everybody needs a little help now and then. Eric's good at getting people to help. Besides, it would do me good, having somebody else around. Especially a woman. I like hanging out with women. Nearly everybody in my daily life is male. I forget who I am sometimes."

"They don't," I said, staring at the last inch of beer in my mug.

"No," said JJ. "They are all very aware you're a woman."

"To be sure," I said, "we're also aware of each others' femininity, and love each other because of it."

"A cheerier take on things," said JJ. "And it's true."

A phone donked somewhere on our side of the table. And, guess what. We had the same text tones programmed into our phones.

"Oh right," said Renee. "I remember now. The rest of them are coming up to see the place."

"Now?" said JJ.

"Now," said Renee. "They've just parked in front of my condo and wonder why the lights are out and nobody's home."

"I'll settle up," said JJ.

"Which coat do you want?" Renee asked me, helping herself to the one she hadn't been wearing earlier.

"I'm glad you know the way. I'm totally lost," I said.

"That's us, no sense of direction," said Renee. "And here we are." She kissed Eric and led the procession upstairs, where she opened the door and flipped on the lights. Once inside, she collected coats, piling them on her bed.

After a few minutes, JJ and Emily joined us. JJ put their coats on the obvious pile in the bedroom.

"Welcome to the family, Emily," said Eric, when Renee had rustled up enough chairs for everyone. "The large, extended family."

"Our sisters and their respective out-laws," said Renee. "It's nice to have you all here, in my little apartment. Especially you, Emily."

"Awww, thanks," said Emily. "I seem to say that a lot."

"No problem," said Renee. "Well, assuming most of us go back to Denver before bedtime."

"Can we get a tour of the lab?" asked Max. "I understand if it's too late at night, or a holiday or whatever. I'm not sure the security folks at my building would be thrilled by a midnight tour."

"We can do that," said Renee. "Eric, you know where the wine is."

And so we whisked off to the campus, parked right by the door, and visited Renee's lab. Some of her stuff was open on the bench, where the grad students were carefully cleaning each piece that was to go into the vacuum system. That day, thankfully, they were off doing something else. Even grad students deserve a holiday.

Renee lectured JJ and Max and me about what it was she was trying to measure, while walking up and down the beamline, pointing at mostly enclosed boxes and peeking into ports in the big chamber.

"This looks like my lab," I said.

"Or mine," said JJ.

"Mine is full of dirt samples," said Max.

"Not all that exciting, I guess," said Renee, locking up behind us. "Merry Christmas," she told the guard as we let ourselves out.

CHAPTER FIFTY

Housewife

The tour finished, it was getting late, so we went back to the Rectory, set Emily up on the couch, and went to bed. Perchance to sleep. We were all of us tired enough, what with being up very late the previous day, and all the fun of Christmas itself.

By mid-morning everybody had appeared, hair more or less in order, sore muscles if any stretched out, and halfway down the second thermos of coffee we started to talk.

"So," Renee said, looking at me.

"So," I said, looking at her.

"We hafta decide where Emily is going," said Renee.

Eric set down his mug, and Emily leaned in to listen. "From what you said last night," Eric said, "it might be good for you to be away from the action for a while," he said.

Emily nodded. Renee pushed the ever-present box of tissues across the table to her, and she took one.

"Welll," said JJ, looking at me. "Our house is... full of professors who could use some organizing."

"It's true," I said.

"And I have a spare bedroom in Boulder," said Renee.

"We also have five salaries to help pay for a housewife," I said. "Just to be practical for a moment."

"I feel like a bride being auctioned off," said Emily. "It's been so long since anybody wanted me around, and now there are two options."

"Why don't Ravyn and I consult the rest of the... Order," said JJ, "and we'll come up with a plan."

So we retired to our guest room, closed the door, set up the tablet on the desk and crowded into the field of view. We dialed Rachael, but there was no answer after several rings. So we dialed Andi, who picked up.

"Oh look, it's JJ and Ravyn," she said. "How's stuff?"

"Stuff's good," I said. "Is everybody around? We have a little proposition."

"I looove being propositioned," said Andi. "As you know. Lemme just..." And there was a pause and some blur on the screen and a momentary glimpse of three women, and then more blur and the ceiling in the dining room.

"Oopsie," said Rachael. "Let me, um... there. Hi."

"Hi," we said.

"So what's up?" said Joy. "Ready to come home again? We've missed you."

"You just missed my..." said JJ.

Joy was laughing and nodding.

"So it's about Emily. She's a homeless person we brought in from the cold on Christmas," I said. "She and Eric think it would be good to be far away from her former life for a while..."

"So the question is," said JJ, "do we want a housewife? Housekeeper? Whatever."

"Wife? Or keeper?" said Joy, just because she's Joy.

"Am I my sister's keeper?" I misquoted from somewhere. Genesis, I think.

"Who are you, Becca?" said Rachael. "She was always scraping people up off the street and bringing them to visit for a while."

"We could use some help being organized," said Andi. "And the more the merrier, up to some point we haven't reached yet."

"How did I ever manage to live in that house alone?" I asked nobody.

"We could... there's an extra bed here someplace, I think?" said Rachael. "Is it still in the attic room?"

"I think so," I said. "I haven't been up there in a while."

"Or maybe she'd like to... um..." said Joy, because she's Joy.

"I think it would be good for her to have her own room," said JJ.

"Well, we need some help around the house, and we can certainly afford to have a sixth person, so, um, sure, why not?" said Andi.

"Sure," said Joy.

"Oh boy," said Rachael. "We always said we needed a housewife," she said.

"We did," I confirmed. "Let me go get her and introduce her around."

JJ and I took the tablet downstairs, thumb over the camera lens, and propped it up on the dining room table.

"Emily, meet Joy and Rachael and Andi," I said. "Left to right."

"Huh. Somehow I was picturing Andi being a guy, and was wondering how that worked," said Emily. "But I'm forgetting my manners. Hello! And thanks so much for..."

"Oh, hush," I said. "We need somebody to help out, you're available, it's pretty simple."

"It really is," JJ said.

"You're making me cry," said Emily.

"Last chance to bail out," said Andi.

"I'm in if you'll have me," said Emily.

"Woohoo! I can't wait to meet you in person," said Rachael.

When we disconnected, and Emily was done with her little cry, JJ said, "Now I wonder if there's another seat available on our flight home."

"Home," said Emily, and started to cry again. So I held her while JJ got the computer to tell her about flights.

"Score!" said JJ. "We're really doing this?"

Emily nodded, mid-sob, and JJ pressed a button on the tablet with a flourish.

"Sweet. We can even sit together," said JJ.

CHAPTER FIFTY-ONE

Going Home

We all had breakfast together one last time at the Rectory. Eric went to work, and Renee herded us all into the van.

"It's been good," I told her, embracing at the door on the way out to the car.

"Yeah?" she said. "I wasn't sure it would be, but it is. Keep in touch, you."

I resisted the urge to kiss her. "You have our contact info. We can talk sometimes."

"I'd like that. Now in the van with you."

The trip to the airport was uneventful. We hugged Renee goodbye at the curb and she drove away.

"And you miss her already," said Max.

"Yup," I admitted.

"I do too. She's a good one," said Max.

"Yup," I said. "And I know I'm not her, and she's not me, but there are connections I had no idea I was missing. I know now."

"Renee is very... I dunno how to say this... Sticky, maybe," said Max. "To know her is to be involved in her whirlwind of emotions."

"Sounds like somebody else I know," said JJ, putting her hand through my elbow. "Let's go inside and check in. It's cold out here."

Emily had a backpack that was ready for anything, and she traveled light.

"It's been forever since..." Emily said more than once. We checked her in, explained security procedures, and the five of us went through security and got on the train together.

"So efficient," said Max. "There's an hour for dinner before we leave."

"And there's a brewpub right here on the concourse," said Laurie.

"I could do with a beer," I admitted.

We squeezed into a booth. "It's good we're little people," JJ said.

The waiter understood about deadlines and people flying off to other timezones on schedules over which he had no control, so the food was prompt, hot, and filling.

"More beer for you ladies?" he asked.

We declined. He left the check. "Mine," said JJ.

"I'm a little reticent about spending your money," said Emily.

"Pff," JJ pffed. "The pay scale is designed to support a family. We have five incomes like that. It's really no problem."

"The waiter's nice," said Laurie.

"But is he gay?" my mouth said. "Besides, I ain't no lady."

"It's more polite than fucking wench?" said JJ.

I had to laugh. "Nowadays, who knows?"

"Our flight leaves before yours does," said Laurie. "It's a pleasure to know you both. And good luck especially to you, Emily."

We all stood up and had a round of hugs, they sorted out their carry-ons and left. There didn't seem to be pressure to leave the restaurant, so we hung out for a while.

"So," said Emily. "I dunno where to start. It's a whole new life for me, and I'll get to meet the rest of you when we get there. But I want stories. How did you end up in such an odd arrangement? I'm assuming it's an odd arrangement, even in Boston."

"Where the Boston Marriage was invented," I said. "Rachael and I kinda had that going for a while. It was all legal and everything, a year or two before we could go anywhere else that it counted. We met in grad school, the same university gave us both tenure, we eloped to Provincetown..."

"It's kind of a gay Mecca right on the end of Cape Cod," said JJ.

"...bought a house in suburbia with a picket fence and everything."

"Can we walk down to the gate while we talk?" JJ asked.

We waved to Max and Laurie who were about to board their flight. Our gate was at the other end of the concourse, but we still had a half hour.

"So introducing somebody else once, Rachael said at this point in the narrative that we started working on the 2.3 kids thing..."

Emily looked confused, so JJ said, "The average household has a house in the 'burbs, a picket fence, 2.3 children and most of a dog."

"Thanks for the Cliffnotes," said Emily. She put her hand through JJ's elbow.

"... and discovered we were lesbians and something was missing," I finished. That line works much better if delivered uninterrupted. I could see Emily would fit into the household banter, feeling free to interrupt with questions.

Emily laughed politely.

When it was our turn to board, JJ stood on the aisle seat and we did a bucket brigade, swinging each person's bag up to her, and she into the overhead bin, in one fluid motion. "D'you want the window?" JJ asked.

"Can I sit in the middle, between you?" Emily asked.

"Of course."

She slept fitfully on the flight, sometimes with her head on my shoulder, and sometimes on JJ's. We explained things and told stories about the others when she was awake.

"Sorry I'm so sleepy," Emily said.

"The couch isn't so comfortable?" JJ asked.

"It's fine. It's better than anything else I've had in... Well, a while."

"I hope Rachael found the spare bed wherever we stashed it," I said. "She was there then, she should remember as well as I do. It was a trick getting it up that last flight of stairs, with just two little people to push."

"We'll work something out," said JJ.

Emily smiled. "You're very good to me," she said.

"Oh, hush," I said. It's what I say to the cat when he hisses at me after I don't even touch him.

When the plane landed, we waited until there was room, and then swooshed the bags out of the overhead as we'd put them up there. JJ and I had checked a suitcase, so there would be a wait for that.

"A new novice for the Mother House," was the first thing out of Joy's mouth when she found us at the luggage carousel. "You must be Emily."

"This is Joy," said JJ. "We'll be having a quiz on people's names after while, so take notes."

Emily laughed.

"Bathroom," JJ said. "Maybe our suitcase will be here by the time we get back."

"I'll watch your pack if you want," said Joy.

Andi and Rachael flitted by, coming out of the bathroom as we went in.

At last we were all together, with luggage.

"This is Andi," I said.

"I'm the blonde one," she said.

"I can see that," said Emily.

"And Rachael," said Rachael. "I hope you'll feel at home. They let me in, after all."

"Returning to the fold, or something," I said. "Time was, it was your house, too."

"It's true," said Rachael. "And I'm still a little remorseful about how that turned out. Here's to happier times."

"To happier times," I said. "Dammit, I need a beer."

Rachael laughed. "When we get home."

"Speaking of home, are we driving? Or taking the train?"

"I totally hate driving to the airport," Andi said. "The car's in the lot at the last subway station."

"They rearrange all the airport roads more often than I come here," said Joy.

"You need to travel more," I said.

"I need a cushy grant like yours that would pay me to travel," said Joy. "Are you always this quiet?" she asked Emily.

"Oh no," said Emily. "I learned a while ago when I'm in an unfamiliar situation to shut up and listen."

"That's kinda profound," said Joy. "Hey, everybody, I think Emily gets to be our new emitter of profundities."

"Emitter," said Emily, skeptically.

"Of profundities," said Rachael. "I like it."

"No pressure at all," said Emily, with a nervous laugh. "Just don't look too hard for anything profound."

"How was the flight?" Rachael asked, when we had settled into the back seat of the bus, and stowed the luggage.

"It's been a long time since I did that," said Emily. "And the security stuff is a little frightening."

"Theater, mostly," said Andi. "Mostly it's just to convince you that they're doing something other than just violating your privacy."

"And collecting a complete set of naked pictures of everybody in the country," said JJ. "I guess I don't mind that much, at least if my students don't hack into their collection."

"Or my ex," said Emily.

"Yeeeeah, that could be ookey," I said. With, of course, a glance at Rachael. Who is my ex, at least in some ways, but is also the person least likely to hack into anything.

"Oh, right," said Rachael. "It turns out we had an extra Charlie Card, and put some cash on it so you can ride the subways."

"Wow, thanks..." said Emily.

"I'm sure it'll be confusing, but here's the map," said JJ. "Blue to Orange, all the way to the end."

"Planes, trains, and..." said Emily.

"Automobiles come at the end," said Andi.

We managed to get six women, two suitcases, a backpack, plus carry-ons, coats, etc. etc. to the platform at the end of the line without losing anybody or anything. "Now up the escalator so we can cross over the tracks, and down again to street level," said Andi.

"And my car is over there," she said, making it blink tail lights in welcome. When we approached, the trunk flipped open, so we stowed luggage and squeezed inside.

"It's just a mile," said Andi, "But a ride is great when it's cold or you have luggage."

"And here we are," I said, as Andi parked in the driveway next to Rachael's car. Mine's in the garage. "Welcome to our house," I said.

"Dot, dot, dot, of ill repute," Joy added.

"Thank you all so much for taking me in," Emily said quickly before anyone could shush her. "It's amazing what you're doing for me."

JJ found her keys and opened the door, leading the procession. The luggage went to the basement, where it was mostly emptied into the laundry basket, and then upstairs where the remaining stuff was hung up or put away.

Rachael reappeared, clomping down the stairs from the attic, followed by Emily.

"It might get a little hot up there," she was saying. "There are little windows at both ends of the attic. If you leave the doors open it might give you some circulation."

"It looks cozy and wonderful," said Emily.

"And we put some stuff in the slow cooker," said Andi, "since it's hard to guess how long it'll take, picking people up at the airport."

"So tell me about the spices," Emily was saying to Andi, when her bowl was half empty.

"How'd it go?" Rachael asked us at the other end of the table.

"It's, like, whoosh," I said.

"Renee and Ravyn are remarkably alike, way more than you'd expect, even given identical initial conditions," said JJ. Spoken like a physicist. Initial conditions indeed. "It was cute watching them finish each others' sentences, and bringing back riffs from when they were fifteen together."

"A couple too many of those riffs, maybe," I said. "Remembering Alkaburkey."

"Albuquerque," said Rachael.

"They both pronounce it that way," said JJ. "And I'm not sure I wanna remember what we did in Alkaburkey."

"Like..." prompted Rachael.

"Like flashing each other with a 'My boobs are bigger than yours' argument," said JJ. "You might, maybe, expect that from teenagers. Young teenagers. Not from when they meet again after all these years."

"And, um, stuff," I said. Just to not quite get it all on the record.

"And, um, stuff," said Rachael, catching my drift, and mercifully dropping the subject right there.

CHAPTER FIFTY-TWO

Fitting In

To: renee@ravynscroft.org
  From: Ravyn@ravynscroft.org

Lemme start by saying thanks, again, for a lovely visit. You're really something, and I like what you've done with your life while I wasn't looking. Eric is... amazing. And it was good to get to know his sister & her partner.

Emily seems to be settling in. It's intersession, so people's schedules are even more disrupted than normal. JJ has a public outreach thing going where she plays with the lecture demonstration equipment, of which there's quite a lot. She's having a great time. But the lectures are in the afternoon, so the rest of us shower quickly and go, and JJ can have coffee at her leisure with Emily.

So imagine with me, JJ gets out her old laptop, which is the most recent one we're not actively using, spiffs it up, discovers the battery still holds a charge, and sets it up for Emily. Who hasn't actually had a computer or sat in front of one except for a few minutes at the library, for years.

"So the wifi password..." said JJ.

"The what now?" said Emily. She says that a lot.

"Poke that little antenna pattern thingie," she said, pointing at it.

"Right..." said Emily.

"It's a list of little radio networks the neighbors have for their computers to talk to."

"Huh. Most of them have locks next to them," said Emily. "And I bet the one marked ravynscroft is us."

"Yup," said JJ.

"Whiiiich would be why I need the password you were offering. Eventually I do catch on."

"The wifi password," JJ said again. She's very loyal to Emily, shepherding her through all the changes in her life.

"So, um, hold your horses," said Emily, poking at stuff. "Ah. A box with a blank I can type in. Hit me. You're embarrassed. You're never embarrassed."

"Well, I'll let you guess who thought it up," said JJ. "Ready?"

"Ready," said Emily.

"fuckme6waystil2sday," said JJ. With her hand covering most of her face. I was sitting across the room trying to stay out of it, but it was a funny situation.

"Sounds like a Joy special," said Emily. "The unprintable words are like her belongings or something. Ooo, it remembers, so I don't have to type it again."

"And we can set you up with an e-mail address," said JJ. "I just did this for Renee a month or two ago, I wonder how I did it."

Emily watched JJ think. Or just sit waiting for the clock to strike. It looks much the same. I swear she thinks in her sleep sometimes, because she has amazingly detailed ideas first thing in the morning.

Emily fit right in. She was up before the rest of us the morning after we got home. She found the coffee and made some, started putting together an assortment of likely breakfast foods, jury-rigged a sugar bowl out of one of those old coffee cups of Mom's that was in the back of the cupboard. And professed to be unperturbed by people parading through her kitchen on the way from shared bedrooms to the shared bathroom, often swapping partners on the way. Everybody remembered her jammies that first morning, but I'm afraid the second and third produced a nearly complete set of wardrobe malfunctions.

Emily has the most wonderful laugh when we do something silly in front of her.

Andi pressed car keys into Emily's hand and begged for a ride to the train station.

"What a great idea," I said. "Door to door service. Or something."

The day passed without incident, and Andi and I wandered down to JJ's lecture when it was time. She had a geyser set up; a six foot tall glass thing with a large glass tube dangling from a pan to catch the eruption. She had it pre-heating with an industrial strength Bunsen burner. We helped her put warning tape on the first three rows of seats on that side of the hall. It won't do to scald the audience.

The lecture was lots of fun, and when she was done she answered questions for an hour or so and then came to get us.

"Oh," said JJ.

"Oh?" I said.

"I forgot to tell Emily about the phone. We'll have to walk."

"Raitch?" I asked.

"Rave?" she answered.

"Does your phone remember our land line's number?"

"There's no actual phone hooked up to..." JJ said.

But Rachael dialed it, put it on speaker, and Emily picked up.

"We'd like a ride," said Rachael.

"And we're impressed you..." I said.

"...Found a telephone in my attic room," said Emily. "Not hooked up to anything. Huh. So I plugged it into the jack in the kitchen and hey! it works!"

"Turns out to be cheaper to get internet if you let them sell you TV and a land-line phone," I explained.

"I think I remember the way to the station," Emily said, and hung up.

"We should get her on the household mobile phone plan," said Joy.

"In case she gets lost," said Andi.

But she didn't get lost, and we got a ride home. "So I was trying to cut open a package I found in the freezer," said Emily, back in her kitchen. It was already her kitchen, after a day and a half. "These scissors are obviously left-handed, which I am not."

"It's a bitch finding those things," said Rachael, who is left-handed. "The orange ones are right-handed."

"Ah. Thank you," said Emily.

Anyway, Renee, I figured you'd like to hear how Emily is doing.

love,
    Ravyn.

To: emily@ravynscroft.org
     From: renee@ravynscroft.org

heeeey! they tell me they hooked you up to the family e-mail server.

renee

To: renee@ravynscroft.org
     From: emily@ravynscroft.org

They sure did (hook me up).

Could you hook me up with the recipe for your never-ending pot of stew? I could use that around here some days when people are coming and going at odd hours.

Emily

To: emily@ravynscroft.org
     From: renee@ravynscroft.org

um... i'll look it up next time i'm in denver. after having a house stuffed full of people, it's kinda lonely with just eric and me there. people stop by sometimes to talk or to visit, so it's handy having something like stew already cooking. i guess i sound like a preacher's wife or something.

if those housemates of yours ever mistreat you, give 'em what-for, from me. there's so much for ravyn and i to envy about each others' lives and choices, but having a housekeeper probably tops the list.

renee

To: ravyn@ravynscroft.org
   From: renee@ravynscroft.org

heeeey. thanks for the updates. i kinda feel like i know the rest of your household just from the stories you and jj tell about them.

and thanks for coming for christmas. it was great having a house full of people, but even greater because one of them is you. i spoze we should prolly work on doing the grown-up thing. it was funny, though, seeing how shocked jj was by the 'mine are bigger than yours' thing. just like janet when we were kids.

we'll always have alkaburkey. right?

take good care of emily. and thanks for setting her up with her own e-mail address. she's already pinging me for recipes. when did i become the matronly one?

don't be a stranger. too many people (including us) are too far from their families. either physically or socially. again including us. let's fix the social part, and work on the physical part as opportunity presents itself. one thing in this business is travel happens to us a lot.

love,

renee

To: renee@ravynscroft.org
   From: Ravyn@ravynscroft.org

Renee,

Yeahthat, about all of it. Let's work on staying in touch this time. As for the physical closeness, I know you would be disappointed if I didn't ask just what kind of physical closeness you had in mind. With my eyebrows raised, of course. Do we *want* to always have Alkaburkey?

No pressure, but... you know (or can find out) where we live.

love,
   not even ironically.
   whodathunkit?
   Ravyn

CHAPTER FIFTY-THREE

Two Sandwiches

One winter's evening about that time, Emily was sitting on the couch with the big old clunky laptop JJ had set up for her. People were arriving, changing clothes; the household was winding down. Those first few days of the new term are always grinding for the faculty folks, and of course Emily was still adjusting to the huge transformation in her life.

"Oh fuck," said Emily.

"OK, sure," popped out of my mouth before I had a chance to shut it. It's a thing we say around the place. Not that it's appropriate for Emily, since she's living in the attic and not on the second floor with the rest of us. "Uh... sorry," I added.

There were tears running down her face. I handed the tissue box to JJ, who was sitting beside her on the couch. Emily sniffled for a while and wiped her eyes.

"What's up?" I asked her.

JJ did one of those elaborate nonverbal communications to the effect that Emily will tell us whatever she wants to in her own sweet time, back off.

"So... it turns out I can get the Denver newspaper on the computer," said Emily, gesturing palm-up at her screen. "JJ said I could subscribe if I wanted to, so I spent a little of your money doing that."

"Whatever you want," I said.

"And now..." Emily put one hand under her nose and wrapped the other around herself. "Fuck."

"OK, sure," said Joy, walking into the room and sitting down.

JJ growled silently in Joy's general direction.

"It's Mrs. D," said Emily. "She died. I feel like... I dunno what I feel like. She was good to the street people."

JJ closed her laptop, borrowed Emily's computer, closed it and set it on top of her own. She scooted a few inches closer and put an arm around Emily's shoulders. She offered another tissue.

"People should be there for her," Emily said, between sniffles and sobs. "And I'm a thousand miles away."

"If you want to go..." JJ said, "we could arrange that."

"Just like that?" said Emily. "How... very odd."

"Just like that," said JJ.

My phone came out, my thumb found Renee's number, dialed, and put her on speaker. JJ retrieved her laptop.

"Ravyn? What a surprise," said Renee, when she picked up.

"I know, right?" I said, wondering whether forty-something professors said things like that. "I have some bad news and a favor to ask."

"Oh?" said Renee.

"Yeah, a friend of Emily's has died in Denver. She'd like to go to the service."

"And she needs a place to stay," said Renee. "Done. There's a guest room at the rectory, as you know. Who, if I may ask? If it's somebody in the neighborhood, maybe Eric knows them."

"Mrs. Diefendorfer," said Emily. "Gretl, I think her first name was. She was good to the street people."

"Hey Eric?" Renee said, off mic. There was some mumbling.

"Hi," said Eric's voice. "Yes, Gretl was one of the flock at St. Bart's. And she was always taking in homeless people. You're welcome to stay here for the funeral if you want. We're doing it on Thursday morning."

"Thank you, soooo much," said Emily. She had learned to thank people quickly because we usually shushed her before she finished. "I haven't ever taken an airplane trip alone," she said, stealing a glance at JJ.

"We can get you a seat," said JJ. "And you're looking at me," she added, looking up from the screeen. "You want me to go with you... I... guess I could do that?"

"Thank you, soooo much," Emily repeated, throwing her arms around JJ's shoulders.

JJ smiled, just a little bit, clearly pleased to be able to help. "Ravyn," she said. "Can you teach my class on Thursday?"

"Um..." I said, consulting the calendar program on my ever-present laptop. "I guess so, sure." There wasn't anything that couldn't be skipped or rescheduled.

"We're doing this?" JJ asked Emily. At her nod, JJ concluded a deal for airline tickets.

"You're very good to me," said Emily, embracing JJ again when the computer was closed.

So when the day came we helped Emily pack, disabusing her of the notion that she needed to take everything she owned. Andi dropped the rest of us at the train station, paid for parking, which she hadn't done since Emily had come to live with us a month before, and they were off.

JJ's class was one of those where you demonstrate angular momentum by whirling around, talking about ice skaters in spins, and I had forgotten how dizzy the whole thing made me. Crowd control can be a little iffy for a professor a head shorter than everybody in the class, especially if she absent-mindedly boosts herself up onto the edge of the demonstration table in a little dress. So I started a little conspiracy with the one girl in the class, a kid named Allie. I guess it was a little much for her, and I felt terrible when she dashed away in tears at the end of the hour.

JJ and Emily were due back that night, and kind of without thinking about it much, we left the east bedroom empty. The two of them were snuggled up tight there in the morning, so we let them sleep. It was a little... odd... seeing Emily in JJ's arms. I wasn't entirely sure she was gay, and she had carefully kept to herself at bedtime, sleeping alone in the attic.

I went to JJ's office at lunchtime with two sandwiches I had made for just this situation. How did it go...

Sad, was the answer. Emily needed a shoulder to cry on. Skin to convince her she's alive. Renee really understands those things so we slept together, Emily and I.

I'm not sure how much of that conversation was out loud and how much was interpolated based on shrugs and the waves in JJ's hair. They slept together at our house for several nights while Emily found herself again.

CHAPTER FIFTY-FOUR

Electric Sweat

"Hey," said Joy one night. "It's the deeps of February, everybody has the blahs, we should have a party."

"Just what kind of a party did you have in mind?" Rachael wanted to know.

"Invite all the lesbians we know? I dunno," said Joy.

Emily pulled the ever-present shopping list out of her pocket. I found a pen I had parked in my hair earlier, freed it, and handed it to her.

"Well, there's my student Margaret," I said. "If Alice happens to be visiting..." She's a green-haired very soon to be post-doc from the Midwest, who's considering an offer to come work with us whenever she finishes with her thesis. She was the not-quite-gum-chewing kid in the back row who asked all the right questions when I was there giving a talk about our lab and our work.

"Isn't Margaret, um, coupled? with Cilla? She's kinda sorta my student," said Joy.

"Are they?" I asked. "I mean, they were, but, ahem, Alice."

If Alice hasn't had her own hurricane yet, she will one of these years. She has the personality to match. "Fuck normal," seems to be her mantra. "I'm really really gay."

Which, um, I, wouldn't know, officially. Ever again.

"And of course there are the rest of the Very Serious Business queer studies faculty," said Rachael.

"How many women..." started JJ.

"That's not funny," said Rachael, and everybody laughed.

"Not a lot of fun at parties, I'm thinkin," said Andi.

"We could invite Renee," said JJ. "If we're having one of *those* parties."

"Far away and pretending to be straight," I said.

"Not as much of either as you'd think," said Emily. "She's, like, four hours away, and…"

"Recognizes skinhunger when she sees it, might be a good way to put it," JJ said.

"Yeah, exactly," said Emily. "So we… kinda…"

"Snuggled," said JJ. "With the consent of the management, let's just say."

I was looking at the lock of Emily's hair that was in front of her ear, bent gracefully back over her shoulder, and miraculously stayed right where she had put it. She's like that herself, Emily. Kind of neutral brown, flexible about most everything, but utterly steadfast and reliable even while being soft and feminine. The rest of us are brash or loud or stompy to make up for the soft voices and short stature. Emily is just Emily. The place works when she's running it from the kitchen. Or, it turns out, from the east bedroom.

Anyway, we had a house full of people over. Everybody invited her labbies and students and graders and other hangers-on. A lot of those folks are men, it turns out. We invited Kat and Christy, who had separately sampled our household goings-on and then ended up together. And, as it happens, Hurricane Alice was doing the long distance thing with a local chick who was not somebody we'd met before, proving that we don't in fact know all the lesbians in the metro area. So they came. To the party, I hasten to add, before Joy makes a lewd fill-in-the-blank.

Emily snapped to, gave everybody cleaning or shopping or cooking assignments, got the stew into the slow cooker, a great spread of cheeses and crackers and wines, filled somebody's grandmother's fondue set with molten cheese and what amounted to croutons to dip in it. The house isn't all that big, so we dined in the dining room, or at least handed out food there, and the young-uns and an occasional superannuated professor danced, very chummily, in the living room.

"Electric sweat," is how JJ summarized the atmosphere.

It's not possible to keep your hands to yourself in a crowded room like that. I hope everybody was okay with that, or at least found someone to her liking.

Or his. Some of them were male. Some of the women are bi. I mean, sure, a lot of us are, in principle, but don't actually wanna hang out with the boys more than just at work. Though, I hafta say, my guy Jason has some really interesting physics ideas, and knows how to turn them into computer code.

Where were we? Electric sweat. Right. And twenty degrees but between snow storms outside, so sometime after 2am we herded the last of them out the door. I think the train stops at half after midnight. They all seemed to know where they were going and with whom. The canyons between the snowbanks were so empty in the morning, after being packed full of cars for a block in all directions.

"I didn't know you could dance," Emily murmured in my ear.

By then I was half asleep, so I just let my mouth do the talking. "I can't," I said. "In a crowd you have to go with it. I think I had a bowl of guacamole in one hand and a bag of chips in the other."

"It was a great party," said Emily.

"It really was. We should to it again sometime."

"After I recover from this one," she said.

When morning came, much of my hair and one of my arms were on the other side of her unmoving body. There was a smile on what I could see of her face, so I let her sleep until I totally had to get up and pee.

"Does anybody else remember Alice's friend's name?" I asked everybody who appeared wanting the bathroom or coffee.

"Who's Alice?" people would ask, but then they would nod when I mentioned the hurricane thing. "Why do you ask?"

"They're asleep on the couch," I would say.

"What? No," my householder would say. And she would go peek and come back. "Sure enough. I thought we sent everybody home."

CHAPTER FIFTY-FIVE

Augmented Seventh

I came home one afternoon, decided to walk from the station just because it was a little nice out, and so I let myself in the front door after twenty blissful plodding minutes alone. Sometimes my life is a little too full of people, to be honest.

"Um, hi," said a very young-looking woman who was sipping iced tea in our living room.

"Hello," I said. "I'm Ravyn. I live here?"

"I'm Miranda," she said, carefully putting the tea glass on the coaster and bouncing out of her chair. She stopped about an arm's length away from me.

So I shrugged off my backpack, put it next to my foot for the moment and accepted the hug she had pretty obviously intended to give me.

"Um, so..." I said. "Wait, this one sounds familiar..."

"Yeah, so..." said Miranda. "I, like, met Rachael once when I was a kid? Rachael Cohen? I think my mom stayed with you guys for a while, uh, a year ago maybe? Lia MacDonald."

"Oh of course," I said. "What brings you to Boston?"

"My thumb, curiosity, some kind of random program," said Miranda. "Lack of willpower to resist, maybe. So I called Rachael and she invited me for dinner."

"Sweet. Welcome," I said. "I'm just getting home from work, as you see. You have everything you need for now?"

"Emily set me up, yeah," said Miranda. "She's even washing my clothes for me."

"Lemme just go change," I said. "I'll be back in a flash."

So I lifted my heavy backpack again and went to find some casual, weather-appropriate clothing. The urge to wear something risqué was firmly suppressed, by the simple principle that accidentally flashing the younger generation is not a thing. By the time I returned, other folks were drifting in, some were calling Emily for rides, and the evening rush was in progress.

"More tea?" I asked Miranda.

"This is confusing," said Miranda, watching the traffic in the front hallway and stairs. "How many of you are there?"

"Uh, six," I said. "It depends a little on how you count and when..."

"And I thought our house was crowded with just four of us," said Miranda. "And then... we all kinda went off in different directions."

"We heard some of that tale from Lia," I said.

"Hi, I'm Rachael," said the latest arrival. Miranda hugged her, too. "I think I remember meeting you when..."

"I was a kid," said Miranda. "We lived next door to..."

"Stefan and Becca, yeah," said Rachael. "They had a kid your age, right?"

"Yeah, Jim and I were in and out of both houses all through growing up," said Miranda. "Well, until it turned out I'm a girl and he's a boy and then stuff happened and we never did manage to catch up again. I kinda miss that girl."

"There are past versions of myself that I miss, too," I said quietly.

"Is everybody home at last?" Emily asked when she breezed through with a laundry basket full of Miranda's clothes. "I've lost track. You want to fold this stuff, Miranda?"

"Sure," said Miranda. "Uh... I'm not sure I can find my room."

"Come with me," I said.

Miranda put the laundry basket's cutout on her hip and we went upstairs. "That way, up one more flight," I said. "And, um, sorry about all the..."

"People changing," said Miranda. "I was kinda expecting that based on my mom's reviews of your little bed-and-breakfast thing."

"Oh good," I said, and she clumped up the stairs. "Wear clothes, everybody, we have company," I announced in a loud voice for anybody who might be considering something else. Which, really, would most likely be me, and I was already covered. In several senses of the word.

I snagged a chair from the bedroom JJ and I often shared and took it down to the dining room.

"Oh thank you," said Emily, "I'd been meaning to find another chair, but..."

"Things are a little nutty," I said. "I get that."

And then like one of those modern musical pieces that sounds like chaos but resolves itself to a nice chord in the end, in a couple minutes everybody was seated at the table while Emily dished out bowls of stew.

"I was expecting cooler weather," she said.

"It's wonderful," said Miranda. "Thumbing is... nice, I guess, but home-cooked meals are fabulous."

CHAPTER FIFTY-SIX

Jin

We came home from wherever one evening to find Emily, amused, gathering up wine glasses from the living room, one of them bearing lip prints in strange lipstick.

"Counting noses," said JJ, "I'll make a wild guess that Joy has company upstairs."

"Not that much of a reach," said Emily. "Apparently Little Miss Ex has reappeared in the life of our... uh... whatever she is."

"Tell us everything," said Andi, applying the bottle to four clean glasses, and the one Emily was keeping for her own use. "But first, how did you wrap this cheese? I'm tearing it all to bits trying to open it."

"Under-over?" said Emily, like that explained something blindingly obvious. But she managed to open it even after it had been stretched and deformed by Andi's attentions.

"Jin," said Emily. "I think that's what she said her name is. She has those super obvious puppy eyes for our Joy. Though it's a bit of a surprise to see her, because I heard Joy thought she was boring and crazy, both at once."

"Interesting combination, I guess?" I said. "Maybe it maximizes the impact if you can go from apathy to pathos in one tiny step. Do we know anything else about her?"

"Just that hearing Joy talk about her made Andi drool that one time," said JJ, grinning. "It was cute, and also kind of disturbing, seeing, as you put it, super obvious drool and puppy eyes on our friend's face."

"Yeah, well," said Andi. "I, uh, know Joy better now."

"So to speak," I said. Joy wasn't around to double down the entendres.

They didn't seem to be returning, so we finished our wine, ate the supper Emily had put together (with two helpings already missing, I noticed), and tried not to pay too much attention to those who weren't there.

"Beethoven?" suggested Rachael, thumbing her phone, and finding the stereo remote on the table near her elbow.

"It's a bit too, I dunno, *Clockwork Orange*, don't you think?" I said.

Miranda laughed, sitting in her homework corner.

"What?" said Andi and Rachael at once.

And then they started to laugh, first Rachael, and then Andi, with a blush for good measure.

"I think I have the soundtrack version here someplace," Rachael said, and sure enough, there were the sounds of Wendy Carlos in the 1960s, synthesizing Beethoven, warping gradually from a very good imitation of a symphony orchestra into electronic mayhem in ten minutes or so.

"Right," I said, when the snickering died down. "I'm going to bed. They've left two beds for five of us. Is everybody okay with that?" As usual at this point in the evening, Miranda gathered up her stuff and went to the attic.

I don't usually have to ask; they either figure it out for themselves, or JJ does something magical and everyone's happy with the results.

Other than the one closed door and the sleeping arrangements, it was a typical night at Ravynscroft. Until there was a crash and a screech and some muffled cussing behind door number two.

It was awkward, extracting myself from between two people, untangling the covers, and finding my glasses so I could read the clock. Just after midnight. "The witching hour," I said.

"Sounds like some witchery gone wrong," said Rachael, somewhere near my elbow.

So we opened the door. Joy found the lamp, and turned it on. I could see this was a problem that would keep us up the rest of the night. Focus on the now, Ravyn, and do try not to panic too much. How we got here is not your concern.

Joy and Jin were on sitting opposite corners of the bed, facing away from each other, breathing heavily. Jin held a wad of tissues to her face, trying to stop something from bleeding. She looked up at us, standing in the doorway, five faces and... the night clothes we generally slept in, what with the overactive heating system was not much at all. Convenient for some things, to be sure, and thermodynamically advantageous if you're a person who has hot flashes. But if something happens in the night, hey, you're naked.

"We'll... just..." Andi was suggesting. I was sort of expecting JJ or Emily to take charge. "You want a ride home?" she asked Jin.

"When I stop bleeding all over your sheets," said Jin. "Sorry about that."

"I'll just go... put on some clothes then." It was Andi's car that we used the most, if only because it was big enough for all of us in a squeeze, and so it tended to be parked at the end of the driveway.

Emily and Rachael found Jin's clothes and determined they were... compromised, shall we say, so they sized her up by eye and went for something from our collection she could wear home.

"You okay?" JJ was saying, sitting on the bed beside Jin.

"Ummmm..." said Jin, tentatively removing the compress from her face. "Maybe?"

"We found you some clothes," said Rachael.

Jin stood up, inhaled sharply, and sat down again. "Guess not," she said.

"This is way too familiar for me," said JJ. "I think we're taking you to the emergency room."

"Um, 'kay," said Jin.

"Can you find her a wraparound or something?" JJ asked Rachael. "It's so much easier to get into with a dislocated hip."

We all, except Joy, accompanied her to the emergency room, where JJ took charge. Once we'd walked her in with her arms around the shoulders of two of our gang, JJ sent Rachael and me out, because... Well, I wasn't entirely myself. I hate it when my peeps are hurt. Even more so when they hurt each other. Even though Jin isn't, strictly speaking, one of my people.

Rachael hailed us a ride home and she tried to get me to sleep again.

Joy was still sitting right where we'd left her, staring at nothing with the lamp on. Miranda was sitting right beside her, wearing pajamas, with an arm around Joy. Raitch went to talk to them after putting me to bed. I heard their voices murmuring in my sleep.

CHAPTER FIFTY-SEVEN

Hurricane Alice

I kinda had the impression that there were always a couple people between Joy and me after that. Not obvious enough to say anything, just, huh. There's stuff I could say to her but there never seems to be an opportunity.

Meanwhile, life went on. It does that, life.

So we had this problem in the lab we just couldn't figure out. The interaction chamber needed to be isolated from the beam source, so we could work separately on either end of things, but then opened when we were ready to run the experiment. Which calls for a gate valve; every vacuum system pretty much has one. But it was tricky because cesium vapor tends to plate out on everything. I figured if we put the actual mechanism inside the vacuum boundary it might help. Right? How hard could it be?

Tricky, was the answer. So I asked the professional, my sister.

To: renee@ravynscroft.org
    From ravyn@ravynscroft.org

Hey, Renee,

So I have this problem with my experimental setup I'm having trouble figuring out. I'm attaching a folder full of pictures and diagrams and specs and stuff. If you could advise, it would be most helpful.

Otherwise, how are things? We had a heck of a party last week or sometime, I forget, with everybody's labbies and students and folks we knew. The best part was watching the younger generation of riot grrls interacting with the grey haired "How many women does it take..." "That's not funny" crowd.

"Yeah?" said Hurricane Alice after being politically corrected. "Fuck that. I'm gay. I don't care who knows it."

And yes, Nancy is gay also, but she would never put it that way, and she comes from a generation that had to care who knew.

Alice is fun but dangerous; she swings through town now and then, and we're thinking of hiring her to work on... this experiment, actually. She tends to leave a trail of broken hearts and damaged relationships in her wake. For the moment she's more or less happily getting her action at a distance with a local chick we hadn't met before. Who says we know all the lesbians in the metro area?

Thanks for taking Emily in for the funeral last month. She was really shaken by the news. JJ says you're doing well.

thanks, love, and stuff...

Ravyn

To: ravyn@ravynscroft
   From: renee@ravynscroft

dear ravyn,

interesting little problem you have there with the experiment. there are some engineers at a company here i tend to consult on stuff like this. if there's money in your grant for these kinds of things, they can fix you right up. i'll hook you up if you want.

your party sounds like lots of fun. didn't we go to some of those when we were kids? or was that later, in college, when we, when i, was old enough to get drunk and do regrettable things. and, apparently, forget who else was with me.

i know a certain somebody else who might be described as a hurricane, but who'll never have one named after her, being a person of unusual name too far down the alphabet. i wonder if the weather channel, who are naming other kinds of storms nowadays, take suggestions. winter storm ravyn has a nice ring to it, don't you think?

love,
   renee

So Renee put me in touch with her favorite engineering team, and I sent them the specs we'd worked out, they asked some questions, and we decided a face to face discussion would be useful.

"Jay?"

"Rave?" she answered.

"When you have a chance, could you get the airlines to bid against each other for the privilege of transporting me to Denver?"

Joy snorted elsewhere at the dinner table.

"Suuuure," said JJ. The magical phone came out. Emily sorta likes having the lights low at dinner time, and since she discovered the dimmer JJ installed, she's loved experimenting with it. The light from the screen on JJ's face made her seem... Well, I wanted to interrupt and, um, stuff.

"Dong!" said my phone. Someone had replaced JJ's text alert tone on my phone with her actual voice, saying "Dong!"

So I got it out of my pocket and I had a reservation. "It finally donged on me," I said. "If I let JJ do what she likes doing anyway, the whole trip works better."

"She donged on you," said Joy.

There was giggling around the table, ending with JJ staring into my eyes, her smile fading.

Emily emitted a fully theatrical sigh. "Go. I'll wash up here."

"We'll help," said the other three housemates.

"She said *dong,*" JJ whispered in my ear when we got upstairs. There was more giggling.

"D'you think I'm a hurricane?" I asked JJ, later. "I was explaining my lab equipment problem and mentioned our party and Hurricane Alice, and Renee said I'm not so very unlike that myself."

"Well, meeting you again seems to have brought up lots of issues for Renee," said JJ. "Which she might arguably have wanted kept buried where she put them."

"True," I admitted.

"Did you really..." JJ asked. "When you were kids, I mean."

"I, uh," I said. "Yes."

"Dang," said JJ. "Or should I say Dong."

"We didn't have toys, so no," I said, and we laughed away the tension.

"Ravyn?" said JJ.

"Mmm?"

"Treat her gently, okay? For me, if not for your own relationship with her," said JJ. "Renee's kind of... Well, she built her life on the flood plain."

"No dongs," I said. "Got it."

CHAPTER FIFTY-EIGHT

You Really are Fifteen

The day rolled around at last. JJ agreed to teach my class, since I'd taught hers when she went to the funeral with Emily.

The rest of the gang were going to work, but they made room for my luggage in the car, and I stayed on the train, transferred in the usual way, and thence to the airport. A few hours later I turned my phone on, and texted JJ and Renee that I'd arrived. I found a bathroom, some coffee, my suitcase, and a door on the 4th level, and I called Renee to tell her the number. I was a little nervous, there being just the two of us together, which, except for a few hours in Alkaburkey, hadn't happened in thirty years.

And there was her car. She hopped out, we stuffed my suitcase into the trunk, we curtseyed together to the random stranger who remarked there were two of us, and we were on the road.

Renee was all business until she pulled at last onto the toll road, which was nearly empty. "Um, hi," she said. "Welcome to Colorado."

"Hi," I said. "Thanks for coming to pick me up. JJ did sort through the public transportation website and wrote me out a script for getting from point A to point B, but it's hella complicated."

Renee laughed. "It's getting easier, though."

"Not stopping at Eric's?"

"Nope," she said, glancing at me. She checked out my dress. "We gotta be in Boulder tomorrow morning." I checked out her dress. "Somebody set up appointments with some engineers for then."

"Sorry," I said.

"Pff," she pffed. "I don't usually see him on Tuesdays anyway."

"It must be..."

"Weird."

"...not living in the same..."

"...town as my husband? Yeah." said Renee. "Maybe I should move in with him."

"Ya think?" I asked.

"I think," she said. "I do love my condo though."

"It's nice," I said.

"I wish you lived closer," she said, not looking at me. There was plenty of road to watch.

"I actually don't think you do," I said.

"True. But if you did, we could take turns living in the condo," she said.

"Whee. Like wearing identical dresses to school."

"Something like that. Seems like I could both be here and there with him," said Renee.

"I am not you," I said. "Ravyn," I added, pointing at myself. "Renee," I added, pointing at her.

"You wanna be me," she said.

"And you wanna be me," I said. "But we're not."

"Dammit, Ravyn," she said.

"Dammit, Renee," I answered.

She grinned at me kind of crookedly, just like my reflection only swapped right for left. "I missed you, all those years," she said.

"I did, too. I didn't really know how to say..."

"Yeah. Me neither. Not much needed saying, it turns out."

"Or everything. Dunno which," I said.

"Why is it that I can't tell the difference between the inane and the profound?" asked Renee.

"Woh. Profound. Or is it silly? I can't tell."

"Eggs Ackly," said Renee.

"Are we fifteen? Or forty-five?"

"I have it on good authority that you've been fifteen all your life, Ravyn," said Renee.

"You've been talking to JJ," I said. "How about you? Did you grow up? Or are you Peter Pan?"

"Oh, I grew up, all right," said Renee, suddenly serious.

There was a long silence. I didn't dare interrupt her thoughts. It was April, it was starting to be springtime, so she had stashed her coat in the back seat. I unbuckled and carefully removed my own, and buckled in again. Which led me to a glance to see how the shoulder belt on her side of the car split her cleavage. They don't really make women's clothing with this in mind, I don't think.

She glanced at me while I was looking at her boobs.

"Just thinking about shoulder belts, women's clothing, and boobs," I said, squirming uneasily in my own rig.

Renee shrugged, which moved the belt and drew my eyes. "Maybe when we're done getting your valve engineered, we can ask the boys about it," she said.

"Yeaaaah, no," I said, with a shudder, which bound this against that. "There has to be a better design."

"There's this thing about practical problems," said Renee. "If you want the best solution, you hafta talk to people about them. Even if they're guys and it involves your boobs. Which are, incidentally, bigger than mine," she added, checking mine out. She glanced back at the road, laughed, and put her tongue out at me. Like when we were fifteen.

"Nuh-uh!" is the answer to that, so I said it. When we were fifteen, of course, we were each claiming ours were bigger. How things change when you live with them for another three decades.

"Here we are," said Renee, laughing. "Gotta pay attention to the traffic for a few minutes."

"Traffic is totally nonlinear in Boston," I said. "It's like the Reynolds number for fluid flowing in a pipe is right at unity, on the hairy edge of going from laminar flow to turbulent. Anybody sneezes, and it's all over."

"It's laminar here, for the most part," said Renee. "But people are idiots."

"Andi tells me that in Boston, if you do something stupid in front of somebody else, they have eyes, they'll stop."

"Yeah, this is the wild west. Shoot first, ask questions later," said Renee. "Condo," she said, pulling up and killing the engine. The sun had sunk below the mountain as we drove toward it.

We retrieved our coats from the back seat, my suitcase from the trunk, and she went up to open the door and turn on lights and heat, while I followed more slowly, wrestling luggage up the narrow staircase. I remembered going down it with an arm around JJ at Christmas time, so it's not all that narrow, but the suitcase was less manageable than my lover.

She closed the door behind me. "So..."

"So?" I asked.

"Um," we both said.

"One bedroom or two?" she finally asked, not looking at me. "I'll just close the curtains. I never close the curtains, even when Eric is here." The place is really stunning, with transparent walls each of which had a curtain or a shade between the plexiglass layers.

"I, um... What do you want?" I asked.

"Everything. Nothing. I wanna know what it's like being fifteen again. I wanna show you what it's like being forty-five."

"Renee," I said, interrupting.

"Mmm?"

"You're not helping. Two bedrooms, since there's a question about it."

"Thank you," she said, in a voice I hadn't heard since we were ten. She looked at me again, with a tiny smile.

"Sure," I said. "I want a hug."

So she walked over and hugged me. It was good to hold my own flesh and blood in my arms. I mean, sure, the Little Sisters of the Holy Fuck are fun to hang out with, and there are lots of hugs and stuff, but they're not family. Well, they are, but not like Renee. They're not me. Well, I mean, she's not either. But... I dunno what I mean.

"Food?" asked Renee.

"Lemme freshen up a little. Is that bar we ate in at Christmas still around?"

"I'm sure," said Renee. "That'd be grand. Bar food. I never go out by myself, seems like."

"Me neither, but then I have five..."

"Fucking wenches," said Renee.

"I wasn't going to say that, but Joy totally would, at my house. I rarely have the choice of eating alone, out or otherwise. It's nice."

"I imagine," said Renee.

"Aw, honey, don't cry. I didn't mean anything by it."

So we had another hug. And then we changed out of our dresses into jeans and astonishingly similar t-shirts, given that we really hadn't exchanged much of anything in twenty years. Thirty.

"You really are me," she laughed. "Or should it be *you are I*? Nominative. Something."

"Something. Food. At least our coats are different."

She locked the door behind us, and at the bottom of the stairs, turned me the right direction. It was dark, I had no idea.

"How is it that I have a sense of direction and you don't?" she asked.

"Come to Boston. We'll see about your sense of direction then," I said.

"Here," she said.

"It was facing the other way last time I was here."

"We went in the other door," she said. We went outside again, farther along the street, and in again.

"Right. I recognize it now," I said. "Without JJ and Emily," I added.

"Aw, honey, I didn't mean anything..." she said, quoting me earlier when I'd made her tear up. We had a hug.

"There..." said the waitress.

"...are two of us," we said together. "What's on tap?" Renee added.

So the waitress performed the beer list and we ordered.

"Beer and burgers. Something we never ate together before," I said.

"Except maybe at Christmas?"

"Doubt it," I said.

"I don't recall. I went out with Eric and JJ and Emily to the brewpub in Denver."

"Renee?"

"Ravyn?"

"JJ's not me, either."

"True," she said. "She doesn't even look like you."

"How's everything?" asked the waitress.

"Identical," we said together, without even stopping to consult.

"I can see that, yeah," she said, noting that both of our plates had a dab of ketchup and three French fries left.

"Sweet waitress," I said as we left.

"I didn't check her out," said Renee.

I looked at her. We used to girlwatch together when we were kids. Hey, everybody was watching us... We basically figured out that watching boys watch us embarrassed them, but if girls watched back, there might be something there. The high school version of the secret lesbian handshake. Or something.

"Who are you really, and what did you do with the Renee I used to hang out with?" I asked her, a little more than halfway home.

Thank goodness, she laughed. "You know, I could ask you the same thing. We went different ways."

"You still feel the desire," I said. For me, I didn't say.

"Yes."

"But you don't do anything about it."

"Well, there was Alkaburkey," said Renee. Odd, given how few women there are in physics, that we wouldn't have bumped into each other at conferences over the years.

"And I've seen you looking at men sometimes," said Renee.

"True," I admitted.

"And you don't do anything about that," she said.

"Not yet. Not for a long time now."

"But you kind of see the issue," said Renee.

"I guess. It's different."

"Each person, each love, each relationship is different," said Renee. "Surely that's obvious, with way too many women living in your house."

"Yeah," I said. My lip quivered and a tear escaped from my eye.

"Sorry, no offense intended. My tongue..."

"...kinda runs away with itself sometimes. I get that," I said. "And yeah, they really are all different. Oddly enough, they all seem to like sleeping with me."

"Duh," said Renee.

"Duh?" I asked.

"You're damn near irresistible. Attentive, good with fingers and tongue, willing to give stuff a try, creative, full of ideas and fun. What's not to like?" she said.

"I'm blushing," I said, and it was true.

"And I'm going to kiss you now." And she did that.

It was... It was many things, perhaps most of all confusing. "Oh God," I said. "I feel like I'm fifteen again."

And rather than hauling off and snarkily remarking that I've been fifteen for thirty years now, she stood there in my arms, just far enough away that we could watch each others' faces.

"Butterflies in your tummy," she said.

"You totally wanna…" I said. But she put a finger to my lips.

Some of this is dialog retold from our affair as baby dykes. But it's also a contemporary play by play from that night. Finishing each other's sentences? Yup. Describing our arousal to each other? Yup. I was a bit surprised Renee kept it up as far as she did.

Rather than reciting the next line, I moved back about three inches. "Any of my housemates? I'd be on top of her in bed by now," I said instead.

"This, right here, is delicious, don't you think?" said Renee. She kind of melted against me somehow, our curves still separated by four or more layers of fabric.

"It is, you know?" I answered. "I was about to ask if we're fifteen or forty-five, but I think I know."

"Yes," she said. "Both."

"One more kiss," I said, and helped myself. "And then to bed. In there." My shrug was intended to indicate the guest room where my luggage was.

She smiled as we let each other go; sadly, perhaps, but also relieved. I know because I could feel the same conversation among the insect life in my own stomach.

"Towels…"

"Found 'em."

"What time?"

"Nine," I said. "Your time," I added, grinning.

"Kay," she said, swept in for another kiss good night, helping herself to a boob grope. I was grinning, leaning back against the closed door. She had previously dropped the shades in between the plexiglass panels to make the walls opaque. The floral pattern was appealingly Renee-like.

CHAPTER FIFTY-NINE

Ask the Experts

I woke up in a strange room, having trouble remembering where I was, who I might be with. I found glasses and then a clock and it was only six, so I lay down again. Thankfully there was a decent robe in my luggage, so in time I put it on and went to shower. Renee's door was still shut. But then I have two hours' advantage on her; by now it's chaos at home, and she's still sleeping.

"What do Ravyns eat?" Renee asked me when I emerged from the bathroom.

"Did I wake you up? I blame timezones," I said. "And I imagine, given the initial conditions and all, that Ravyns eat pretty much what Renees eat. I'll poke around and put breakfast together while you shower, if you like."

"Oooh, a useful houseguest, how novel," said Renee.

And so I stood in my sister's kitchen, wondering where to find stuff. "Identical is as identical does," I murmured, "or so the saying goes." I wonder if I was quoting our mother or something. Our lives really have been different; the wheel turns, and anybody who knows one of us can tell which is which.

Pancakes struck me as a breakfast kind of a thing I don't do very often, so I looked at the closed doors of the cabinets, and almost without thinking found everything needed, right where I would have put it given this kitchen.

The resemblances are way more than skin deep.

"What do Renees eat on their pancakes, we wonders, we does," I said when she flitted through the kitchen on her way to getting dressed.

"Ooo, pancakes!" was the unhelpful reply.

But I found some jam and some syrup, so that would probably do, and indeed it did.

"You found everything okay?" she said, reappearing.

"It was uncannily right where I expected it to be," I said. "Are you sure we're two people?"

She put a hand on my shoulder. "There's no mirror. Yup, I'm sure. Besides," she said, "your glasses are stronger than mine." She took them off her nose and handed them to me. Then she went back to her room to find her own. I had put in contacts at the end of my shower, so I hadn't yet missed my glasses.

"These are good," said Renee.

"Thanks. It's been a while since I made pancakes. Now days Emily mostly does the cooking at our house; but even so, there's rarely time." I stopped talking before I explained to my sister why there isn't time for much breakfast in the mornings at our house. The more civil members of my household, if they're reading this, may now applaud.

"Let me just say," I said, as we finished clearing up, "I forget how dry it is here. I hope engineers like unmanageable hair."

"I, um," said Renee. "Yeah, that's no problem, as they would say. Actually it is, but they do like my hair fluffy."

So we got our briefcases out, I went through the spec sheet I had sent to the company, and she drove me into the rising sun, through the traffic or what passes for it in this town, and we pulled up ten minutes before our appointment. My appointment. Renee of course also does business with these guys, so she knew where the entrance was, and introduced me to the receptionist.

"Obviously you're identical," he said. "Why the different last name?"

"It's a long story," I said, unwilling to go into it for the present audience.

He escorted us to a conference room. I sat down, spread out my papers, and waited.

Renee thumbed her phone, which I know from previous experience she hates, and put it to her ear. "Jim? Renee. I understand you have an appointment with Ravyn, my sister." She put him on speaker.

"She's your sister? When?"

"Five minutes ago," said Renee, laughing, and disconnected.

"Tell me who you are," I repeated, "and what you did with the real Renee, who hates cell phones."

"Useful tool," she said. "Hi, Jim. This is Ravyn."

"You are identical," said Jim, "just to blurt out the most obvious thing as soon as it occurs to me."

Renee took off her glasses, we checked in with small eye movements born of doing this countless times before, and said together, "She's my evil twin."

Jim laughed. "Well, Renee's a heck of a negotiator, so I seriously hope she's the evil one. I'd like to stay in business for a few more years. Let me round up some folks and we'll talk. Can we get you a muffin or some coffee?"

"Sure," said Renee. When he left, she continued. "You always accept what they offer. Jim gets discombobulated easily and one more thing to do means he's not thinking about how much your gadget is going to cost them."

Three more copies of Jim filed into the room, folders under their arms. Even though it was 9:15 in the morning, ties were beginning to come a bit loose at the neck.

I sort of wanted to ask Renee out loud why it is that men wear nooses around their necks, but thought better of it. After all, I actually did want these guys to make something for me.

The receptionist brought in muffins, a thermos of coffee, and some paper cups.

"We don't do styrofoam in Boulder any more," Renee said. "Though it wouldn't surprise me if it was invented here."

"Right. Sorry we're a little late today," said Jim. "I assure you we take deadlines seriously, and will deliver product on time and under budget if it's humanly possible."

I believed him and I told him so.

"So here's what I have in mind, just in summary. All the details are in the stuff I e-mailed you last week," I said. I opened up the laptop, took the cable Jim handed me, and found it wouldn't plug in.

"Ah," said one of the engineers. "Hang on a sec."

I took advantage of his absence to ask the assembled wisdom why blueberries are green when you put them in muffins. Disarming the enemy, or something. Renee smiled.

He returned with a fistful of adapters and we found one that would let us plug that into here.

They asked some detailed questions, they made some suggestions that I had in fact thought through, and one that I hadn't. "Why not make this gate valve part of the vacuum boundary?"

Well, why not, indeed? I was asking them to create for me a valve that would work in vacuum, when maybe it would be okay if the mechanism was in air, outside the vacuum chamber. Surely the engineering problems would be much easier if they did that, not to mention keeping the vacuum pumped down. Vacuum mechanisms require lubrication, and it's tricky, making sure they never ever see hydrocarbons because the vacuum grease won't adhere to the surface if they do.

"What an interesting idea," I said.

Renee and I looked at each other. She borrowed some of my drawings and had a look at them. "Do I get an acknowledgement in the paper for this?" she asked, smiling. "Well. I think it might work your way," she said at last. "Can you give us a couple minutes to review this?"

So the engineers went for coffee. They took the thermos thing and refilled it, and then refilled our cups for us as we huddled under a pile of fluffy curls.

"I think he's right," I said. "It's so much easier this way."

"And the interlock that prevents you from opening..."

"No difference; there's a computer in the loop anyway."

"Ah," said Renee. "I was wondering how you'd done that. It'd be a pretty fancy mechanism."

"Exactly," I said.

"Exactly," she said. And we were fifteen again.

"Okay, we do it your way," I told the engineers when they came back to the table. "I'll hafta resubmit specs and stuff, I guess." I was really hoping to get the order in that day.

"Allow me," said Jim, borrowing the projector cable, swapping the adapter for a different one, and plugging it in to his computer.

And there was a spec sheet, like the one I'd sent them, but all the numbers were different. Substantially smaller, especially the one on the bottom line.

"You guys just engineered your way out of a fat contract," I said.

"Out of one that was pretty iffy into one we can actually do," said Jim. "I like contracts where I understand what's going on."

"I can see that, yeah," I said. "So..." I added, getting up and walking to the screen.

"Yes?" said Jim.

"What's this *RSM discount* item at the bottom?"

"Renee Susan Menendez," said Jim. "She spends so much of the national treasury here that we give her special rates. If you're with her, we'll do the same for you."

"I'm not exactly..." I said.

"Hush," said Renee. "Thank you very much," she said to Jim. "We'll check this over carefully, of course, but I think it'll do."

"Great!" said Jim, and he leaned across the table to shake first my hand, and then Renee's. He handed me a USB stick with all the documents on it. "We'll be in touch..."

"Next week," I said. "Thanks for talking to me."

"Anything for Renee," said Jim. "I'm looking forward to building this thing for you."

"Thanks," I said, when we were in Renee's car again.

We looked at each other, smiled, and said, "You rock."

"Seriously," she said, "You've got a deal with some very competent engineers. They'll make you a fine valve, make your experiment the best it can be."

"I need to e-mail this stuff to my labbies," I said, still holding the thumbdrive in my hand.

"Bandwidth is good at the campus," said Renee, so we went there. Parking is, always, a hassle on campus, so she found a spot on the street a few blocks away and we walked.

We were in her office in the tower. The elevator dinged as I typed furiously on her keyboard, trying to bundle everything up and put it somewhere the lab guys (and girl) could grab. It was too big to e-mail.

"Hi, Renee," came a male voice from the doorway. And then, "Oh, my."

I glanced up from the keyboard long enough to catch Renee's eye, and we said, "She's my evil twin" together.

"Ah. The sftp site is perfect," I said. Her colleague laughed and went away. "And I'm done. An e-mail to the gang..." So I narrated as I typed. "To: atomic-cafe at physics dot etc. etc. etc. From: Ravyn."

"Huh. You use your first name for an e-mail address, too," said Renee.

"There's only one of me there, by that first name. Unlikely there'll be another."

"Well, exactly. The guys mostly use their last names."

"Yeah, they do. Huh." And I grinned. "I suppose it's another thing that makes me look unprofessional or some damn thing, like not wearing pants to work. Or getting a haircut, ever."

Renee was laughing so hard she almost fell out of her chair. While at the same time keeping her knees together, her skirt in order, and her hair perfectly coiffed. Mine kind of comes apart and gets rebraided or whatever several times a day.

Speaking of which, I did it up again while she watched. I swear she was watching my boobs move around, which they do, when you're braiding hair above your head.

"Now what?" I asked, wondering if she wanted to do something about...

"Beer?" she said. "We could have lunch in the Alferd E Packer Grill," she added.

"K, whatever."

"He's the only person ever convicted of cannibalism."

"Sooo they named the grill after him."

"Exactly," said Renee. "They have Packerburgers..."

"Because of course they do," I said. I was about to suggest that if she wanted to eat a girl...

"You're looking at me like..." said Renee.

"Like..." I prompted, when she stopped.

"There was this girl I knew once," said Renee. "She looked at me like that when..."

"I remember," I said. "You used to say *Don't look at me in that tone of voice.*"

She laughed. "I had forgotten that."

"Am I looking at you in that tone of voice?"

"Kinda, yeah," said Renee. "Makes me want to kiss you."

"Go for it," I said, hustling her into a corner outside the student union and kissing her.

"Woh," she said, smiling, when I stopped sucking on her tongue.

"Nice," I said. "For you, too, I hope."

She nodded.

There was a lull in the conversation for beer and burgers. From time to time somebody walked by, did the doubletake, and it was all high school lunchroom again. But we finished our food, decided not to have a second beer, and let somebody else have our table. We walked through the campus in the general direction of Renee's car. Apparently. I wasn't keeping track, just following my sister. Soooo much like high school.

"Dammit, Renee, I wanna mess up your hair," I said, when we were more or less alone.

"Dammit, Ravyn, I wanna mess up more than your hair."

But we were laughing again.

"It's really hard to seduce somebody when you're both laughing," I said.

"I missed you," said Renee.

"I missed you, too," I admitted.

"You missed my fingers in your twat," said Renee, smiling innocently.

"Yeahthat," I admitted. "There's only one Renee in the known universe."

"You've got lots of, um, attention," said Renee.

"Yeah, life is pretty good this year," I said.

"For me, too," she said. "Give or take a complication or two. Like you. Or JJ."

"Can I have another kiss?"

So she did that.

"Mmm," she said. "Packerburger."

"If you'd rather eat girl..." I finally said out loud.

And she laughed, tossed her hair, still unmessed up, by me at least.

We walked back to the car and she drove us home. When we arrived, I sat in the car with her for a moment. "With all the excitement I forgot..." I said.

"It's our birthday, yeah," said Renee.

"Yeah. Happy birthday, Renee."

"Happy birthday, Ravyn. That bottle of Scotch you got me for Christmas is still going... we could have a nip."

And so we did. I used her computer to check, and everybody at the lab seemed pleased with the changes to the design.

"So, let's see... food," I said, checking out the freezer and the fridge. Which were mostly empty. "We could buy some stuff and I could cook for you..."

"Or," she said as we settled into the car again, "we could eat girl."

"Now she says it," I said aloud, "when we're not where we can actually do anything about it."

And she laughed. We bought a swordfish steak, some bok choy, a bottle of red wine, and some wasabi. Char, wilt, reduce, voila. Silence the smoke alarm. Fifteen bucks for two, and it's very tasty. We also came home with two little cupcakes. She found a candle that was way too big for the cakes, lit it, and we blew it out together. Wishing, at least on my side, for a better relationship in the coming year. I kissed her happy birthday. With tongues, which is how she likes it.

And the tablet went plink.

"It's JJ," said Renee, poking at the *accept* button and setting the tablet against the ever-present stack of books on the table.

"Hey! Happy birthday!" said JJ from the screen. And then it zoomed out to show the rest of my household, except Joy, in bed. Of course. Singing happy birthday to us. Joy joined the pile of women on the bed.

"How did it go?" asked JJ.

"I have a contract," I said. "Renee really knows how to kick engineer butt."

"At least you didn't say *suck dick*," said Renee.

Giggles and sounds of mock dismay came over the little speaker from my bedroom.

"You're coming home tomorrow?" JJ asked. "Your class went okay this afternoon, but..."

"Yup," I said. "Renee's teaching, so I'm using public transit. Wish me luck."

"We'll let you two get back to birthday..."

"Suits," said Joy, squealing.

"Ahem, quite," I said, and disconnected. "She's always like that," I told Renee.

"I can see it would be fun, for a while?" she said, with the rising intonation of a twenty year old coed.

"Yeah, exactly?" I said. "If you're twenty."

"Well, they keep telling me you're perpetually fifteen, so that works then," said Renee.

"We're the same age, you and I," I said.

"Nuh-uh," she said. "I'm twenty minutes older."

"Or maybe you're me and I'm you and *I'm* the one who's older," I said.

"This is where... Oh, fuck it," said Renee. She pulled her dress all the way up, like when we really were fifteen, and lovers, and... bad girls. "My boobs are bigger than yours," she squealed.

"Nuh-uh," I said, standing up and showing her mine.

"Jeez, we really are fifteen," she said, going into her bedroom to change. With, to be sure, the door open, because she's almost always alone here. Or was it an invitation?

If it was, I declined it, went to the guest room and changed my own clothes. With the door open, in case... Jeans, t-shirt, still pulling it down when I turned around to see her dressed in just the same way, leaning against the door frame, arms folded under her (covered) boobs, hair neatly braided, grinning.

"I think mine really are bigger," I said, giving her another look. "And that's not a good thing."

"Keeping our girlish figures," Renee said, completing my thought. She didn't show me her boobs again. "There's some really good wine, or some Scotch," she said. "When you're decent."

"I'm always decent," I lied. "Even when I'm naked."

"I remember," she said. "It was not that long ago that the woman I actually invited to my hotel room got out of bed, let you in, put on the dress you took off, and left us together. You were more than decent."

"I'm glad you think so," I said. "I'm sorry it complicated your life."

"Well, I know more now about how to stay married," said Renee. "Pretending I'm not attracted to women is not part of it, at least for me. Can't be; it's important to be totally honest."

"Yes," I said.

"I'm still not entirely sure where it's going. Or what Eric wants to do about his own latent homosexuality. Maybe it's enough to go on vacation someplace and girl- and boy-watch together."

"Could work," I said. "I used to do that with Rachael. I didn't think she actually wanted to fuck the men we ogled. But she did."

"Aw, honey," she said. "I'm sorry I made you cry."

I hadn't even realized there was a tear running down my cheek. She held me for a while. "My life now is good," I said. "It was tough, getting here from there."

"Yeah," said Renee. "Making stuff up as you go along can be..."

"Lots of fun," I said, grinning.

"Fraught," she said. She was not grinning.

"Aw, honey," I said. "I'm sorry I made you cry."

She laughed through her tears and got hiccoughs for her trouble. "Dammit, I hate hiccoughs."

"Maybe you've had enough," I said, sliding the wine bottle farther away.

And she started to giggle and sob both at once, hiccoughing in between. I went around behind her chair, and when she leaned forward, I hit her back gently with my fists. It seemed to help.

Renee stood up, took her glass, and went over to stare out the window at the twilight. I brought my wine and stood behind her, one arm around her. I felt her diaphragm jump a couple times. I put my nose behind her ear. So I was out of the way when she sipped her wine. Well, my nose almost went in the glass.

"I'll behave myself," I said, letting her go. I tugged my shirt down. She checked out my boobs.

"Dammit, Ravyn," she said, grinning.

"Dammit, Renee," I said. It's the Right Answer.

"I mean," said Renee. "I dunno what I mean exactly. It would be nice. You would be nice. Eric... Well, yeah. Eric."

"Not advice; I wouldn't do that. But you and Eric should come to Massachusetts on vacation, go to Provincetown, have a few gay flings, forgive each other, and go back to being straight in the City. Did I say should? Could."

"We totally could," said Renee. "I dunno if Eric would go for it. Maybe we need another weekend together up at the tree line. One of his parishioners has a cabin up there where we..."

"Fuck," I said.

"Well, yeah. But try to screw..."

I laughed

"...our heads on straight," Renee finished.

"She said *straight*," I said, with a Butthead chuckle.

"You really are fifteen," she said. She was smiling.

"Yes'm," I said. "I really are."

There was a silence.

"We're really different, in some ways, you and I," I said.

"It's true," said Renee. "More alike than I thought, but also more different."

Another silence.

"You're really not going to sleep with me, are you?" Renee asked.

I shook my head no, kinda sadly.

"It's probably for the best," she said, with a sigh. "But I want a hug and a nice sloppy wet French kiss good night."

So we did all that. I didn't tell her how much I wanted to rub her back with massage oil, How much I wanted to hold her boobs in my hands, how much I wanted her fingers in my twat, as she put it. How much I wanted to sate her skinhunger, and mine, together. JJ would be proud of me.

We left our bedroom doors open. I, for one, slept naked. The satiny sheets were nice on my skin; the comforter just the right weight. It wasn't Renee in my dreams. Which is probably a good thing.

CHAPTER SIXTY

Home, Exhausted

Shower, breakfast, pack suitcase. Renee is as groggy and uncommunicative in the morning as I am, so grunts and thanks for the coffee was pretty much all we said.

"Thanks for putting me up," I said. "I know it's... weird."

"Come again. I kinda like you, now that we're all growed up and stuff," said Renee. "And, um, stuff."

"And, um, stuff," I echoed. Much of which should probably be left unsaid.

"So, Ravyn," she said as we started moving to the door. "There's a bus that leaves from 14th and Walnut."

"14th Street and Walnut," I echoed, so I could remember.

"Don't worry about remembering. I'll take you there on my way to campus. It's like halfway, you could walk, but then you'd have to know where you were going."

So we went to the transportation hub... just an elaborate bus stop. She figured out how to buy a ticket and did that. And then we hugged as the bus pulled up. The driver put my luggage underneath. I told him which airline.

"I didn't want to burst in on you like this," I told Renee.

"Of course you did. You like messing things up."

"OK, true enough. But it's good to see the workings of the life you've built for yourself, and with Eric."

"Thanks."

"You really should come out our way and take Eric to Provincetown. They have sailors, sometimes..."

Renee laughed. "It's hard to imagine him... like that."

"Which would be why you need to witness it with your own eyes," I said. "And I'm done giving advice. It's good to see you, and I really mean that."

"It's good to see you too."

The bus was ready to go, so I boarded, waved at her through the window, dried my tears, and settled in as far from the hacking, coughing pestilence as I could.

Of course bus travel isn't lonely nowadays since everybody has phones. I even remembered to charge mine, and then to pack up the charger again. It was time to start reconnecting with my old life, leave my sister behind to get on with her own life, without interference from me. Some people have family in their lives, even through middle age. But not for me.

So I texted JJ to tell her I was on my way. There's a time difference, so it's like mid-morning there or something. There was no response, and that's probably why. And I texted Emily to tell her the same thing.

"Cool," said Emily. "Anything in particular you want to eat? Off to the store."

I'm sure those words would make sense if I woke up a little more, or if I were immersed in my normal life... "Um, surprise me," I texted back. I was in one of those states like after an all-night run at the lab where the phrase "Saturday afternoon" makes no sense. But my phone knew my itinerary, the bus would get me to the airport in plenty of time, and all I had to do was get through security. And find the gate.

It seems like I've been through the Denver airport enough lately to do it in my sleep. Must. Stay. Awake. At least long enough to board the airplane. Dunno why I'm so sleepy; I think I slept well at Renee's house.

Maybe it was the prospect of going from complicated family dynamics with Renee, back to really different complicated dynamics in my own household. Being away for a couple days made me wonder how it ever works. But it seems to. I thought at first everybody was being extra nice, but that's really not it; there's only so long you can live in a situation where you're not yourself, on your best behavior. But people seem to only do outrageous things to other people who actually like being done to. Or whatever.

Maybe I was tired because, even though JJ is a dear, and a great teacher, still I'd have to try to figure out what she told my students, what I would have told them, and how to make up the difference during the next lecture or two.

I found the spot where we ate at the airport at Christmas time, with Max and Laurie and JJ and Emily. I texted a picture of me alone at the table to JJ and Emily. I thought about sending one to Max, but, somehow, no. I don't know her that well, for one thing. And she's Renee's friend anyway.

That put my finger on the weariness: A whole three day trip hanging out with Renee and not confusing our identities even once. Well, not very much anyway. You'd think, since I'm the one who's in this head and she's not that it'd be obvious. But I think at some level she wants everything I have, and I want everything she has. One way would be to pass through each other, adopt each others' envy of our respective sisters, and then just go home being who we are, each of us, glad at least that somebody wants what we have.

Because we both have pretty kick-ass lives, really. They're just really different, which is odd, because so much of who we are, or at least who we were, is identical.

I texted JJ and Em to tell them I was boarding, got on the airplane, settled in with a sweater, and went off to sleep. At least Boston is the end of the line so they'll wake me up when we get there.

Thankfully there was a delegation from the mother house at the airport to catch me, get me home, and pour me into bed. After stripping off my travel clothes, and jointly coming to the conclusion that I was way too tired for anything further. JJ was spooned with me in the morning, which was nice, and my skinhunger was mollified for the moment.

The craziness of Ravynscroft in the morning got me up, fed, coiffed, dressed, and out the door. I zombie-walked through my day, thankfully not expected to actually do much that involved wits.

And no sooner than my first day was winding down and I wanted to go home and crash, JJ reminded me... did I ever know this? that her student Allie, the one I'd picked on in her class when I was subbing, was doing a skating show. So, we went. Every one of us, with the regular visitors.

Watching her graceful curve across the ice was thrilling, unexpectedly so. And then seeing her calculating in her head the workings of that next jump that... didn't land well. But she got up, went around for another try, and nailed it the second time. Our whole row was on our feet cheering.

"Drinks? I'm buying," said JJ.

I'm sure I'll be dead in the morning, but hey, why not. At least this way I'll have people to make sure I get home okay. And pour me into bed, like they did last night when I came home exhausted from the airport. Conquering heroine, they said. It's true I have a contract for my widget, thanks mostly to Renee and her pet engineers. If I only had a wit or two, I could savor the moment.

I ended up sitting next to a guy in the bar who introduced himself as George.

"You were one of the judges," I said, proud that I made the connection.

"Yeah. I used to skate, but I'm twice their age," he said, waving at the other end of the restaurant where the contestants were having dinner together.

"Indeed," I said. "This," I said, pausing during the obligatory flip of hair away from my beer, "used to be all black."

He had the grace to laugh. "You in physics, too?"

"Yup. JJ took my class while I was away this week. I took hers, the one Allie's in, while she was away last month."

"Sounds convenient," said George.

"Well, except I picked on Allie, and made her cry. JJ's still after me for an apology. Perhaps after another half a beer." I took a mouthful. "Or maybe next week when I'm not exhausted. Travel does me in."

"Where to, if I may ask?"

"Visiting a vendor for my lab in Denver. And my sister. It was... very strange, on both counts. But I have a contract, and they should deliver the widget by the time we actually need it, so that's something."

"Family. Can't live with them, can't ignore them completely."

"Well, we did, for a long time. But I ran into her at a conference last fall, and, ever so tentatively, we're getting reacquainted. She really knows how to negotiate with engineers, so that was helpful."

"It's nice when adult siblings can be helpful, as adults," said George. "And I can see... Perhaps I'll go chat with the contestants. They seem to be finished with dinner."

He was kind enough to hold my elbow so I wouldn't fall or trip on something going across the room.

"Well done, everybody!" said George, who stood at the head of the table. "Here's to another performance in the can."

I went down on one knee next to Allie's seat. "Allie," I said, somewhere close to her ear.

She turned. "Oh, it's you, Dr. P."

"Call me Ravyn. And I wanted to say I'm sorry about last... gosh was it two weeks ago already?"

Allie nodded.

"And I'm also sorry about how long it took me to apologize. Picking on you in public was way out of line, unprofessional, and ... And I'm really tired and can't come up with more pretty words. If I stay here, I'll be crying on your shirt pretty soon."

She stood up, pulled me to my feet, hugged me, and I actually was crying on her shirt.

After some blubbering, she said, "Dr P... Ravyn. Stop it. You're making me all weepy."

So I pulled myself together, fought with the white noise in my head, wiped my eyes on the napkin she offered, and smiled for her.

"That's better," she said. "And I think we're even now." She grinned. "It's kind of like an even trade? Only better? But not by much. Because I didn't have to embarrass you myself; you even took care of that for me. You guys are really a full-service physics department."

A sentence like that makes one think back to all the things one has ever done with a student and regretted later. "Oh, my," was what I said. Given the choice of laughing or crying, I chose to laugh.

And then of course she wanted to know why.

"So many reasons," I said, and left it at that. "You should be having fun with your friends, not comforting some old lady."

"Hey," she said. "Don't talk about yourself that way."

"Yes'm," I said, sheepishly, and left them there, with George still holding court at the other end of the table.

I found the household in the bar, all by myself, but then had to ask Andi and Raitch to help me find the bathroom. Where they were kind enough to put me back together. JJ, ever the practical one, settled up with the bartender, and we stumbled off to the train station. It probably would have been more fun if I'd actually been awake.

CHAPTER SIXTY-ONE

Brinksmanship

And, home. JJ and Joy had been filling both of my ears with sweet nothings whenever the noise level on the train permitted.

So here's the scene: the six women who live here, and two men who regularly drop by to visit the two who are actively bi, were all in the kitchen. Some of them were talking about the liquor supply and further plans for the evening. I was... well, lusting, not to put too fine a point on it, for pretty much anybody female in the room.

I may have said out loud something to the effect of, "I am so horny." I might have said, "fucking horny."

"We can," said JJ, looking at the guys and then back at me, "fix that."

Emily laughed nervously.

Andrea took Ben's hand and towed him upstairs.

Rachael turned John around, pointed him at the doorway, and pushed, following him closely.

The other three of them took me upstairs to bed.

Stuff... happened. It was every kind of wonderful, a really good approximation of exactly whatever I needed but couldn't find any words for. It wasn't even all that late.

The guys went home and we gathered in the living room. What with it being between bedtime and bedtime, we were, um, relaxed. "It feels good," I said, "just to be myself, in my own skin, not having to worry about Renee, her desires, her reluctances, and just be."

"Let your hair down," said JJ. She tossed hers.

"So tell us more about Renee," said Rachael.

"She's... so much more like me than I expected. And yet in other ways, less alike than you might think," I said.

"It's uncanny, watching Renee do Ravyn's gestures and fidgets and wordplay," said JJ. "And being able to read Renee's mind from Ravyn's body language."

"And she knows exactly where all my buttons are, and presses them with mad abandon," I said. "Well, no, carefully planned to create increasing frustration. She's unavailable when there's opportunity, but as soon as the situation prevents it, she's making passes at me."

"I should totally take notes," Joy said.

"If you want to learn to torture me, she's a good teacher," I admitted.

"So how's she doing?" asked JJ. "I worried about her going home to Eric after Alkaburkey."

"Albuquerque," said Rachael.

"She seemed to be okay at Christmas, and in February when Emily and I were there," said JJ.

"She still seems to be okay," I said. "She made some kind of a comment about knowing more about what it takes to stay married, without elaborating."

"Yeah, probly don't need details on that," said Rachael, not looking at me.

"Probly not," I said.

"And what's up with her never ever including a capital letter in her e-mails?" Emily said. "I have an all-lower-case recipe for the fabulous stew she always seems to have going at the rectory."

"I know, right?" I said. "And who says *I know, right?* any more?"

"Most of my students," said Andi.

"And mine," said Joy.

"Anyway, so I... suggested, carefully without recommending it, that if they felt like it they could come out our way, blow off some steam in Provincetown, and stop in on the way home, jointly or severally," I said. "She sorta started to say something a couple times, at first snark, and then a more adult *Oh no no no* kind of a reaction, and then finally realizing that I might have a point and wasn't just trying to pick at her sore spots."

"Reminds me of you," said JJ. "When we manage to get to speechless."

"Sometimes somebody says something outrageous," I said.

"Fuck you," said Joy, and she smiled when I looked at her.

"In your dreams," I said. "And then Ravyn the founder of the House of Ill Repute goes, like, suuuuure."

"Suhweeeet," said Joy.

"And then the mature Ravyn thinks back to what I just told Joy about how to torture me, and I'm like wait a sec there..."

"It's only emotional abuse, and consentual," said Joy.

"All right then," I said.

"Mostly," said Joy.

"Um..."

"It's the brinksmanship that's sexy," said Joy.

"Is that named for the Brinks robbery?" asked JJ. "And what's this *man* thing?"

"We, uh," said Rachael, glancing at Andi.

"... fuck men," said Andi, picking up the cue.

"Just did, in fact," said Rachael.

"Yeah, not so much," I said. "Renee seems to, though."

"Another way to tell who's who, I'd imagine," said JJ.

"It's true," I said, looking at her. "It's kinda profound, even."

"Or really really obvious," said JJ, chuckling. "It's hard to tell sometimes."

"She said *hard*," said Joy. Because, of course she did.

I yawned. "It's been a long week," I said.

"You gonna do something with that mouth?" Joy said.

"I prolly owe you people," I admitted.

"Nobody's keeping score," said JJ.

"I remember trying to figure out how many scorecards we'd need once," said Andi.

"It's late," said Rachael. She stood up, took Joy's hand, and went upstairs. Pulling Andi by the other hand.

"I'd love to," said Emily, snuggling in between JJ and me. "I'll pick up the wine glasses in the morning."

There's not quite room for three of us to walk up the stairs together. I was gonna say *abreast*, and I could have, because Joy was already distracted.

"It's Friiiiday at last," I said, trying in vain to latch the bedroom door.

"You know that won't work," said JJ.

And I'll admit it was a thrill, having the door swing open just as I was taking off the last of my things.

CHAPTER SIXTY-TWO

Occupancy

"Hey, guys," said Rachael, one evening after supper.

We all pulled our attention out of whatever we were doing.

"So you prolly heard on the news or someplace," she said. "There's some town nearby... Uh, Somerville? Medford? Anyway, they're having a tilting match with the local university (not ours, thank heavens)."

If she'd been her normal self, Joy might have interrupted to say "Thank fuck," just because she's Joy. She'd been rather joyless since... Jin.

"Seems they, or the locals near the campus plus the town council or whatever they have there," said Rachael, "don't like living next door to a house with a dozen undergrads in it."

"Oh yeah, I heard about that," said Emily. "I'm still a little hazy on the geography around here."

"It's between here and work," I said. "If we drive, we usually go through their campus."

"Gotcha."

"Anyway," said Rachael, "The town coped with this by passing a new ordinance making it illegal for more than four unrelated people to live together. Five. Some number I forget. I remember the news story talking about other towns having similar ordinances, notably Boston vs. the undergrads in various campus neighborhoods."

"There's six of us," is what came out of my lips. I've been looking for that telepathic symbiosis all my life, and partially found it when Rachael and I were a thing.

"Yeah, exactly. That's where I was going with all this," said Rachael. "Are we legal? I dunno."

Emily curled into a tighter ball on her corner of the couch. JJ swapped places with Andi so she could snuggle up to Emily, put an arm around her, give her a shoulder to cradle her head on.

"Um, so..." said Joy. "I didn't think you guys wanted to hear about Jin all that much, but this might be related." She was watching her hands which were wrestling in her lap. It's a thing I do when I'm nervous.

There was a sinking feeling in my gut. Like this wonderful thing we'd built, six queer women of various kinds, all living and loving together in whitebread suburbia... Like it might all fly apart. The seams were certainly straining.

"I got this e-mail from Jin, after..." said Joy. She didn't need to finish the sentence. "She's... mostly fine, by the way, if you're worried. Thrilled, in other ways, but you probly didn't want to hear that."

Andi was doing the puppy-eyed drool thing, looking at Joy. It's... disturbing.

"Oh, and this is amusing, she told me about countering her neighborhood door-to-door evangelists with details of our nights together."

We laughed. "I imagine they fled quickly," said Rachael.

"She told me once, a long time ago," said Joy, "that finding out her ex was suffering made her pants happy."

"Jeez," I said.

"I know, right?" said Joy. "I guess I should have realized she's kinda vindictive. That's... so... foreign to who I am that I never thought of it."

"Until..." said JJ. Joy does have a way of starting a story and ending up in the gutter halfway there.

"Until she sent me this e-mail. In which she mentions this ordinance or whatever it is." Joy ran all the fingers of both hands through her short hair.

"All right, maybe we have a problem," said JJ. "Dunno if our town has one or not. We should probably find out."

Emily began to cry. "I knew it was too good to last," she wailed.

"Em," said JJ, in her take-charge-of-the-classroom voice. "It'll be okay. I promise you that. You in particular."

"I'll try to believe you," Emily whimpered.

"Joy, why don't you ask around and find a queer-friendly lawyer we can hire to sort all this out?"

"OK, I probly owe you guys that, since I... tempted fate or whatever," said Joy.

"And the rest of you? Don't anybody panic, okay?" said JJ. "Can you do that for me?"

"Maaaaybe?" I said, giving Joy the side-eye in a way that was a little too obvious.

"Ravyn, stop that," JJ said to me. "It's your house, so I can't make Rachael take you for a walk to calm you down."

"Yes'm," I squeaked, watching my own hands wrestling in my lap.

"Raitch? Thanks for the heads-up. I read right past that on my news feed and didn't see how it was relevant to us," said JJ.

"Suuuure?" said Rachael.

"Wow, it's bedtime already," said JJ. She stood up, pulled Emily to her feet, and said, "G'night. Don't kill each other before we sort this out, okay?" And she walked Emily up the stairs, into the east bedroom. I heard her hip hit the door, forcing it to latch.

Joy and I looked at each other across the room. Rachael, bless her heart, took her estranged wife to bed, leaving Andi to... do whatever it is she does with Joy, about which the less I know, the better. For one night, at least, it was like old times, Ravyn and Rachael against the world, making lesbian love surrounded by hostiles in suburbia. Which used to make us friskier. Raitch somehow managed to conjure up some echoes of that.

CHAPTER SIXTY-THREE

The General Theory

JJ had been restless in the night; not awake really, but getting her hair tangled up in everything and hard to sleep with. Obviously something was bothering her, and it wasn't physics-related. We got home from work, and I was still feeling like there was a serious conversation kind of hanging fire, but it's a bustling time of day around the household, what with five professors coming home, dropping their stuff in various places where it might or might not be findable again, and hoping to... well, revive.

"Welcome to the nest," said Emily.

"Have I mentioned lately how wonderful it is having you around?" I said to her. I put my arms around her in the kitchen.

"Uh, excuse us," said the others. We were in fact blocking the way.

"Every week or so," said Emily, smiling. "I'm glad you appreciate me."

"I'm gonna go change," said JJ, so I followed her upstairs and we did that. Most of our stuff is in what used to be my bedroom. Other people have their clothes hung in other closets, though there's a lot of mixing, and people wear each others' stuff without specific permission. For a while when she moved in Rachael's underwear was in one room and her hang-up clothes in another.

I was standing before the closet with a sundress in one hand and jeans in the other, trying to decide.

"Thanks," said JJ, snatching the dress, pulling it on and scattering hair everywhere.

There was nothing to do but put on the jeans and find a suitable shirt.

JJ was laughing, doing some kind of imitation of Tree Pose, one bare foot on the other knee, reaching for the overhead beam and missing, going up on one tiptoe hoping to... but no. She collapsed onto the bed. She would have been miserable if she'd made the pose; it's uncomfortable being a short person. Besides, this way I could mistake her discombobulation for an invitation.

I mean, usually if we were doing it, JJ and I? I'd be the one on my back in a little dress with my knees up, and she'd be sensibly clothed and on top. So it was... interesting.

"You girls want dinner sooner, or later?" said Emily from the doorway.

"I'm hungry," said JJ, looking up into my eyes.

"All right, then," I said and allowed myself to be stood up and walked down the stairs with Emily, while JJ followed, pulling her dress into place around her.

"Just six of us tonight?" Emily asked the assembled multitude.

"That's a crowd even without guests," said Andi.

"Especially if everybody's in the kitchen," said Joy, laying hands on Rachael, turning her around, and marching her into the dining room.

"We could enlarge the house, I suppose," I ventured. "It's kind of chummy sometimes."

JJ looked at me, not smiling. "We should probably talk," she said.

Uh-oh, went my stomach. If there are more ominous words in the English language, I'm not aware of them.

"Oh kaaaay?" I said. "Should I worry?"

"Meh," said JJ. "Worry? No. But."

Well, maybe those words are more ominous.

"After dinner," said Emily, who had managed to produce a meal, or at least dispense it, in a remarkably short time.

I spent the meal chatting with Andi, trying not to look at JJ too often, but of course wondering what she was thinking. I'd been doing that a lot lately, it seemed like. The wondering.

Well, the chatting too, we're a very verbal bunch of folks. But it seemed increasingly obvious that JJ had something to say, and was having trouble figuring out how to say it. Or how to say it nicely and spare everyone's feelings. Or something.

Dinner complete, dishes washed, I poured the rest of the wine into people's glasses and we went to the living room. Andi and Emily and I sat on the couch, Rachael and Joy, who'd been kind of close together all evening come to think of it, sat in the cushy chair together, leaving the desk chair for JJ. I snagged the bottle of rum, in case we needed more lubrication.

JJ usually wears a t-shirt and shorts when it's warm enough, and often folds herself into a straight chair with one or both feet on the seat, and coffee, or in this case wine, perched on a knee under her nose. The dress made this posture quite striking, until she noticed us looking at her. "Fuck you all very much," she said in mock annoyance, set her wine on the desk, stood up, frumped her hair while the skirt settled, and sat down again, knees more or less together, bare feet swinging free. I swear, furniture, even our furniture, is designed for people with longer legs than ours.

"So," said JJ.

"So," I said. "Out with it."

"I kinda think..." JJ started. "No, I think I really do think... and that sounded weird." She laughed. She set her wine down again, bent forward at the waist, flipped hair as she sat up again, and took a sip of wine.

"I have what amounts to a general theory of relationships. Well, in the special case of groups of women like us," said JJ.

I strongly suppressed the urge to interrupt with "Isn't that special?"

"Do tell," I prompted, instead. But I was thinking more about myself, and my recent self-examination that turned up the notion that I'd been trying to become whatever I thought JJ wanted me to be, just like I'd done with Rachael before her, and arguably with Renee when we were teenagers.

"We're all of us adults who have a pretty good idea of who we are, what we want out of life, and we've found a way to get most of those needs met," said JJ. "Here, together."

There were um-humms around the room, after everybody considered her own situation. JJ was looking at Emily especially, and Em nodded. She's the most recent addition to the household, and has the largest change in her living situation. If she's happy, maybe we have something here.

CHAPTER SIXTY-FOUR

Nobody Wanting Anything

JJ looked around the circle, frumped her dress again since we'd made her uncomfortable looking at how she inhabited it, and returned to looking at Emily.

"There's a lot of love in this house," she said. "And I think it's safe to say... Well, I'll venture to say it anyway, even if it's not, that each of us loves each of the others. All the two-way relationships are as different as their participants, of course, some more intense and some less, I suppose, if they're even comparable."

"Andi tried to figure out how many pairs there are once," my mouth unhelpfully reminded everyone.

"Fifteen," said Andi. "Now hush." She smiled at me. I do like her smile... she's one of those who shows teeth way up past the gumline when she grins.

"And we really are very different people," said JJ. "It kind of boggles the mind how different, and yet how well our culturally verboten solution seems to fit everybody who actually lives here. I mean, most of the lesbian community even seems to be invested in pair bonding, with just two people in every relationship. I think we've boggled more of the old campus lesbians' minds than we have straight people's."

"Boggle boggle boggle," said my mouth, quoting some old BC comic or something. Lord knows what. "I should shut up now," I remarked.

"So, let's see," said JJ. "We have two bi women, as Andi reminds us whenever we forget. And some much less bi people, who are more comfortable calling ourselves lesbians, though I think we all have men in our histories."

I need a history-ectomy for that, punned my entertainment committee, thankfully without it flying out of my mouth.

"Some of us kinky, some of us not," she said, casting a glance first at Joy and Andi, and maybe Rachael, and then at Emily and me. "Some of us clothes horses," she said, looking at me, uncharacteristically wearing jeans and a grey *My Way or the Highway* tank top, "and some of us indifferent. Others bent on eventually borrowing everything in our size." She flounced the hem of her dress again. "One of us very sure of herself," she said, looking at Joy, "and another wanting so very much to be whatever somebody wants her to be." That was aimed at me, with the tiniest of glances from JJ's eyes.

"Sowwy," I said, in a little-girl kind of a voice.

"And yet, we all seem to be able to get along, mostly, with only occasional eye-rolls and fits of exasperation. And we can figure out things to do together with whoever's available."

She paused to consider each of us in turn. I think I remarked once that if JJ looks at a girl, she stays looked at. I certainly felt that happening. Despite the fact that she was the one in the little impractical dress.

"And, even more weirdly," said JJ, "it seems to scale. When Ravyn and I found Emily trying to make a go of it on the streets, and kinda sorta fell for her despite having no idea if she was even a lesbian, everybody rearranged enough to make room for her, and we all made it work."

"Aww," said Emily.

"And I think we even gave you time to figure out whether or not you wanted in, without undue pressure," said JJ.

"Yeah," said Emily. She blushed. "I've never met anybody who's at all like any of you," she added. "Well, except Renee, of course."

"Story of my life," I said.

"The hospitality, just taking me in off the street, is breathtaking," said Emily. "And ever so gently, first with JJ, making sure I had enough skin contact to feel alive at the funeral for my old... patron, I guess you could call her. And then when we got back, everybody else, one by one, figuring out, helping me figure out, who I am. And stuff."

"Can we talk about sex?" said Joy, "Because we're talking about it without using the word."

JJ laughed. "I figured you'd be the one to ask that," she said. "But the point, really, is that my therapist had it right. Women who love women tend to go all the way or not at all. I think having all of you around helps each of us avoid the merging thing. Maybe especially Ravyn, who's exceptionally moldable. Malleable. Changeable. Something like that."

"I've been thinking I need to be more assertive about what I actually want," I said. "Instead of just going with whatever somebody else wants. I did that a lot with Rachael when there were just the two of us here: nobody wanting anything, waiting for the other person to voice an opinion."

Rachael crossed her legs.

I continued, "I really did it with Annie, my roommate in undergrad. I probably even did it with Renee back in the day. Though I maintain adults are not all that responsible for who they were as teenagers."

"And what have we learned from this?" JJ asked.

"What did you *want* me to learn from this?" I said, grinning. "Seriously? Left to my own devices, I come up with something that's prolly wrong, but I like the sex."

Thankfully, JJ laughed, flounced her skirt in my general direction, and drained her wineglass. "Buuuuut," she continued.

Ruh-roh, went my stomach.

JJ was looking at her knees, hands flat on her lap just above the hem. "There is a hint of trouble in paradise. Joy's kinky, and we're good with that, except it kinda wigs Ravyn out. She doesn't mind if it's just sex, maybe with some ropes, all consensual and everything. But then Joy brings her ex around."

"Um..." said Joy.

"And yes, people are allowed. Several of us fuck our exes in this house." JJ glanced at Andi and Rachael, and then at me. "But Ravyn, who after all owns the house we all live in..." There was a sharp glance in my direction. "Even though she'll deny it... has certain issues with pain."

"Yeah, there was that time we took Jin to the emergency room, after..." said Rachael, glancing at Joy. "And while most of us, pointedly not including Joy, were trying to comfort the one who was actually injured, kick some ER butt, get her some medical attention, reconstruct what had happened in the east bedroom? JJ in her wisdom sent me out of the waiting room to tend to Ravyn's panic attack. Somewhere else. Anyplace else."

My right hand was trying to climb into my mouth to catch the whimper before it came out. My left hand was flat on my ribcage, outboard around beyond my right boob. When I glanced at Joy, she was examining a tendon in her wrist. I don't recall if it's the one she strained that night.

"I mean, sure? In principle?" JJ said. "Do whatever consenting adults want to do together. Torturing Jin maybe was a little much? Though she got off on it, no question. And her revenge, which seems to be a part of your thing together..." JJ waved a hand to indicate Joy and her absent ex. "It seems to involve legal complications for the rest of us. It's like the

Puritans who had this terrible sinking feeling that somebody, somewhere, was having a good time, and they needed to put a stop to it. I'm not saying the Salem witches were lesbians, but they were lesbians."

Both Joy and I laughed at this, and then eyed each other warily. "I'm always gentle with you," she said.

"And it *is* good, what we do," I said. "For me, at least."

She bent her head in agreement.

"In a vanilla kind of a way, I guess?" my babbling mouth went on. "It's kind of thrilling, knowing that... I dunno what, but it could get much more intense... and then it doesn't? Maybe? Does that make any sense?"

"It doesn't hafta make sense," said Joy. "As long as you like it."

I considered this for a while, comparing and contrasting my own, very mild, expectations, with Jin's, which were apparently utterly wild. "I guess so? I mean, that's good, because my sexuality never made any sense to me." I stopped to fluff my hair, entangling fingers behind my right ear. "And Little Miss Exhibitionist here never thought I'd say this, but maybe it's better with the door closed sometimes."

"Hokay," said Joy. "Though Andi gets off sometimes at being left tied up naked where somebody else will find her."

"That was kinda sexy," I admitted, watching Andi blush.

"It was fucking *hot*," said Andi.

CHAPTER SIXTY-FIVE

People Don't Want To

"So are we good then?" JJ asked.

"When you figure out the other two bedroom door latches," said Joy, grinning. "Though I'll miss all the open doors."

"It's not like they lock or anything," said Andi. "It's just... Well, think of it like this. Maybe it's hotter if the details are left to people's imaginations."

"And why am I thinking about sound effects?" said Emily.

"It's all a little too undergrad dorm," I said. "And I know I suggested it. I've been putting off fixing the doors and latches for years now."

"Yeah," said Rachael. "They never worked even when we first moved in."

"Which suited the critters just fine, though now and then a restless something joined us in bed at the wrong moment," I said.

"It was almost strategic sometimes," said Rachael.

"The cat does seem to like sitting on my enlarged bladder in the morning," said Andi.

"But it was sweet, learning that we had the whole house to ourselves, just us," said Rachael. "No real need for bedroom doors, unless we had visitors."

"Yeah, there was Lia," said JJ. "I always sort of felt bad that she was in a den of... is it iniquity? And didn't want to be, not really."

"So we traded places," said Rachael. "I think it worked for both of us."

"I'm not sure it was good for Lia's sanity," I said. "Though I'm not sure it wasn't, either. She kind of had to suffer through her demons and grief in her own way."

"As did we all," said Andi. "In some cases with a little help from our friends."

"Seriously, there are kind of a lot of things we're not really wanting to talk about in this household," I said. "It's good we got one of them out in the open."

Joy looked at me warily. There was another silence.

"Uh-oh," I squeaked, in my little-girl voice.

"Aright. I know we're kinda talked out for right now. Should we have regular meetings to Talk About The Hard Stuff?" JJ asked.

"I guess?" I said. "I mean, if people want to."

"The point is kinda that people don't want to," said Rachael. "And that's a problem."

Emily sort of folded herself into the corner of the couch.

JJ glanced at her, got up, pulled Andi up to a standing position, and took her place beside Emily, with an arm around her shoulders.

Andi, since she was up, went to find the tissue box and the waste paper basket, which she put next to Emily and JJ.

"You told me you'd always take care of me," said Emily, between sniffles.

"And I will," said JJ. "All this is just... growing pains or something. Nothing to worry about, much."

"I hope," I said.

"Yeah," said Joy. She was still looking at me uneasily.

"Thanks," said Emily, not looking up from the tissue she was using to blot her tears.

People moved uneasily. Emily stabilized for the moment, JJ looked at the rest of us. "Tell ya what," she said. "Based on my reading of the situation, I'm sleeping with Emily, and I really think Ravyn and Joy need to... work something out. You guys good together?"

Rachael and Andi nodded, exchanged a look, and nodded again.

"Ruh-roh," I said, trying to smile for Joy.

"It'll be fun," said Joy. "What could go wrong?"

"Pretty much everything?" I said.

CHAPTER SIXTY-SIX

What could go Wrong?

"Fuck," said Joy.

I mean, that could make a whole chapter, right? Buuut you know me, I am a woman of many many words, and I can say that in a thousand.

~

"Well, this is awkward," I said, when Joy latched the door behind us.

"Yeah," she said.

Babble generator, engage! "It reminds me of that first time my college roommate and I... like..."

"Fucked," said Joy, because she's Joy.

"Except then we talked about absolutely everything and didn't actually intend to..."

"Fuck," said Joy.

"Now, it's pretty clear we're sleeping together, but not so much what we're talking about," I said. "I guess... I dunno, I think I wanna make love with you, make it all better. Bond, somehow. Can we do that?"

"Well, there's making love, and there's fucking," said Joy. "And while they kinda look the same, and maybe involve the same two naked people doing the same things to each other, emotionally they're very different."

"May I kiss you?" I asked. Sleeping with Joy often went straight to the naked bits.

"I'd like that," said Joy.

So we sucked on each others' lips and tongues for a while. When I turned my head in response to a car going by outside, her nose found my ear.

"Let's just..." said Joy, turning me to face the window. She braided my hair, found a tie on the nightstand, and affixed it. Then she dropped the braid in front of my shoulder. She laughed and stuffed it into the top of my shirt, tickling my boobs.

I was kind of expecting her to take me out of my clothes, but there they were, still on. My body was responding to her being there, in my space, I in hers, so close and yet so far. There's a certain blushiness to her face when she's turned on, and she was doing it.

"I... um..." I said, into the hesitation.

"For once I'd like to, I dunno, talk about sex with the legendary Ravyn Perkins, wench, with our clothes on," said Joy.

"Alrighty then," I said, and leaned up against the headboard, letting my jeans stretch and feeling them pull in various places. The braid found its way into my shirt again.

She sat beside me, sort of half turned toward me.

"So what I was saying earlier about the difference between fucking and making love..." said Joy.

"I was kinda hoping you'd explain that," I said. "It was hard to follow."

"What I mean is..." Joy started. "Well. We have a lot of sex here. Maybe not you and I, exactly... how long has it been?"

"I dunno... last week sometime?" I said.

"I think you were wearing flannel. Might have been longer," said Joy. "Anyway. Lots of times people don't actually want anything profoundly bonding, they just wanna get off and get some sleep or whatever,"

"Sure," I said. "The bonding thing happens anyway, I think. Which is why JJ..." I was going to mention the multiple lovers to avoid the emotional merging thing lesbians seem prone to.

"Sometimes, after you're done having Deeply Significant Sex with JJ, she comes to me and we wrestle naked and fuck with mad abandon and laugh," said Joy.

"We... only end up laughing when her flexible snake thing folds over," I said.

"That's one tricky," Joy started, pausing. "Dong," she said at last, thinking better of whatever adjectives she'd considered.

She shifted, turning toward me, and the way her left boob wallowed toward her armpit told me she'd ditched her bra since she came home from work. The other one was having none of that, and the button between used the excuse of the extra tension to pop open.

Joy watched me looking at her boobs, and... smiled. She reached out one finger, put it under my chin, and lifted my eyes to hers.

I took her hand in mine and sucked on her thumb for a moment, and then kissed the tattoo on her wrist before releasing it. I thought for years the tattoo was a flower, but it's pretty clearly somebody's vulva.

"You win," said Joy, so I climbed on top of her, and we undid the rest of our buttons and snaps and zippers.

The moon was rising, big and orange and full, and shining across the bed. We snuggled up tight, inflaming and satiating each others' skin hunger, sharing all of everything.

The grey twilight in the room turned to day, and brighter than day, bright primary colors displacing each other, fighting for our attention. I held onto her for dear life, as I tumbled off the earth I knew, and in the process pulled her in with me.

"I love you," I said to her, finally. I snuggled all my skin up to hers.

"You know what?" said Joy. "I love you, too. And all of... *that*... stuff we just did? Had a lot to do with it. I dunno what I mean."

"I understand," I murmured, somewhere behind her ear.

"Also, we're kinda drunk on the aftershocks," she said. "Tell me again in the morning."

And I woke up in the morning with my nose in her armpit, mouth dry from the rum, head achey (see above under rum, of which, given the fraught conversation, I may just possibly have had more than I needed). Taking inventory of friction injuries and rug burns. My one hand was pinned in the small of her back and numb. The other was wrapped around one of her breasts, so I didn't want to move, try to retrieve my hair, or anything else, until she was ready to wake up.

I tried figuring out where her hands were. One was over yonder on the pillow. The other one, at the end of the arm along her body between us, lay on her thigh right where it was between my legs. She could...

And she did. That first twitch, waking with a start, was a little much. So I squeezed the breast in my hand. Her eyes opened, she yawned and stretched, and moved the hand in my snatch some more.

"So whaddya think?" she asked. "Are you still in love with me?"

"I still love you," I said. "I don't think I'm in love, though."

"Kiss me," she said, so I did.

"I love the taste of a hangover in the morning," said Joy. "Well, not really."

"Did we settle whatever it was that JJ sent us to our room to work out?" I asked.

"Yeah, not so much," said Joy. "We, like, fu…, uh, more like made love, and behold it was very good."

"It's true," I said.

"I'm not sure it settles anything, but at least we like each other for a while," said Joy. "Yawanna fuck?"

"Not while I taste like a hangover," I said.

"Probly good, yeah," said Joy.

"Maybe after you wash all my sweat away," I said.

"Do you tease all the girls like this?" said Joy. But she was smiling, so that's a good thing, right?

She washed my hair, which is a big deal. I washed hers, which is much shorter but just as wild. "Minty fresh!" she said when she kissed me, since I had snuck a gargle on the way into the bathroom. And then we walked, at least half-naked, into a kitchen full of people, took coffee upstairs again, along with several towels, and she spread my hair out to dry and made love to me while we waited.

It was...not overwhelmingly electrifying or anything, just two lesbians connecting. But both the hugeness of the previous night, and the warm light of morning civil sexuality seemed to serve to reconnect our nesting hormones to the rest of who we are. Somehow. There really aren't any words for any of this stuff. But it was warm and fluffy and reassuring, and it was okay that we're very different people, with very different sexual preferences, and ranges of people we share them with.

I kissed her tattoo again, sometime around ten in the morning, and blew it dry, watching goosebumps rise. "It's a picture of Jin's crotch, isn't it?"

"It is," said Joy. "People think it's an iris or some other kind of flower. We were… a forever thing, once. She has one like it. I'm surprised you managed to place it."

"I didn't get a good look that night, but she was in no condition to be modest about it," I said. "Is it okay to talk about her?"

"Yeah. I think she's why JJ sent us to bed together last night."

"She seems kind of vindictive," I said. "And, to be sure," I added, looking at Joy's tattoo again, "hot."

"That's all true," said Joy. "She was... kind of like, meh, whatever, with no clear idea of what boundaries are or where hers were. So when we needed a thrill in the bedroom to stay together, I just kept pushing until she kind of exploded or something. I've never seen anybody quite like that."

"Blood... I mean, dislocated joints..." I said, with a shudder. "And even if it makes her happy, I think trying to wreck whatever nice things there are in your life makes her even happier."

"As I said, she told me once that watching her ex suffer made her pants happy," said Joy.

"Um, huh," I said.

"I know, right?" said Joy. "I gather he was quite the turkey. Mine was just boring as fuck."

"Mine is..." I said.

"Rachael, in all her living colors," said Joy.

"She seems much happier with other people around she can fuck," I said.

"I think," said Joy, moving a hand just so, "you are too."

"You girls interested in lunch?" asked JJ, with a little knock at the open door. "We thought we'd go out for once."

"OK, sure," I said, jumping up, scattering damp hair everywhere. "Where? I could eat." I stood in the bedroom with JJ and Joy, waiting for the verdict.

"Um, you might want some clothes," said JJ. She grinned.

"It's been good. Sending me to bed with Joy got me laid, twice," I said.

"Made love to," said Joy.

I whirled to look at her. "You've changed. Usually you'd just say *Fucked* and that would be that."

She laughed. "Clothes. JJ seems to be wearing shorts. Is it warm out? I don't even know."

"Seventy-five, yeah," said JJ.

So we got out shorts and t-shirts.

CHAPTER SIXTY-SEVEN

What is it you Really Want?

"Is Mexican okay?" asked Rachael. She knows my favorite local restaurant well. With six of us, they wouldn't put us at the two-seat table next to the kitchen.

"Ravyn's grinning. I think that's a yes," said Emily.

"Or maybe it's just, like, I dunno..." said JJ.

"Fuck," said Joy, because she's Joy. And because she's not far wrong.

The manager put together a nice big table in the middle of the dining room. "Saturday lunchtime is kind of slow, then?" I said.

"Sí, Señorita," he said. He's bilingual, but it's part of the schtick of the place to speak a little Spanish to the customers. And a lot to the kitchen help, many of whom are unsteady in English.

When everyone was seated, the arrangement was unusual. At home, typically Emily is at the kitchen end of the table, JJ and I facing each other on either hand, then Andi and Rachael, with Joy at the other end. Or Rachael; they reverse positions sometimes. Miranda squeezes in somewhere in the middle. Here, Joy and I were together on one side of the table, JJ and Emily on the other, which left Rachael at one end and Andi at the other.

"Hellooo down there!" said Andi to Rachael.

"I wonder if they have..." Emily was saying, so she and JJ studied the menu together. I guess spice is an issue for both of them; Mexican and Chinese cuisine use different ones, and some people are really sensitive to, like, cilantro or cumin or something.

Juan appeared at the corner of the table, and tried to engage me in Spanish, but I'm really rusty on a good day, and there were not a lot of words in any language in my head. Joy was holding my hand under the table, and, um. I'd try to say things, but no traction.

He brought us the margaritas we ordered, and asked if we were ready to order. Rachael shrugged and ordered a spicy burrito.

JJ and Emily looked up at him, with that deer in the headlights expression--it was cute. "Um, come back to us?" said JJ.

Andi likes this gooey Mexican seafood creation from Ixtapa on the Pacific Coast that they have, so she ordered that.

"I, uh, will have what she's having," said Joy.

My turn. "Um," I said.

"She'll have that, too," said Joy.

I nodded. She squeezed my hand under the table.

"And you ladies?" Juan asked JJ again.

"We'll do that, too. Both of us," said JJ.

Juan wandered off, satisfied for the moment.

"Never let it be said I'm too proud to let somebody else do my homework," said JJ.

"And it feels like date night or something," said Rachael. "People ordering for their sweeties."

JJ and Emily looked at each other.

Joy and I looked at each other. "I do think you're blushing," I said.

"Woh," said Andi. If somebody is blushing at our house, it's almost always Andi.

"This really is an interesting dynamic," said Rachael.

"Isn't it, though?" said Andi. "Usually we're all about the indecision. So, I mean, ordering and all..."

"Yeah, but you all ordered the same thing," said Rachael.

"Usually we all just do what JJ tells us to," I said, finally putting together a complete sentence. "Odd that it was Andi this time."

"Wait," said JJ. "What now? I missed something."

"You're practically drooling on Emily," Rachael said. "It's really very cute."

"I never thought I'd see the day when our Zen master... mistress... fuckit, wench? Was all google-eyed over just one of us," said Andi.

"Probably the wrong culture," said Rachael, "but, yeah. Maybe we should have those fraught household meetings more often."

"I, uh," I said. People turned their heads in my direction. Joy squeezed my hand under the table, and all the words drained out of my mind. "I dunno what I wanted to say."

"Ravyn, speechless," said Rachael, smiling.

"This is beyond cute," said Andi, "It's kind of... I dunno... alarming?" But Juan and a helper interrupted to deliver five platters of steaming seafood, and a burrito.

"¿De quién es esta?" said the helper, so I indicated Rachael. "Gracias."

"De nada," I said. Apparently my Spanish was not as affected as my English by... stuff. Well, by the reality that is Joy.

She released my right hand so I could eat, and the blissful high receded a bit. Which... in itself was odd. I think we'd had hands on each others' bodies almost nonstop since Friday night.

"Um," I said, later. When everybody had a tummy full of seafood. Except Rachael, who ate a burrito. The restaurant was essentially empty except for us and the waiter. "I think I did it again."

JJ looked up at me.

"I think..." I started. "I may be wrong, but this is so much like all the other times in my life I felt this way, kinda giddy, kinda butterflies mixed in with the seafood. Bad metaphor, but you get what I mean."

"What are you talking about?" said Joy.

"So JJ was kind enough to point out," I said, nodding in her direction, "that I'm really eager to please, eager to become whatever I think somebody wants me to be. So when JJ said maybe you should have this out with Joy... I said, okay sure. Because JJ wanted it. Joy's nice and all, and I love her, and the rest of you. That's not the point."

Joy laughed. Oh good. I was hoping I wasn't hurting her feelings.

"And Joy, uh, kinda blew in my ear and I followed her around like a lovesick puppy," I said. "Without even thinking about what I want, let alone trying to get it."

"You were the one who wanted to skip all the talking and..." said Joy. "I was gonna say fuck, but really it was making love."

"It was," I said. "And it was nice, and it was significant, and now I can't remember who I am. Who I was. Why we were having a disagreement."

"Kink," suggested Andi. "versus Vanilla. Or something."

"I kinda don't think that's even relevant?" I said.

"I was gonna say," said Joy. "That's more about fucking than making love."

"Do you understand what they're talking about?" Rachael asked JJ.

"I think we've learned something," said JJ.

"The Little Sisters of the Holy Fuck are one thing," said Joy. "But actually having a big plural marriage where everybody makes love to everybody else... that could be absolutely wonderful. It's, like, just naked bodies versus naked souls. Or something."

"It could also be terrifying," I said. "Especially since some of us are always going to be farther along than others. I mean, say you're having Deeply Significant Meaningful Relations while I'm... uh... doing some imitation of that backwards and in heels, because... Well, because you want me to be there with you doing just this."

"What is it you really want, Ravyn?" said Joy. "Never mind about me for a while."

"I... uh... really have no idea," I said. "And I can see now that's a problem. I mean, I want everybody to be happy, to be fulfilled. What we have is everybody getting her itches skritched, which is pretty good, but."

"You're still talking about everybody else," said Joy.

"Welll..." I said. "All my life, I had this notion I was transgressing boundaries that were probably there for good reasons. Whatever I was doing was wrong, somehow, maybe in several different ways, but I liked the sex. I imagine there are people who think what we have here is just more of that, and maybe sometimes they're right. But what I really want, I think, is to be in love with all of you, each pair of us in our own unique ways..." I paused and glanced at Andi.

She smiled and said "It's still fifteen pairs."

JJ laughed and turned back to me.

"And I did learn a thing or two from Joy," I said, moving to touch her, thigh to thigh, right arm around her shoulders, left holding her left hand in my lap. "I can feel the warmth and love suffusing my body, just from the contact with somebody I made love with two hours ago."

Emily draped herself over JJ and nodded, smiling. "Suffusing. I like that," she said. "It's almost like you guys are poets or something. I was a little worried about living with a bunch of scientists, and I've seen you arguing about the major arcana of tiny things. And then you sit around the table, talking about love suffusing our bodies, our souls." She smiled and sighed contentedly, and snuggled closer to JJ.

CHAPTER SIXTY-EIGHT

Asking Questions

"Aright," said Joy one night from her end of the dinner table. "I have a name. When's a good time to meet with her?"

"What are we talking about?" I asked.

"Lawyers," said Joy. "A woman in my department had a complicated situation, sorting out a nonstandard living arrangement that was dissolving. She was pleased with the way things turned out, especially with the lawyer."

"Sounds good," said JJ. "I think I'm free most of the time until mid-terms. How's Thursdays?"

"Ugh, midterms," said Andi. "Don't remind me."

"Thursdays work for me," I said. There were murmurs of assent around the table.

"Anytime," said Emily. "Like, duh." She smiled, though her lip was a little wobbly if you looked closely.

"Do we want to have just a few of us visit her the first time? Or all of us?" JJ asked.

"I'd think having everybody there to answer questions would be good?" said Joy.

"Okay, that makes sense," said JJ.

"Lawyers scare me," I said, for once voicing the concerns of the butterflies in my tummy.

"This one's on our side," Joy pointed out.

"True," I admitted.

Thursday afternoon we all got in Andi's car and went looking for the law firm's office. The app on her phone got us to the parking lot no problem.

"Now's the tricky part," said Joy. "Lemme pull up her e-mail..."

"I think it's gonna rain, please hurry," said Emily.

"Go in the door at the corner," Joy read, so six wind-blown women did that, much to the surprise of the dentist's receptionist.

"Oh," she said. "You want the door on the inside corner." The building is kind of L-shaped, wrapped around the parking lot.

So we went out into the gathering... not quite a storm just yet, found the indicated door, and went in again. "Up the stairs," said Joy, so we did that. "Then left." Some of us went one way, and some the other. There's a landing halfway up the stairs, and for some people that confuses left for right, apparently.

"Look for a door inscribed Lakermann and Hart," said Joy, peering into her phone screen.

"Lakermann, Hart, and Smith," said Andi. "Maybe I work here."

"Close enough," said Joy.

"Hi," said the receptionist.

"Hi," said Joy. "I'm Joy Wainwright? And we're here to see Dora McNaughton? I think that was her name?"

Funny thing about nervous people, even into middle age, we up-speak like undergrads.

"I'll let her know you're here," said the receptionist. "Would anybody like coffee?"

Would anybody like coffee, she asks...

"How many?"

"Six, please," said Emily, finally in her element. "One with cream, one with sugar, one with both." She's been paying attention to our sleepy morning routines.

The lobby area had four chairs, but we did what we do at home, and squeezed six small women into them. Kind of like what we'd been doing in the car. It's a thing we do, too many people in not quite enough space. Which, come to think of it, was why we were here, waiting to see a lawyer.

Dora came out of her office, dressed in a neat navy blue suit. "You," she said, waving a hand at all six of us, "must be Joy Wainright."

"I'm Joy," said Joy, extracting herself from partially under Andi and standing up. She offered a hand which Dora shook.

"The conference room will do nicely," said Dora, showing us in.

Emily sat near the door and helped the receptionist pass out coffee when it arrived.

"Sooo," said Rachael, when the door closed. "We saw this article on the news a month or two ago, about an occupancy ordinance in, uh, Somerville or Medford or one of those towns, and some controversy between the university there and the town about living arrangements for their students."

"Yeah, interesting case," said Dora. "It was Medford, and they actually passed a new ordinance."

"So since there are six of us living together in a house in Melrose, one of whom has a jealous ex," said Rachael, casting a sidelong glance at Joy, "we're wondering if we're legal, or whether the neighbors or somebody could make trouble. Not because we're gay, of course (they totally would) but because we're, like, a rooming house or whatever."

The word "six" appeared on the yellow pad in front of Dora, spelled out. Underneath that, "Melrose", the name of our town.

"Right," said Dora. "Let me ask some questions, and I'll do a little research, and we'll get back together in a week or so and we'll find out. Sound good?"

We nodded around the table.

"We told you about the fees?" Dora asked.

"That's no problem," said JJ. "Thanks."

"So there are six of you living in a house in Melrose together. Give me the address?"

I rattled off the address, which she wrote down.

"I can look up the zoning status. Tell me who's who? It's a little overwhelming."

"We have that effect on people," said Joy. "Reading from your right to left, Joy, Rachael, Andrea, Ravyn, JJ, and Emily."

She wrote down the names.

"Oh. You probably want last names. Wainright, Cohen, Smith, Perkins, Jong, and Barber."

"And who owns the house?"

"That would be me," I said. "Ravyn, if you've lost track already."

She smiled, drawing a star and the word "owner" on her pad next to my name on the list. "Mortgage?"

"But of course. It hasn't been 30 years yet," I said. "These kind folk, the ones at the university at least, all chip in a bit toward the payments."

"Anything else I should know?" asked Dora.

"OK, we should tell you that Rachael and I are married," I said. "We lived apart for a while but never did any of the paperwork, and eventually she returned to the fold."

"I'm sure that counts," said Dora. "They did a very thorough job of scrubbing the statutes and ordinances when same-sex marriage became legal, so I'm not worried about whether your marriage is valid for our purposes."

"Well, that's a small comfort, at least," said Rachael.

"It might actually help," said Dora. "I'll look up the ordinances for Melrose, but we'll see. Any other questions?"

"Does it matter that five of us are employed? Outside the house, I mean," said JJ. "We chip in for Emily's room and board and whatever stuff she wants to buy. We took her in off the streets of Denver, where, being homeless, she was having some serious situations."

"I can only imagine," said Dora, looking at us with a little more respect.

"Weee, should probably tell you..." I started, in a small voice, looking at my hands. "We all, like, sleep together, or whatever."

"Consenting adults," said Dora. "I can win that one in any court in the Commonwealth. See you all in a week?"

We shuffled out. Emily gathered up the coffee cups, put them on the tray the receptionist had left, and brought it out to the front desk as we left.

"So now we stew," she said, when we were in the car. "This is so much more genteel than when I got evicted."

"Hey," said JJ, who was sitting extremely close to Emily in the back seat. "Nobody's getting evicted, okay?"

"I hope you're right," said Emily.

I glanced over my shoulder to see tears standing in her eyes. "JJ is always right," I said, hoping it was true this time.

CHAPTER SIXTY-NINE

Expensive Hobby

A week later we repeated the drive, knowing more or less where we were going this time. "I could get used to taking Thursday afternoons off," said Joy.

"Kind of an expensive hobby," said JJ.

"I guess," said Joy.

We took the same places at the table, to help Dora keep track of who's who. Of course we were all wearing different clothes, and there were some altered hair styles as well, if she uses those to identify people. It's hard to know what other people care about.

"Okay," said Dora, handing out six copies she'd made of a two-page document. "I found the relevant ordinance. Your place is zoned for single-family residential use. There's a definition of *family* for purposes of occupancy."

People were reading ahead. "What's all this stuff about servants!" snorted Emily.

"Well, you're the housekeeper," said JJ. She moved her chair closer to Emily.

"Right," said Dora. "There are two definitions. One is *A group of people related by blood or marriage...*"

"So that'd include Ravyn and me," said Rachael.

"*Plus Necessary Domestic Help, such as servants or nurses,*" said Dora.

"You're certainly necessary," said JJ to Emily. "I dunno how we ever did without you."

"*And further including, if the unit is owner-occupied...*"

"Which it is," I interrupted.

"*...not more than three lodgers or roomers taken for hire,*" Dora finished.

"So that brings in JJ, Andi, and Joy," said Rachael. "We're in! They even chip in some money for the mortgage and the upkeep of our trusty housekeeper."

"So..." I started and everybody turned to look at me. "Just supposing my sister moved in. You know, sometime in the future after Eric dies or whatever. We're related by blood..."

"I guess that counts," said Dora. "I'd argue that in court. Anyway, the other definition is up to four unrelated individuals plus necessary domestic help. So one of you professor types would have to become the gardener or something. I don't think we need that since you fit the first clause."

"Oh good," said Rachael. "I do like gardening, though."

"Also?" said JJ. "Are you still convinced it doesn't matter that we all, like, sleep together?" She cast a sharp glance at Joy who, in any other circumstance, would have interrupted to say "fuck".

"I can still win that in any court in the Commonwealth," said Dora.

"I always get a little squirmy whenever law and being gay come up in the same sentence," JJ said. "I know it *should* protect us, but it was written by white men to protect their own straight white cisgendered interests."

"Which is why I practice law," said Dora. "Rubbing their snotty noses in the equal protection clause." She turned to Joy. "If your ex makes trouble, have them call me," she said. "Are we happy with this? Is there anything else I can do for you ladies?"

"Um..." I said. "What about Miranda? Or for that matter, other guests?"

"Miranda?" said Dora.

"She's a college kid, daughter of some friends, who's living in our attic, going to school," said Rachael.

"She's a guest, sort of?" I said. "She's been here, what, a couple months now?"

"Like eight months," said Emily.

"That long. Whoosh, the months go by," I said. "So I guess we're seven instead of six."

"We could argue that a ready supply of students is necessary to a household of professors, maybe... So she's necessary domestic help or something," said Andi. "Or is that too much of a corruption of the rules?"

"As for short-term guests, for, say, a day or a week or something, I'm sure they'd be covered," said Dora. "I'm not so sure I can make an argument for a live-in student unrelated to any of you."

"I knew it was too good to last," Emily murmured, almost to herself.

"Hey," said JJ. "I told you we'll work something out, and we will. Surely there's something to be said on the side of taking in people who need us, right?"

"Well, you'd think," said Dora. "That's not really how zoning laws work. They're about maintaining the neighborhood culture or some such thing."

"Well, Miranda's mom--one of them--lives somewhere nearby. Maybe she has some room?" said Joy.

"I think maybe we saw her apartment when we helped her move? I don't really remember," I said. "Miranda goes to visit now and then, but she always seems glad to be back. Lia's still mourning all the changes in their lives, or something."

"We'll have to think about this one," said JJ. "If you have any legal ideas, do let us know," she told Dora.

"Yes, thank you very much," I said. "I think... I mean, it's good to know what the rules actually are, so we can work on complying before somebody else decides to call us on it. What happens if they do?"

"I suppose they'd file a lawsuit against you, or get the zoning board or somebody to investigate," said Dora. "If they do that, I'll be standing right there when you open the front door to them."

"That's good," I said. "I... really hate conflict."

"I'll let you know if I think of anything else," said Dora.

We stuffed ourselves into the car for the ride home. "I can't believe we forgot about Miranda," I said.

"Yeah, me neither," said JJ. "I guess we all sort of think of her as yet another student rather than a member of the household or whatever."

Emily was pressed in between JJ and me in the back seat. She began to whimper quietly. JJ put an arm around her.

"All right, everybody," I said, when we got home and were milling around in the kitchen. "We're going to have to talk this out, whenever Miranda..."

"What about me?" asked Miranda, from somewhere over beyond the few members of my household who are taller than I am.

"We need to talk," I said. "And I've always hated that sentence. Sorry." But everybody moved into the living room, and after some hesitation over who should sit where, Miranda settled into her homework corner, sitting on the floor next to a stack of books. We took the chairs. "Aren't we a bunch of old ladies with creaky knees and stuff," I said. "And I seem to have been drafted to speak for the bunch here."

So I explained the situation with the occupancy ordinance, our visit to the lawyer, which had happened while Miranda was in class, and, uh, stuff.

"Whoosh," said Miranda. "So you're saying I should leave."

"Oh no no no no," I assured her. "We just have to think of some kind of a plan."

"Or maybe I should leave," said Joy. "Since it's my ex who seems to be making trouble for us. I didn't think vindictive people existed."

"What planet are you on?" said Miranda. "I seem to have a sign on my back that says, *Grumpy? Vindicate Here.* Or something. It's on my back; I can't read it myself."

"Um," I said, or something equally eloquent.

"I dunno what to do now," JJ admitted.

"Well," said Miranda, "Joy and I had this little talk on the night in question. Maybe we should have another one?"

"I remember," said Joy. "It was good." She managed a smile, the first such thing I'd seen in hours.

"Get a jacket, it's chilly outside," said Miranda. She accepted Joy's hand, pulling her up from the floor. She stretched her back and cracked her neck. "Much better," she added.

"We'll be back... in a while, I imagine," said Joy as she closed the door behind them. "Gus? You wanna go for a walk?" She got out the leash and took Rachael's dog along.

"Maybe there are just too many of us to have a heart to heart conversation," Andi suggested. "I, for one, have no ideas that would be helpful. Maybe those who are on the cutting edges need to do the labor of figuring out how it should work."

"Maybe," I squeaked, feeling small and as if I had lost control of a careening automobile.

"Miranda's family kind of pioneered a different way of thinking about their conflicts," said Rachael. "Maybe she has another trick up her sleeve."

"She's wearing a sleeveless tank top," I pointed out.

"Was she the one who pointed out that Jin and Joy have matching tattoos on their wrists?" said Emily.

"Ummm, no," I said.

"About the tattoos? Or who pointed them out?" said Emily. "I'm just trying to keep up here." There was a bit of a grin on her lips.

"I think I'm being teased," I said, returning her smile. "It's good, after all that seriousness."

"And before the next round of seriousness," said Andi.

"Yeah, let's burn that bridge when we come to it," I said.

"It's sort of like we have to have a deep, soul-searching group chat every time somebody new joins the household," said JJ. "Whether we need it or not."

"And sometimes it seems to be delayed until it's past ripe," said Andi.

"And, as we found out an hour ago, some, or maybe all, of us didn't really think of Miranda as a member of our little band," I said. "I mean, huh. I wonder why not. She's certainly welcome here, as far as I'm concerned."

"But maybe not the neighbors and zoning board or whatever they have here," said JJ. "I like Miranda. She soaks up our tutoring like a sponge."

"But we never really talked about it," I said. "It was just kinda, you're staying? Cool. Let us help you out with some edumacation or something."

"Her vocabulary is amazing," said Rachael. "I could imagine doing a study of word choice in people with mild brain damage. There are words of five syllables she just rattles off, but some of the one- and two-syllable ones are just missing."

"Linguistic Oddities in my Household, part XVII, by Rachael Cohen, PhD, Professor, etc. etc. etc." I said.

She put her tongue out at me. But it's true, and it's annoying, that as a professional linguist, she sometimes listens more to how we say things than what we're trying to say. I mean, most of it is probably babble anyway, but still.

CHAPTER SEVENTY

Un-Miranda-Like

Miranda came in a few minutes late, dropped off her backpack and jacket, and flopped into her place at the table.

"What's up?" Joy asked her.

Which, that's odd, kind of, because usually we just kinda let her chatter if she wants to, or if she cares to interject commentary into the old lady conversation around the table.

"Yeaaaaah," said Miranda. She dabbed at one eye with her napkin. "Soooooo after the little chat with Joy over ice cream, I kinda went all cyberstalky on Jin. I pretended to be a reporter from the school newspaper and she, like, gave me some time in her office?"

Well, that's even odder, making me wonder why our little shy, retiring Miranda who is normally either being tutored or sitting quietly in her corner doing homework, would dare to try the labyrinth, knowing the beast lurked inside somewhere.

"Anyway," said Miranda. "There's this thing my mom used to say. Sarah, my other mother, not Lia, whom you all know. Work hard, do your homework, cheat a little when you have to. So, I cheated, but only a little."

"You gonna tell us what you're talking about?" I asked.

"I'd like to buy a clue, yeah," JJ said at almost the same time.

"I was kinda expecting she'd just banish the importunate child, but no, she was even kinda nice to me. I pointed out that her tattoo is just like Joy's. She had me shut the door." Miranda slurped her soup.

I sorta felt like the mom I never was, that I should tell her not to.

"Anyway," said Miranda again. "Right, so. Either I'm adorable, or I'm a horrible negotiator. I just kinda put all my cards on the table, mud, embarrassment, everything. She laughed a lot, sometimes nicely, sometimes not so much."

"She may be a snake sometimes, but she has a soft spot for cute kids," said Joy. "I think it's the lesbian mom thing,"

"I... huh," said Miranda. "I had two of them, and... she's nothing like them. Except maybe for the stochasticity of her response."

"Sto... what now?" said Emily.

"Randomness," I translated.

"Yeahthat," said Miranda. "Holes in my head, remember?"

"Yeah, sorry," said Emily.

"So, I dunno, really," said Miranda. "She might decide I'm cute and I can keep on living here, for whatever she cares. Or she might decide Joy deserves the chaos and... do something. What would she do, anyway?"

"Uh," said JJ. "We did ask the lawyer that question. Maybe she sues us. Or she files a complaint with the zoning board or something."

"And we'll get a sternly worded letter, and a month will go by, and..." said Rachael.

"When does that happen?" I asked. "Do they have regular meetings or something? The zoning board, I mean."

"I kinda think so?" said Rachael. "You remember when the plumber across the street knocked down his old garage and had to wait months to rebuild because it was too close to the lot line..."

"I'd forgotten about that," I said. "I do remember his kid using the garage door for a field hockey goal. I finally had to go over there and ask what that sound was. Ka-whoosh! Clunk! Again and again and again."

"Jim and I used to do that when we were kids," said Miranda. "Boy next door?"

"Becca and Stephan's kid," said Rachael. "I was kinda... hanging out? With them, before they moved to Virginia. He was born not long after. Becca used to say maybe I was Jim's father."

People laughed. Miranda did not.

"I... um... huh," said Miranda. "Dunno what to say." She was blushing. Yet another un-Miranda-like response.

"It was a joke," Rachael said.

"Yeah, well," said Miranda. "Not all that farfetched sci-fi, let's say. I gotta lotta homework to do." When she had cleaned her teeth, she retrieved her backpack and went upstairs, not to be seen again that night.

"Um, wow, sorry," said Rachael.

"Tell it to Miranda," said JJ. "Tomorrow or sometime, when things have settled a little."

"I can imagine wanting to be alone after the day she had," said Joy.

"And then coming home to report... I don't know, actually. Mixed results. Ominous gathering storm clouds. More business for our lawyer. Something," said JJ.

"Ya know, being gay is not for sissies," is what slipped out of my mouth.

"Actually, it is," said Rachael. And we had a laugh around the table.

"Seriously, though, we've been breaking rules all our lives, all of us," I said. "Maybe all this togetherness was just too good to be true. Or it's another us against the world kind of a thing. There's too many of those already."

~

In the morning, somehow or other, we were a little late getting started, JJ and I. Work day and all that, so the dance through the kitchen to the bath, quick shower together accelerated by the fact that our housemates had used most of the hot water... All that made it easy not to indulge in any kind of delay.

Miranda was nowhere to be seen, but that's not unusual. As Emily puts it, if you don't need to be around, best stay out of the way in the mornings. Sometimes, I swear, her street name, Auntie Em, really fits. She's kind of the wise, sane, stable aunt who tolerates and moderates all our craziness. And gets us where we're going on time if that's in any way possible.

So along about eleven, when the adrenaline from teaching was wearing off, I was aware of a thought kind of hovering somewhere right off the corner of my field of view, bothering, but not obvious enough to show up if I turned to look at it. Sometimes bugs get caught in my hair and do that buzzy thing right over there just out of sight.

I tried to remember if JJ and I had made plans for lunching together, and couldn't. Often we do, but not every day, what with having other responsibilities and cares to attend to.

The ensuing hour brought a number of shiny things to my attention, but no progress on whatever it was that was annoying me. So at noon, I called her.

"Did we have lunch plans? I can't seem to remember," I asked.

"I could eat," she said, which didn't exactly answer the question, but close enough.

Neither of us seemed to have the lunch bag, so we walked the three blocks to a local restaurant. "So..." I said when we were settled. "Something's bothering me and I dunno what it is."

"I am clue-free," said JJ. "But I know what you mean. It seemed like Emily was a little out of her groove this morning or something. Maybe if we payed as much attention to her as we did to each other?"

"Well, we do that sometimes," I said.

"Maybe not that kind of attention?" said JJ. She was laughing at me and the absurdity of being unable to get our minds out of the gutter.

"Miranda's usually around in the mornings, isn't she?" I said.

"Staying out of the way so she doesn't get run over," said JJ. "Or, perhaps worse from her point of view, invited to join in."

"Well, yeah, sometimes I just kinda grab whoever and shower with her," I admitted. "It could be... interesting... if it turned out to be Miranda."

"And not, maybe, in a good way. Somehow we managed to avoid doing it to Lia when she lived with us," said JJ.

We went back to work, rode the train home in the usual way, texted Emily asking for a ride the last mile, and waited.

After a while she appeared, looking a bit frazzled. I'm not sure what I mean by that exactly. When I'm that way, my hair goes absolutely crazy, way more than usual. Emily's hair was perfect, staying right wherever she put it, so that wasn't the clue.

"Traffic is nuts," she said, when we were in the car and she was driving again.

"In our little town?" I said.

"Yeah, some kind of motorcycle rally or something came through," said Emily. "It was over on Washington Street, but I could hear it with the windows shut. Anyway, she's safe."

"She?" said JJ, just before I opened my mouth to say the same thing. Could mean anybody in the household.

"Miranda," said Emily. "Maybe I didn't tell you this morning."

"Maybe you did?" I said. "I kinda thought all day long that I missed something."

"She left a note to say she's going to Lia's apartment to hang out for a while," said Emily.

"Uh oh." was the first thing that popped out of my mouth.

"I guess the last few days have been a little intense, maybe especially for her," said JJ.

"Ya think?" said Emily. "Also for me, and to some extent for Joy. It's... odd, being on the outside looking in. Again. After living here this long. While the in-crowd debate our future."

When we got home, Emily handed us the note.

Dear Rachael,

Thanks so much for inviting me to dinner when I got here. It's been great seeing how you all live your lives. It's so different, in so many ways, from how it's done down South. And thanks to everybody else for everything else you did for me. A place to stay, encouragement over my education, convincing me that i'm really not a lesbian but asexual (i'm joking about that part (mostly. (i think?))).

And I'm sorry I overstayed my welcome. I've never been good at knowing when it's time to move on.

I'll be hanging out with my mom, Lia, for a while. Probably until the end of the school year at least. Maybe I can get the moms to talk, to each other, like, about me finishing my education. And how to do it without mooching off the lesbian community everywhere I go.

love you all,
  Miranda

"I'm going to miss her," I said, trying not to panic, or to cry, or whatever those emotions were that were clamoring for expression.

"Lia does have a second bedroom," said JJ.

"Full of computers and papers and books and stuff, I'm imagining," I said.

"And candles," said JJ.

I was imagining a brooding presence, in dim light, muttering spells in her own version of molecular biology or whatever it is she does.

"Is it okay if I cry now?" I asked JJ.

JJ held me while I cried out my frustration and grief that the youngest member of our household felt it necessary to sacrifice her place here. And perhaps guilt, that nobody older or wiser could think up a better solution. Though arguably Miranda was the wisest one, having won her street smarts through actually bleeding into the gravel in a gutter.

CHAPTER SEVENTY-ONE

Provincetown

Phone rang one day in June. So I looked at the screen and it said it was Renee. How... odd.

"Hello?"

"Ravyn. Good. So I do know how to use this thing after all."

"Renee. What a surprise."

"Pleasant, I hope?" said Renee.

"Sure. What can I do you for?" Damn. I haven't said that since we were teenagers.

"Directions."

"Where to?"

"The Provincetown Ferry."

"Uh, okay," I said, "Where are you now?"

"The airport in Boston."

"What a surprise," I said.

"I know, right? And I'll stop channeling my students now," said Renee.

"Any further clue about where the ferry leaves from?" I asked. "And Mom just corrected my grammar in my head. What are we? Fifteen?"

"We'll always have fifteen, my dear," said Renee. "Lessee. World Trade Center, it says."

"Ah, right. The whale watch cruises are different. So, um, Silver Line. There's even a stop at the World Trade Center."

"Uh," said Renee. "Did that mean something to you? It didn't mean anything to me."

"How long do you have?" I asked. "I could come down and..."

"An hour," said Renee.

"Guess not. Do stop in on your way home."

"Sure. But right now, how do I get to the ferry terminal or whatever it is?"

"There's this bus thing, with articulated buses? It wants to be a subway but it's not, really. It visits the ground transportation place at all the terminals at the airport."

"Bus, with hinges, gotcha. Called, I bet, The Silver Line."

She pronounced it The. Silver. Line. It's actually theSilverline. But hey. "Right."

"Do I pay?"

"I don't think so. If so it'll be like two bucks. Maybe three."

"I can swing two bucks."

"Exact change, or they keep the diff."

"Let 'em," said Renee.

"So after the bus has collected people from all the terminals, it goes through a tunnel; I think it's a private tunnel for just the Silver Line buses. Other side of the harbor, that's South Boston. Some place along there, it'll stop at an actual subway-style station for the World Trade Center."

"World. Trade. Center. Got it. Wow, I can thumb stuff into my phone while I'm talking. Eric made me get ear phones that'll actually stay in my ears."

"Get there, go upstairs, there's a walkway over to the WTC. The boat dock is on your left as you walk that way, down, obviously, at surface level. There are signs. You'll probably hafta ask somebody."

"Or my phone," said Renee. "If I knew how."

I laughed. "You're with Eric, right?"

"Right."

"And he has a sense of direction, if I recall correctly. Unlike us, I mean."

"It's true."

"Go north. At the station, I mean."

"I'll tell him," said Renee.

"Renee?"

"Yeah?"

"Welcome to New England."

"Thanks."

"Come visit before you fly home. I mean that."

"OK," she said.

"Like, if you get done in Ptown before Eric is ready to go. Or you're done knowing what he's doing there. Or. Y'know. I have a houseful of..."

"Horny lesbians. Yeah, I've met some of them," said Renee. "I'll think about it, thanks. And thanks for the directions."

"Renee?"

"Yeah?"

"I love you. In so many ways."

"I love you too, sis."

And she was gone. I guess she found the place, because there were no further calls.

~

Until...

Four days later, she appeared at the train station, phone in hand, and I borrowed the keys from Emily and went to pick her up.

"Hey," I said, loading her suitcase into the trunk.

"Hey," she said. "Thanks for..."

"Hush," I said, hugging her. But it's a loading zone, and somebody tootled us with vigor. I held the passenger door and made sure her flowing skirt was inside the car before I closed it.

Home. Em unloaded her suitcase. I held her in the kitchen while she cried herself out.

And then, daring greatly, I put my fingers in the hair above her ears, on both sides, and pulled her face in for a kiss. And then another one. With tongue.

She returned it, with passion.

I released her, backing off to the point where I could focus my eyes on her face.

"I'm sorry I cried all over your shirt," said Renee.

"Come with me," I said.

"Yes," said Renee.

"We'll take off my wet shirt anyway," I said.

She laughed, nodding.

I grabbed a handful of hangers from the coat closet. I picked the room with the door that latches. We hung up her stuff.

Sometimes I wonder what consent means, really. That was not one of those times. She cried me a river, not out of reluctance, or regret, or Weltschmertz, but more relief, perhaps, at simply being herself, loving who she loved, being who she was. Knowing, from her own rich experience, that she loved at least two people passionately.

The tissue box was, of course, in another room, so I excused myself to find it. "A lot to cry out of her system," I said, in answer to concerned looks.

"How," she asked, "can there possibly be that much snot in my head?"

And we laughed, together, like the schoolgirls we were no longer.

It was deep into twilight by the time we emerged. I found the lamp, turned it on, only then drawing the curtains, and offered her anything she could find to wear that would fit to her satisfaction. "We wear each others' clothes all the time," I said.

And she laughed. "Like a couple of girls I remember."

The household was eager to meet her. "Um, hi," she said, waving, and then sweeping hair behind a shoulder in the same way I do it.

"Everybody, this is Renee," I said. "Renee, meet the Little Sisters of the Holy Fuck."

"There's potato-leek..." Emily started.

"Unspeakable Soup!" said Renee.

"Ravyn calls it that, too," said Emily.

"It coats your vocal cords so you can't talk," Renee explained. "Yours is delightful. My mom... Our mom, managed somehow to make it kinda flat. This is tasty, with interesting spices."

"I started with the spices in your stew recipe and experimented," said Emily. "Turmeric is amazing stuff."

There was silence for a long while, punctuated by little slurps and people politely not asking questions.

"So, um," said Renee, clearing her throat and tossing hair. When she finished eating she pushed her chair back a bit and folded herself up, one knee near her chin and the other foot underneath her someplace. "I'm, uh, kinda married to a mostly gay man. We..." She glanced at me. "We're vacationing in Provincetown, giving each other permission to, like..."

"Fuck," said Joy.

"Yes," said Renee, unembarrassed. "Fuck women. For once in my life, just go with it. Before we go back to being priest and professor, all properly straight and married and stuff."

"More stuff," said JJ. "Less straight."

"Exactly," said Renee. "Ravyn suggested it. We're blaming her."

"I'm her evil twin," I said.

"Anyway, I know more than I ever needed to know about how gay men..." said Renee, drifting off in mid-sentence. "So Eric agreed to meet me here at the end of the week."

"And a good time was had by all," I said.

"We're probly gonna hafta Talk," said Renee.

"Mañana," I said.

"Exactly," said Renee.

CHAPTER SEVENTY-TWO

Flustered

"So is there always a parade through your bedroom?" Renee asked. We were leaning against the headboard in the morning, with Emily partly in her lap, snoring softly. "I think I remember JJ and Rachael?"

"I don't bother keeping track," I said.

"It's good to see Emily so much at home in her skin," said Renee. "I mean..."

"I know what you mean, and it is good. She's figured out that she's safe here."

"Coffee," JJ announced from the doorway. We left Emily sleeping off last night.

"How do you, like, make up your collective mind about... guests, or whatever?" asked Renee. "I mean, how does this work? How can it possibly work?"

"The house is kind of full-ish nowadays, but we'd invite somebody in for a night or a weekend and if she wasn't jealous after watching her sweetie get laid in a group, she's promising material. There are only so many beds."

"It's that... calculated?" Renee asked.

"Not really. It's like last night. If they're kinky, Joy can usually manage to amaze."

"Yeah, not so much."

"Not so much, check," said Joy. "I was thinkin..."

"Ruh-roh," I said.

"Some of you are bi, right?" said Renee.

"Yeah," said Rachael. "Andi came up with..."

"I just invite Ben around now and then," said Andi. "He behaves himself, and everybody seems to be okay with that."

"Likewise, with John," said Rachael. "It was... hard... getting to this point. As you've probably heard, I left Ravyn because I thought I wanted John and still had this monogamous propaganda tattooed on my ass or something."

"White people are weird. All hung up about who's sleeping with whom," said JJ. "Well, okay, Chinese culture is too. In Hawaii... maybe it's a 20-something culture thing, just kinda being happy for friends finding something they like."

"Yes, JJ-san," said Rachael. "Eventually I learned where you're coming from with that."

"I... huh," said Renee. "I hafta talk all this out with Eric, probably before we go home again. And there, we're married, we hang out together, though we live in different cities."

"Maybe that guy of yours would like..." said Joy, and she stopped, flustered. Joy is never flustered. "We, uh, play with gender identities, and trade sexes and stuff," she added. "Fuck it, peg him."

"What?" said Renee.

"Fuck him up the ass. If he's gay he might like that."

Renee's mouth opened, her eyes went wide, and her mouth closed again. Using a patented Ravyn gesture, she swept a curtain of hair over most of her face, and she peered between the strands at Joy.

"If I may translate?" I said. "Renee is intrigued by your ideas and wishes to subscribe to your newsletter."

Everyone laughed politely. Emily wasn't online when that was an internet meme, but we've used it often enough around the table that she was also amused.

Renee glanced at me, settled her hair, and squeaked, "Yeah that."

"I'm sorry I embarrassed you," said Joy.

Renee squirmed in her chair, folding her arms, unfolding them again, loosening her shirt where it bound, crossing her legs, uncrossing them again.

"But sometimes it's better to just say what you mean," said Joy, carefully not actually looking at Renee, but rather at Rachael whom she had talked through comparable problems before, "We have, ahem, toys. As you know."

"We boggled her mind with them," I said.

"Does that newsletter..." Renee started, and then went through her rituals of embarrassment again. "Does it have a toy-of-the-month club?"

"What an interesting idea," said Joy. "Whose minds are being boggled now?" she added, to the nervous laughter around the table.

"I'm, uh," said Renee, turning to look me full in the face. "Sorry, I..."

"Go," I said, grinning.

So Renee went upstairs again with the kinkier side of the Order. Joy is very careful about exploring a person's limits and pushing her near them but never over. As she says, brinksmanship is sexy.

Emily and I went to the grocery store. When we came back, Rachael and Renee were just getting out of the shower. Joy brought her some clothes. "Great," said Renee, "A t-shirt and a denim miniskirt, shorter than anything I've worn since Ravyn and I were pompom girls."

"Those were freaking little skirts we had," I said.

"And no underthings," Renee added. But she put them on without stepping on the cat who was sleeping wrapped around the half-open bathroom door.

"The cat..." said Renee.

"Freddy," said JJ.

"He's very much in the way," said Renee.

"He gets grumpy if you move him or close the door," I said.

"You guys are pussy-whipped," said Renee, laughing at her own joke.

"It's true," I said.

"And he can see all my..." said Renee, who was still standing over him.

"He's asleep, for one," I said. "For another, he's a cat, and doesn't care about people's, uh..."

"Twats," said Joy.

"Although, he does like sitting on top of me when I'm in bed," said Rachael.

"Putting his little elbows on my pubic bone and purring," I said. "It's disconcertingly like a vibrator."

"He also likes kneading my bladder," said JJ. "In the morning. When it's full."

"The blanket is fuzzy. I think you remind him of his mother," I said.

"Or not to have a mind," said JJ.

"How true that is," said Andi.

"It's like his higher brain function just switches off and he's running on instinct," said JJ.

"I'm, uh," said Renee, struggling to stay inside the little skirt, "not mentioning the unmentionables. Back in a bit," she said, and went in search of her luggage and her underwear. She returned in a few minutes wearing her own clothes.

"So I had sorta thought," said Renee, when she was settled again, "that what you had going was a continuous party or something. I couldn't imagine living like that. With lots and lots of sex and stuff with anybody who walked by."

"I sorta kinda did that when I was in college," I admitted. "It's not nearly as sexy as I thought it would be."

"But I see now it's a different thing altogether," said Renee. "There's a lot of love in this house. You have each others' backs. You've found a situation that's stable, and practical, and still satisfies everybody sexually. It's not what the larger society thinks is the right way to do any of those things, but it works for you."

"It really does," I said. "It's kind of amazing."

"Like, totally," said Andi, and then everybody had to say that, imitating their silliest Valley girl students.

"It was hard getting here, though. We all went through a lot of grief," I said. "Just to get that on the record."

"I get that," said Renee. "I think I've been grieving about loving you, and breaking up, and going off to different lives, ever since we were fifteen."

"Seventeen," I said.

"Whatever," said Renee. And then everybody had to say that, as well.

"And yeah. When Rachael moved out, I was in a dark place that was being seventeen and forty-two both at once. The relationships were completely different, but the griefs were remarkably parallel."

"I'm so sorry about that," said Rachael. "You know that."

"I do know that," I said. "And it's all good, now."

Rachael and I looked at each other the way we used to when it was just the two of us against the world. We smiled, not quite as innocently as we did then.

"I can totally see why you married her," said Renee.

"And I'm glad we never got around to filing for divorce," I said. "I tried hating you, and I just can't do it."

"I am, too. And it's good you don't hate me; I couldn't blame you if you did," said Rachael.

"I know how this dialog ends up," said Andi. "With the rest of us sleeping in two bedrooms."

Rachael and I put our tongues out at Andi.

Renee laughed. "So it's not without tensions, but real life never is," she said.

"If there's anything we can do to help with yours..." JJ suggested.

"Thanks, I'll consider it. Eric will be here tomorrow. Can I, like..."

"Anything," I said, tearing my attention away from Rachael.

"We could use a space to talk," said Renee.

"You're flying out the next morning, right? We can offer you a spare bedroom if you want," I said.

Emily nodded.

"Aww, thanks," said Renee. "I'll talk to Eric and we'll let you know."

"Meanwhile, there's most of another day of..." said Joy.

"What happens at Ravynscroft stays at Ravynscroft," said Rachael, grinning.

"So, five of you are academics, and I happen to know that academics travel. There's a major airline hub near my place..." said Renee.

"Drop in, is what you're saying?" said JJ.

"Please. Now that I know you all," said Renee.

"She said *know*," said Joy.

"Exactly," said Renee. "I tried Ptown, really I did, but I suck at strangers."

Joy merely laughed, instead of taking the obvious pull-quote.

"Yeah, me too," I admitted. "I brought home a girl or two, including one who objected to my then-doorless bathroom (hey, it mollified the cat). And Rachael, probably way too often. Because of the strangers thing."

"Yeah that," said Rachael.

CHAPTER SEVENTY-THREE

Comfortable in your Skin

Mid-afternoon the doorbell rang, so Emily went to open it. Having an inkling, plus the fact that nobody rings the bell here, I dropped Renee's hand, and we stood up.

"Father Maxwell," said Emily. "Welcome!"

"Call me Eric, please," said Eric. "And it's good to see you doing well, Emily."

"Could we offer you coffee? Wash your clothes for you?"

"Oooh, that would be nice," said Eric, retrieving his suitcase from the front porch where he'd left it. "Ravyn, Renee," he said, looking at us.

"Welcome," I said. "After coffee and due pleasantries, we'll leave you to sort things out," I said.

Emily had gone to the laundry room with the suitcase, so I served coffee and made introductions. "JJ you know," I said. "And respectively, Rachael, my official wife, Andi, and Joy."

"Hello," said Eric, mouthing each name as I said it. I guess he's professionally bound to learn people's names.

"Thanks for lending us Renee for a couple days," I said. "We made her an honorary member of the household."

Renee laughed, with just a tinge of nerves.

"I couldn't help noticing the ash tree in the yard," said Eric. He's also professionally able to carry on a conversation about something with pretty much anybody in any situation. "I bet it drops thousands of leaves into your gutters. Mine certainly does."

"Well, Rachael will remember when we got them re-done," I said. Not only conversing, but drawing others into the conversation. "They were collapsing, and dumping all the water next to the basement."

"I remember mopping the floor down there every time it rained more than an inch or so," said Rachael.

"We found a design with a cover on it that lets the water in, but, at least in their ads, no leaves," I said. "I haven't tried cleaning them since the new ones were installed."

"It's a long way up the ladder," said Rachael. "And we're little people."

"We could send our gentlemen callers up the ladder," Andi suggested. "Oh. Am I not supposed to talk about that?"

"I'm glad you did," said Renee. "It's... pertinent."

"That would be our cue," I said, herding the permanent residents, and the dog, out of the room. "Let's go look at the gutters."

So we went outside. Now, I've been doing this since I was a kid, when, to be sure, Renee was around to help with the braiding, but a windy day shouldn't be that much of a problem. But of course there were no hair fasteners and it was too warm for a jacket to put it under, so I just let my hair do whatever it wanted. Finding the lee side of the house meant the breeze was in my face, so at least it was streaming behind me, out of my face. Perhaps it was a coincidence, but the ash tree Eric mentioned was on this side of the house.

Behaving itself, not dropping anything, what with it being June and all. Do they drop blossoms? I don't remember. One has the sniffles sometimes, but my sometimeses are not convertible into actual times and seasons any more. It's one of the lingering after-effects of the whole Rachael thing.

"D'you have trouble keeping track of time?" I asked her, standing there in the front yard.

"Always," said Rachael. "You know that about me."

"I kinda lost my intuitive sense of the passage of time," I said. "One little season of..."

"Angst," said Rachael.

"Grief," I suggested. "And I don't blame you, any more. Never did, really. You did what you needed to do to stay Rachael."

She nodded. I get kinda maudlin sometimes. She knows me well.

"Maybe this is not about me," said Rachael.

"Prolly not. I'm carefully not-thinking about Renee going home tomorrow."

Rachael gathered the household and they did a group hug for me. My hair got into the faces of only two of them, which is kind of amazing.

"I wonder if they need more coffee," said Emily. "Besides, it's probably time to put Father Eric's clothes in the dryer." She went in to tend to things.

"It was fun, I guess," I said, to nobody, to everybody.

"More than that, I think," said JJ. "We have an oversupply of what Renee needed most, and we shared."

"I hope both of them can see it that way," I said. "I care about what happens to her."

"She's your sister. Of course you care," said JJ.

"Well, I was afraid to contact her for years," I said.

"And you've grown a lot, just in the time I've been living here," said JJ.

"You're comfortable in your skin again," said Rachael.

I had to laugh, because the sundress I was wearing was anything but comfortable on a windy day.

"They're right," said Joy. "I am not sure how to say this, but you are... different somehow... from the girl who picked me up in a bar three years ago. Four. Whatever it is."

Knowing how minutely she observes me, my desires and boundaries, I had to listen to Joy even if I could dismiss the others as flattery.

"And it's very cool what you've done for Emily," said JJ.

"It really is," Andi agreed.

Emily returned and said it was okay to come in again.

"Well," said Renee. "Your hair is a fright." She was smiling and laughing, so I figured things had gone well.

"You used to braid it for me on windy days," I said.

"C'mere," she said, and she braided my hair, like when we were fifteen.

JJ found the living room stash of hair toys and handed one to Renee, who affixed it.

"We're still married," Renee announced, when she had finished.

"Hooray!" I said, and the other people present said similar things. Eric was grinning.

"If you'd like some food, I figured we could barbecue," said Emily.

"That'd be grand," said Renee.

So the household sprang into action. Rachael, just as she had when we were a couple here, went out to the deck and set about lighting the coals. She had found a chimney thing that you stuff with newspaper and light, with the coals on the other end, and in a few minutes the coals are lit and you can dump them into the barbecue itself.

"Ravyn?" she called in from the screen door. "Smoke!"

"Dammit, every time," I said, what with that being the next line in the dialog. So I rushed upstairs to the bedroom. There's a window fan that normally sucks air in from above the patio, and was currently filling the room with smoke. So I flipped the switches on it to make it blow instead of sucking. We repeat this drill every week or two all summer long, for decades at a time. Well, with timeout for being depressed and sad. I didn't do a lot of much of anything the summers I lived here alone.

"That sucks," said Rachael. She was putting Gus on the chain, so he could get sniffably close to the barbecue but not close enough to hurt himself or steal anything yummy.

"Now it blows," I said, and we laughed together.

Emily supervised food prep in the kitchen, and Eric helped John and Ben carry a table out to the patio.

"It's nice having big people around," I told Eric.

"Happy to help." He laughed. He and Renee did a lot of laughing that afternoon.

We cracked open a bottle of the good rum after dinner, had a round, talked the guys into moving the table back indoors, and then noticed that Renee and Eric were exchanging glances.

"So, um, why don't you guys take the east bedroom. The door latches," I said. We sent Rachael and Andi home with their plus-ones, which left four of us and two beds. Perfect.

Emily and I packed suitcases for Eric and Renee, and Joy made some donations from the community toybox. "First installment of the toy of the month club," she said, and we all laughed.

Emily was up before I was in the morning, making coffee, figuring out (with JJ's help) when the East Bedroom people needed to be on their way.

Leaving it up to me to interrupt the slumber-or-whatever of my sister and her husband. "It's your wakeup call," I said knocking and opening the door.

"Did I tell you when our flight leaves?" Renee mumbled.

"We're a full-service outfit here," I said. "We figured it out. I'll bring coffee."

"Thanks," said Renee. She was up and mostly dressed when I returned, and Eric soon followed.

"I love you, you know that," I said, with my arms around Renee.

"Thanks for..." she said, but my tongue was in her mouth before she finished. "Thanks for that," she added, when I released her.

Eric stood by, with a huge grin on his face. "Drop in any time you're nearby," he said. "That goes for all of you."

Emily took them to the train while the other three of us showered and put on work clothes. She dropped us at the train on her next trip.

Life goes on, visitors or no.

"I'm impressed," said JJ. "Both of you are really class acts."

"Me, too," said Joy. Though her analysis was probably based on different factors than JJ's.

I mumbled something about identical and runs in the family, but JJ was not having any of it.

The train pulled in, doors open, public transportation to the rest of our lives together. We sat together, what with it being the end of the line and so empty. All three right legs crossed over left. Adjacent hands held. Two of my favorite people. Let people stare at us if they want. I'm happy, right here.

Made in the USA
Middletown, DE
06 June 2021